William Knox

Photograph courtesy of the William L. Clements Library, Ann Arbor, Michigan

William Knox

The Life & Thought of an
Eighteenth-Century Imperialist

by Leland J. Bellot

University of Texas Press, Austin & London

The publication of this book was assisted by a
grant from the Andrew W. Mellon Foundation.

Library of Congress Cataloging in Publication Data
Bellot, Leland J   1936–
   William Knox.

   Bibliography: p.
   Includes index.
     1. Knox, William, 1732–1810. 2. Statesmen—Great
Britain—Biography.
DA506.K58B44   973.3′1′0924 [B]   76-44006
ISBN 0-292-79007-4

To Marlita

Contents

Preface

Nearly a half century has elapsed since Sir Lewis Namier first issued a call for the biographical study of "ordinary men": "We have written about Parliamentary leaders and great administrators, and more or less ignored those whom they led and with or through whom they had to do their work, the individual members of Parliament, the Civil Servants, etc."[1] Certainly in his own lifetime Namier— through his meticulous structural studies of Parliament, his initiation of the mammoth *History of Parliament*, and his countless essays —made a prodigious contribution to redressing the scholarly balance in favor of those figures of the second and lower ranks who individually and collectively played crucial roles in the politics of eighteenth-century Britain. Scores of historians, including Namier's disciples, have taken up the challenge and have extended the study of "ordinary men" into many other historical eras and areas of investigation. Still, only a few years ago, a historian of the first British Empire (the subject which had originally engaged Namier's historical interest) could complain that too often studies of imperial administration were concerned essentially with institutions and economic theories "without investigating the undercurrents of personalities and politics which operated to produce a particular program" or attempting "to establish the origins of measures for the colonies in terms of the concrete experiences of the men who participated in policy decisions."[2]

One can hardly maintain that William Knox has escaped historical notice. He was not only a significant participant in the most important events of late-eighteenth-century British political and imperial history, but he was also a prolific and candid commentator, who has enjoyed the distinct historical advantage of having most of his commentaries survive in a variety of published forms readily available to modern researchers. Indeed, it sometimes seems (to this author, at least) almost impossible to pick up a work on the so-called Age of the American Revolution without finding some acknowledgment of Knox as a primary source of evidence and even some treatment and analysis of this or that aspect of his personal role in one contemporaneous event or another.

These partial reproductions of Knox's life, career, and thought, however, have produced and perpetuated a composite portrait which remains at best incomplete, inconsistent, and even contradictory. Although Namier singled out Knox as a worthy subject "for a study of the eighteenth-century Civil Service," a recent student of subministers during the period of the American Revolution has specifically excluded Knox from classification as a civil servant and has categorized him instead as a minor politician.[3] Or again, while several scholars have expressed the highest regard for Knox as an imperial theorist and publicist, others have denounced his colonial thought as wrongheaded and even unworthy of contemporary imperial issues.[4] Indeed, several decades ago Knox's imperialism so aroused the righteous wrath of a respected scholar and unstinting admirer of the modern British Commonwealth that he described one of Knox's pamphlets as "desperate wickedness" and loaded this undersecretary in the American Department with an inordinate burden of responsibility for the American Revolution: "But in the end the ministry had to resort to Catherine the Great of Russia and Hessian troops to implement the programme of William Knox."[5]

The essential purpose of this biography, then, is to provide a comprehensive narrative and an integrated interpretation of the whole person who was William Knox—the interactions of his being and becoming, his thought and his behavior. The biographical approach, of course, has its limitations as well as its advantages: what the scholar gains by concentration in depth must be balanced against the loss inherent in precluding the widest scope. Every effort has been made not only to trace the evolution of Knox's life and thought within the proper historical context but also to incorporate to advantage the critical omniscience of scholarly hindsight; nevertheless, the scope and perspective of this biographical study have been consciously focused and projected from the point of view of the subject.[6] Whether Knox's perceptions, attitudes, and behavior were indeed typical or even representative of his contemporaries is a question which can be answered definitively only in appropriate general histories. But hopefully a better understanding of William Knox, as both historical actor and witness, will contribute substantially to the comprehensiveness and cogency of the history of eighteenth-century Britain and of the revolution which sundered the first British Empire.

In the course of my research and writing I have benefited from the assistance and encouragement of so many scholars and friends that I regret I cannot acknowledge them all individually. My foremost debt is to the late Professor J. Harry Bennett, Jr., of the University of Texas. He first interested me in the subject of this biography; he guided the early stages of my research; and shortly before his untimely death, he read the drafts of several chapters, providing invaluable scholarly criticism. I can only flatter myself in the belief that he would have approved the final product. Professor Stanford E. Lehmberg of the University of Minnesota sustained my work during a trying period with generous encouragement and scholarly counsel. Professors John A. Schutz of the University of Southern California and Peter Stansky and John C. Miller of Stanford University graciously took time from their own work to read and comment upon the entire manuscript. The knowledgeable suggestions and painstaking attention to detail of these scholars permeates the whole of my work. To them I am indebted beyond return for the merits of this study; I alone, of course, am responsible for its defects.

I also wish to express my gratitude to those who assisted my research either as individuals or as members of scholarly and philanthropic institutions. Dr. Howard H. Peckham and his staff at the William L. Clements Library, Ann Arbor, Michigan, especially William S. Ewing, Curator of Manuscripts, made my research trips to Ann Arbor as pleasant as they were rewarding. The Clements Library also generously provided me with microfilm copies of several documents and rare books. The staff at the Henry E. Huntington Library, San Marino, California, allowed me access to their extensive collection of manuscripts and rare books. In England, through the courtesy of the Keeper of the Public Records and the Trustees of the British Museum, London, the vast and indispensable manuscript collections entrusted to their care were generously and efficiently made available for my research.[7] Through the kind permission of the Earl of Dartmouth, I was allowed to use the Dartmouth Manuscripts at the Staffordshire Record Office, Stafford. The Colonial Dames of Austin, Texas, awarded me a grant for microfilm copies of several pamphlets from the collections of the British Museum and the Library of Congress. My faculty colleagues and the administration of California State University, Fullerton, as well as the University Foundation, continually provided me encouragement and crucial assistance in the form of several financial grants and a semester's leave to concentrate upon refining the raw materials unearthed in my research. At various stages Mary Dalessi, Shirley de Graaf, and Garnette Long typed drafts from the impossible cipher of my longhand manuscripts.

Above all, I am indebted to my wife, Marlita. Over what must have seemed an interminable period of time she persevered and endured, even though she was continually put through the ordeal of oral readings of the rough draft. Without her quiet understanding and sacrifice my work certainly would have become impossible.

L.J.B.

William Knox

1. "The First Rudiments of My Political Education": Childhood & Youth in Ireland, 1732–1757

William Knox was of Scots-Irish descent—one of that ubiquitous race which contributed in so many ways to the creation, the shaping, and even the disruption of the first British Empire. For William this ancestry was a predominant, conscious factor in the development of his personality. Even in his later years, after he had been assimilated into the society of English gentry, Knox made his Scots-Irish heritage the salient feature of a personal narrative which he composed either as an introduction to a formal memoir or for the private instruction of his children.[1]

In the opening lines of this autobiographical fragment, William recounted the family tradition of kinship with the great Scots Presbyterian reformer John Knox, a claim he repeated on more than one occasion. William's paternal grandparents had left Scotland and settled in County Antrim, Ireland, within the Protestant enclave of Ulster Plantation, some time during the last years of James I's reign or the beginning of Charles I's. William's outstanding recollection of his grandfather was his conversion from steadfast royalism to an equally intense dedication to the "principles of Whiggism"—a legacy which, of course, would allow William to claim the primary credentials for access to the Whig oligarchy which dominated eighteenth-century political life.

By William's own account his grandfather had embraced the cause of Charles I as a matter of principle, in defiance of the hostile attitudes generally prevalent among his Scots-Irish neighbors. During the civil war he served as an officer in a Royalist cavalry troop. After being captured by Cromwellian forces at Carrickfergus Castle in 1648, he still remained loyal to the Stuarts, preferring to see his lands confiscated and granted to new proprietors rather than renounce his allegiance. At the Restoration, however, the house of Stuart sacrificed the claims of loyalty to expediency and confirmed the Cromwellian land grants in Ireland. Staunch royalism was

3

transformed into an equally fervent hatred of the Stuart line. William's grandfather embraced Whiggism, and during the Glorious Revolution he had the satisfaction of seeing his sons take an active part in the expulsion from Ireland of "James the second of the race he detested."

According to William's genealogical narrative, his father Thomas, the youngest of several children, distinguished himself in youth by an apparent calling for the church. Some time after the revolution he was sent to the University of Glasgow to study for the Presbyterian ministry. However, both his clerical vocation and his stay at Glasgow were terminated by the untimely "detection of an Amour with a bedmaker." He turned his attention to medicine and entered the University of Edinburgh, "where he received his Diploma about the time Bishop Burnet was scheming a union between the churches." He returned to Ireland to establish a medical practice in Dublin, but he was quickly forced by poor health to quit the city for the countryside. Subsequently he married Nicola King, the youngest daughter of John King, Esq., of Gola, County Fermanagh. For a while the couple lived at Clones in County Monaghan but finally settled in the town of Monaghan. There William, the youngest child, was born in 1732.[2]

Among the many influences which shaped William's personality in childhood and adolescence, the predominant force was unquestionably the awesome figure of his Scots-Irish father. Thomas Knox exercised a strong and pervasive authority over each member of his family. Upon his children he impressed a deep and lasting sense of loyalty and mutual responsibility. As the youngest child, William was the family favorite and correspondingly enjoyed special privileges and immunities. But even such unique advantages in no way diminished the impact of Thomas Knox's formidable character and paternalistic sway upon the mature personality of his youngest child.

Above all, the father's influence was asserted through the form and substance of religious training and example. Some time prior to William's birth, Thomas Knox converted from Presbyterianism to Anglicanism, and from childhood William was reared within the privileged ranks of the established Church of Ireland.[3] Yet the particular formulation of Anglicanism which Thomas Knox personally imparted to his children was nonetheless steeped in the principles and practices of Calvinism. In later years, William specifically attributed to his father's influence his own lifelong dedication to Bible study, Sabbath keeping, family devotions, and private prayer. Without a doubt all the elements of William's mature religious faith—his belief in the omniscience and omnipotence of God the father, his deep conviction of humanity's guilt for the sin of Adam, his belief in the efficacy of Christ's atonement for the sins of humankind—reflect the influence of Thomas Knox's religious training.

Even as a septuagenarian, William retained vivid childhood memories of his father's manner of religious instruction.[4] He recalled that every Sunday afternoon his father would gather together the family and servants for Sabbath services. There before this congregation, the father called upon each of his children in turn to read portions of the Old and New testaments, "upon which he required them to make their own observations as they went on, and in their own words." Then, after all the children had finished their recitations, Thomas Knox supplemented their efforts with his own considerable knowledge of theology, explaining the meaning of the scriptural passages and drawing "the proper inferences" from them. Although young William's first such command performances must have been awesome ordeals, he was a precocious child and evidently was soon able to respond with virtuoso performances, which won him the considerable rewards of his father's approval and the admiration of his siblings.

Thomas Knox not only schooled his children thoroughly in the doctrines of Calvinistic Christianity, but he also imparted to them the conviction that religion was of more than transcendent relevance in human affairs. In later years William remembered that in an era when physicians seemed to be enamored with Deism his father "always blended the duties of religion with the exercise of his profession." Among William's most lasting childhood impressions was the sight of his father "imploring divine assistance in his closet" before going to visit his patients. William explicitly acknowledged his father's teachings and example as the source of his own belief that statesmanship was equally dependent upon religious conviction and political acumen, since "the object of both is to promote the welfare and happiness of mankind."[5]

In contrast, the evidence of maternal influence is singular only in its absence. Within a voluminous literary record which William compiled during his long life, there are only two references to his mother: one is an account of his parents' marriage; the other is his acknowledgment of new responsibilities for his mother's welfare after the death of his father. In both instances William perceived his mother in a secondary role within the sphere of paternal authority. Indeed, the surviving evidence indicates that during the years of William's childhood and youth Thomas Knox's ascendancy over his youngest child was significantly rivaled—or rather reinforced—not by the mother but by the surrogate influence of an Anglican clergyman.

The Reverend Philip Skelton was a remarkable figure among the eighteenth-century Irish clergy, a renowned scholar who spent his life in dedicated service to a pastoral calling.[6] He was appointed curate at Monaghan in 1732, the year of William's birth, and except for a brief absence from 1742 to 1743 he served this parish until 1750. During the first five years of his residence in Monaghan, Skelton lodged with Francis Battersby, who was related by marriage to the Knox family.[7] Skelton, who was as gregarious as he was dedicated, regularly made the rounds of his parishioners' homes; but he seems to have become especially attached to the family of his landlord's devout and erudite relative, Thomas Knox, in whose home he undoubtedly found a challenging and appreciative forum for his favorite pastime of theological disputation. During such visits young William certainly must have received special attention from Skelton, who not only considered children "the sweetest and most pleasing companions" but also admitted that the surest method of securing the affection of parents was by playing with their children.[8]

On the Sabbath, in the somber surroundings of the parish church, little William must have been deeply impressed when his genial companion took the pulpit and was transformed into an imposing and even frightening figure. Philip Skelton was a powerful preacher whose "gigantic size" and strong, expressive voice were combined with a manner and a message which contemporaries labeled enthusiastic and, in a later day, evangelical. Although Skelton's theology was orthodox, his religious teaching emphasized the depravity and sinfulness of human nature. Personally afflicted by doubts about his own salvation, he regularly "explained to his hearers in plain and powerful language the threats and promises of the gospel," summoning visions of "heaven and hell before their eyes." Accordingly, it was not unusual for his congregation to be "insensibly carried away with him, they were astonished, they were convinced."[9]

On Sunday evenings Pastor Skelton resumed a more benign character and gathered the children of his parish into the church for instruction in catechism. First, his charges were required to memorize the tenets of religion as set out in the Anglican prayer book. Once the "original catechism" was mastered, the young catechumens were taught the "proof-catechism," which confirmed and illustrated "the doctrines of the other by texts of scripture." Since Skelton took a special pride in his parish children's reputation for catechistical learning, it is not surprising that bright young William Knox, doubly experienced in such exercises, quickly became the prize pupil of a demanding master.

Beyond a few explicit references to catechistical training under Skelton's tutelage, there are only a few clues to William's formal education in childhood and adolescence. In the town of Monaghan the children of Protestant families enjoyed convenient access to relatively inexpensive education: the Church of Ireland with the assistance of private benefactors maintained a primary school, while a secondary school at Monaghan was supported jointly by the dioceses of Raphoe, Kilmore, and Clogher.[10] Since William testified that his father refused to send any of his children to boarding schools—"considering the improvement in classical learning to be obtained there, as too dearly purchased by the loss of religious principles" at those institutions where Christian training was "ridiculed and rendered impracticable"—it seems certain that William received his early education at the local schools under the auspices of the established church.[11]

Whatever the relative merits of William's early formal schooling in Monaghan, he enjoyed a distinct advantage in continuing under the informal tutelage of Philip Skelton. On at least two occasions, Skelton was employed as a private tutor, instructing young boys in English and the rudiments of Latin and Greek. He had also taught in an endowed school at Dundalk after his graduation from Trinity College, Dublin, and during his ministry in Monaghan he was offered a school "worth five-hundred pounds a year."

Although Knox's mature correspondence with Skelton indicates that their teacher-pupil relationship was not limited to religious instruction, the surviving evidence provides only fragmentary clues to the particulars the master contributed to William's general learning. During much of his adult life, William submitted his own views on politics and literature as well as theology for Skelton's consideration, and Skelton readily obliged with candid criticism of his former pupil's career and writings. When Knox proposed to acknowledge Skelton as his instructor in one of his publications, Skelton expressly consented to the citation. On one occasion, in a reference to the education of one of William's nephews, Skelton paid a rather oblique compliment to Knox's abilities as a pupil when he commented, "The boy's capacity is not like yours, though very [able?], plain, and sound, the very thing for a merchant."[12]

A tract which Skelton published when William was seventeen years old provides the only extensive clue to the substantive aspects of Knox's early education. Skelton's *Ophiomaches: Or, Deism Revealed* (1749) is a lengthy refutation of Deism written in the form of a dialog among an Anglican country parson, a young gentleman, and two Deists, one of whom is the youth's tutor.[13] In the course of an extended and often animated debate, the "simple" parson—drawing upon an extensive fund of ancient and modern scholarship—ensnares his adversaries again and again in the web of their own Deistical deductions, finally persuading the young gentleman of the validity of traditional Christianity.

Specifically Skelton, in the person of the country parson, contradicted such basic Deistic principles as the inherent virtue of humanity in nature and the ultimate supremacy of natural law. He argued instead that God is the ultimate source of all law and justice, because He alone possesses the omnipotence and omniscience necessary to sustain these principles throughout the universe. Consequently, human society and government must depend upon belief in God, while "all the defects of civil society, all the injustice, oppression, rapine, rebellion, faction, all intestine struggles for power, and all the civil wars, that shake or tear society to pieces, spring only from a want of faith in God."[14] Just as God is the source of all legitimate authority, perversions of such authority originated in the inherent depravity of human nature. Man, who "brings up the rear" of intelligent beings, was therefore "made for subjection and obedience insomuch that he must have either a master, or a tyrant over him."[15] In a classic restatement of the Aristotelian-Scholastic argument, Skelton insisted that the condition of slavery among humankind came about when morally informed reason was overwhelmed by unenlightened passion.

In illustrating his argument against the liberty and virtue of natural law, Skelton submitted a typology of human cultures which betrayed the ethnocentric prejudices of his universals. If humans were the least intelligent of beings, Skelton noted, certainly the learned among the English reasoned better than mere citizens; citizens, better than boors; English boors, better than Spanish; Spanish, better than Moorish; Moorish, better than Negro; and Negro, better than their southern neighbors the Hottentots. So much for natural reason. As for natural virtue, Skelton pointed to such barbarous customs among heathens as the exposure of unwanted children: "A cruelty practised," he insisted, "at this day by the *Hottentots* and some other *African* nations."[16]

The ideas, prejudices, even the style of Skelton's writing unmistakably permeated William Knox's mature intellect. Probably parson Skelton imparted these principles directly to the "young gentleman" who was his own pupil. Certainly William must have eagerly read his master's work shortly after it appeared in print. William, in fact, eventually incorporated and applied much of Skelton's teaching in his own publications, not only those dealing with theology but also those treating such subjects as British imperial authority and African slavery.

To the combined influence of Thomas Knox and Philip Skelton one may partly credit the pronounced traits of self-righteousness and contempt for defects in others which marked William's personality. Yet it is no less significant that in maturity these tendencies were sensibly tempered by a tolerant attitude toward human diversity. Perhaps this latent quality of benevolent tolerance can be partially traced to the fact that in Monaghan, during childhood and youth, William lived in a community marked by heterogeneous cultural influences.

Although County Monaghan was located geographically within Ulster, historically and culturally it had largely remained separate from the great Protestant enclave. Under the Tudors and the Stuarts the county had been scarcely influenced by the English and Scots plantations, and by the eighteenth century the people of the region were still mostly Roman Catholics with a mingling of Presbyterians and Anglicans. Following the relaxation of the penal laws against

Catholics in Ireland after 1745, Monaghan's Catholics worshiped openly and even constructed churches throughout the region.[17]

In his later years William Knox was able to recall the religious practices of the Catholics of Ireland, who, according to one of his recollections, place "a candle, and a rod or staff, in the coffin with their dead, and furnish them with a new pair of brogues with their soles chalked, to enable them the better to walk through the valley of the shadow of death, which they think they must pass through in their way to purgatory."[18] Pastor Skelton himself, despite his staunch Protestant orthodoxy, consistently set an example of tolerant charity, even to the point of selling his precious books on two occasions to buy food, which he distributed among his famine-stricken neighbors regardless of creed. On more than one such occasion, William forwarded money to support his former master's charity. Even more significant is the fact that throughout his public career Knox openly advocated the removal of political and civil restrictions affecting Irish Catholics.

William remained no less concerned with the economic disasters which increasingly beset the Irish during the greater part of his lifetime. In the years of his childhood and youth, agriculture and the cottage linen industry were the main economic pursuits of the people of County Monaghan. The medium-sized farms which predominated were mainly devoted to raising flax for the looms of local linen weavers. The domestic weavers of Monaghan shared in the basic features of northern Ireland's prefactory stage of linen industry: they grew much of their own flax, owned their own tools, and marketed their own products; they raised their own food and during periods of decline in the linen trade made their livelihood by farming. Even in an era of casual industrial organization the linen weavers of Monaghan were notorious for abandoning their looms to participate in organized hare-hunting meets. During the period from 1750 to 1800, however, the linen industry of northern Ireland underwent a gradual yet definite transformation. Scarcely apparent during William's childhood, but with increasing intensity during his later years, the effects of capitalistic organization became evident as the self-employed, self-sustaining domestic weavers of northern Ireland found their independence challenged by the development of new methods of manufacture and distribution and by the growth of a class of permanent wage earners.[19] Although William left Ireland before the full impact of this process had become evident, the subsequent decline of artisans in his native land and their emigration to America had a pronounced effect on his ideas and actions during the many years he was in public life.

If the rough form of William's personality and character was firmly etched in childhood and adolescence by the people and physical surroundings of Monaghan, the great city of Dublin supplied the setting and medium for the detailed strokes of young manhood. For William and other aspiring youths of the Anglo-Irish elite, the preeminent attraction in Dublin was Trinity College. The cost of an education at Trinity was relatively small, and large numbers of poorer Irish gentry sent their sons to the university. Even Philip Skelton, the son of a poor Irish farmer, had been able to obtain a degree and then a fellowship at Trinity.

Unfortunately, the information relating to William Knox's education at Trinity is meager. He attended the university some time between the years 1748 and 1755.[20] Although the surviving matriculation records do not indicate that he was ever formally enrolled in the university or took a degree there, the official records are admittedly fragmentary. It was quite common, moreover, for young men to pursue their education by attending lectures without submitting to the matriculation procedures.

Whatever the particular circumstances of William's attendance at Trinity may have been, the university certainly provided him opportunities for an education of high academic quality and unusual diversity. During the eighteenth century Trinity avoided the decline which befell its fellow institutions in England. Although the classics retained preeminence in the curriculum, the range of instructional subjects was expanded by the establishment of a chair in natural and experimental philosophy and another in oratory and history. By 1759 the list of subjects taught at Trinity included oriental, ancient, and modern languages, sacred and profane history, mathematics, theological controversy, and ecclesiastical history, as well as the classics.[21] Trinity received its share of criticism, aimed particularly at its pedantic mode of instruction; nevertheless, its alumni, including Edmund Burke, defended the excellence of the education they had received at the university.

The contrast between the writings of the mature Knox and those of Burke provides a useful insight into the apparent differences in their educational experiences at Trinity. In both his correspondence and his published works, Knox pays a degree of homage to the classical and rhetorical conventions of his age, but the relative dearth of these elements in his writings stands in sharp contrast to Burke's mastery of classical allusions and his facility in the use of rhetoric. When Knox resorts to these conventions his style becomes forced and artificial. His best work draws instead upon an extensive fund of information from modern history, political philosophy, and political economy rather than from the classics. Some of these elements can be attributed, of course, to individual qualities of intellect and temperament; yet, undoubtedly, the characteristic features of Knox's thought and expression were distinctively shaped by his particular educational background at Trinity.

In the capital city of Ireland, politics competed with academics for the attention and energies of the young men attending Trinity. The student enjoyed the right of sitting in the spectators' gallery of the Irish House of Commons, and regular attendance at the debates was a favorite pastime among large numbers of undergraduates. Many students took a more active interest in politics, often participating in the election contests of the capital.[22] These pursuits were of course expected of the offspring of the Anglo-Irish aristocracy, but the diversions and attractions of Dublin politics equally engaged those students like Knox for whom such activities were in no sense an inescapable legacy of family and social status.

It was probably during his stay at Trinity that William Knox was introduced to his first political mentor, Sir Richard Cox—most likely through the medium of Cox's son Richard, who had enrolled at the university in 1753.[23] Knox never indicated the precise nature of his connection with Sir Richard; he only remarked in later years that he had received the "first rudiments" of his political education from Cox. But this statement, taken in conjunction with the details of Sir Richard's role in the Irish political crisis of 1753–1756, provides the sole clue to those factors which shaped William's political attitudes during this formative period.

Prior to the rise of the Irish nationalist movement during the 1770s, politics in eighteenth-century Ireland were usually rather quiet. The machinery of Irish politics was well lubricated by the oil of patronage. The Irish executive was able to maintain the interests of the English government in Ireland primarily through the judicious distribution of favors among key patrons in the Irish Parliament—men who bore the ominous name of undertakers. There were occasions, however, when friction developed between the executive and the undertakers, friction which at times threatened to bring the machinery of government to a fiery halt. Such an occasion arose in 1753 when the British-dominated executive challenged the supremacy of Henry Boyle, Speaker of the Irish House of Commons and the leading undertaker in Ireland.[24]

Although the relationship between young Knox's mentor, Sir Richard Cox, and Speaker Boyle is not entirely clear, it is certain that during the political crisis of 1753–1756 the Irish administration regarded Cox as one of the more obnoxious members of the parliamentary opposition.[25] When the Speaker's party defeated a major piece of financial legislation in December 1753, Cox not only voted against the government, but he also compounded his defiance with impudence by publishing a pamphlet attacking the administration. In the subsequent purge of officeholders who had voted against the government, Cox was removed from his customs post. The executive postponed a direct attack on Boyle, but when the Speaker refused all offers of compromise he was dismissed from the office of Chancellor of the Exchequer in March 1754.[26]

With the dismissal of Boyle, the Irish government seemed to have won the field, but the opposition had not yet thrown their reserves into the struggle. Irish politics always included the potentially explosive element of mass discontent. Normally the royal administration and the Irish parliamentarians cooperated in keeping the populace under control, but when the undertakers felt their position challenged by the English-appointed executive, they were not above demagoguery—embarrassing the administration by arousing the perennial popular hatred of English rule.

Possibly William Knox was an eyewitness to the public disturbances and riots which took place in Dublin in 1754. Perhaps, as an eager supporter of Sir Richard Cox, William even took some minor part in the extraparliamentary campaign which the undertakers, including his mentor, mounted in support of the Irish opposition. Addresses of thanks to those members of Parliament who had voted against the finance bill were promoted in the constituencies, while Speaker Boyle was toasted throughout the country as the defender of Irish liberties against English rule.[27] On May 13, 1754, Boyle received a golden box and an address from the citizens of Cork, the seat of Cox's political influence. A few verses from the address provide a strong hint of Cox's role in the popular clamor:

> But, as a people (be it spoken)
> Oblig'd we give this golden token,
> And what's more precious than the *Box*,
> The motto was composed by *C-x*.[28]

By 1755 the government at Westminster was alarmed by the turmoil and was no longer in any mood to support the disruptive policies of the Irish executive. A new Lord Lieutenant was sent out to Ireland with instructions to pacify the Irish opposition, and by 1756 the new viceroy had worked out a settlement which basically provided for a division of power with Speaker Boyle. Some of Boyle's followers objected to the compromise, but his principal supporters profited handsomely from the settlement. Boyle himself received an earldom and a pension, and for his part Sir Richard Cox was appointed to the lucrative post of revenue commissioner.[29]

Admittedly young Knox's role in this turbulent political episode remains obscure. Nevertheless, his mature political attitudes reflect the unmistakable impressions of the Irish political crisis of 1753–1756. This is particularly evident in his consistent suspicion of latent demagoguery in popular legislative bodies and also in his steady conviction that political stability essentially rested upon the unqualified attachment of men of consequence to government. For more than two decades after 1756, Irish politics settled back into traditional patterns as the undertakers and the executive cooperated in behalf of peaceful rule and a satisfactory distribution of the fruits of office. But William Knox never forgot the lessons of his youthful initiation into politics. And when Irish political stability was once again disturbed in the midst of the American revolutionary war, he would in fact assume a prominent and decisive role in the politics of his native land.

Following his introduction to the rudiments of politics, William was anxious to obtain an official appointment. But eighteenth-century Ireland provided only limited opportunities for native sons who sought their fortunes in public office. It was not that Irish offices were few in number—Ireland in fact supported relatively large civil, ecclesiastical, and military establishments. But these positions were at the disposal of Ireland's English overlords. Not only were Irish Catholics and Protestant Dissenters disabled from office-holding, but even the privileged members of the established

Church of Ireland found the avenues to public offices blocked by the preemptive claims of English political patronage. To a large degree English politicians considered Irish offices an integral part of their own patronage system, and the satisfaction of English political obligations was a prerequisite to the distribution of positions in the Irish establishment.[30]

Irishmen were not entirely excluded from officeholding in their homeland. The stability of royal government in Ireland rested upon executive control of the Irish Parliament, and even in this subservient body patronage was an essential ingredient of political management—indeed, the very subservience of the Irish legislature was an indication of the skill with which English-nominated ministries distributed patronage among the members. Of course such methods of political management were not peculiar to the Irish system. But in contrast to the Parliament at Westminster, the Irish Commons contained a relatively large number of poor men who sought even minor offices, those which English patrons usually bestowed upon lesser dependents.[31]

Thus the prior claims of Englishmen upon the Irish establishment and the competition among the Irish members of Parliament for the residual offices obliged many energetic Irish to look beyond their native land, to the overseas empire and even to England itself, to seek outlets for their ambitions and talents. Edmund Burke, the most famous Irishman of the eighteenth century, achieved eminence in England rather than in his native country. The course of Burke's fortunes had he remained in his homeland is a matter of speculation, but even when his prospects in England seemed dismal in 1757, he anticipated emigrating to America rather than returning to Ireland.[32]

Burke gave up his plan of going to America and instead pursued his destiny at the seat of the empire. But about the same time, William Knox took up the course Burke had abandoned. In 1756 Henry Ellis, a native of Monaghan, was appointed acting governor of Georgia. Although Ellis was eleven years Knox's senior and had been away from home for many years, his father was a leading benefactor of Monaghan. It was probably through the elder Ellis that Knox obtained an introduction to the new governor.[33] It seems equally probable that William was recommended to the Ellises by his old master Philip Skelton, who throughout his life promoted the fortunes of deserving young men regularly, persistently, and with frequent success. Certainly in later years, when Knox himself was in a position to influence the distribution of such favors, Skelton did not hesitate to remind his former pupil of his obligations in this respect.

William's own cursory account only records that in September 1756 he joined Henry Ellis in London and that one month later Lord Halifax, president of the Board of Trade, appointed him acting provost marshal of Georgia.[34] In December Governor Ellis sailed from Portsmouth in the company of his ambitious young townsman. William Knox had completed the first rudiments of his political education in Ireland. His political apprenticeship would be served in America.

2. "Legislators . . . That No King Can Govern Nor No God Can Please": Georgia, 1757–1762

Among the multitude of offices at the disposal of the British Crown in the mid-eighteenth century, William Knox's appointment in the colony of Georgia could scarcely be regarded as a political plum. After twenty years of organized English settlement, Georgia was still a frontier outpost of the British Empire. The philanthropic imperialists, who founded the colony in 1732 to provide a buffer against the Spanish and the Indians, as well as to offer a haven for English indigents, had realized neither of these goals by the 1750s. Few debtors in England exchanged the certain evils of English prisons for the unknown blessings of the American wilderness. Migration from the colonies adjacent to Georgia was discouraged by the trustees' original prohibitions against large land grants and slaveholding within the settlement. Even with the removal of these restrictions, the colony failed to grow and prosper. When royal government was finally established in the colony in 1754, the three thousand widely scattered inhabitants, both whites and blacks, were virtually at the mercy of their Spanish and Indian neighbors.[1] Georgia was in fact a liability rather than an asset to the empire.

During the fall of 1756, as Henry Ellis and William Knox made preparations in London for the long journey to Georgia, the defenses of imperial frontiers were cause for mounting concern and debate at Westminster. Even while the memory of General Braddock's disaster in the American wilderness was still fresh, Whitehall was shocked by the report that Fort Oswego had fallen to Montcalm in August. With the Ohio Valley in the hands of the French and their Indian allies, the northern and western frontiers in America were exposed to immediate attack. A concerted assault upon the southern settlements, possibly in conjunction with France's former ally, Spain, also seemed imminent.

Little wonder that Ellis and Knox were distressed by the vulnerable condition of Georgia even before they left London. They had taken considerable pains to inform themselves in detail about the circumstances of the colony. In a memorial which Ellis submitted to the Lords of Trade two months before he and Knox sailed for America, the new governor drew up a comprehensive assessment of the deplorable state of Georgia's defenses: frontier forts in ruins, few men and even fewer arms available for military service, and little hope of support from the friendly Indians.[2] Ellis applied for an immediate requisition of five hundred stands of small arms and provisions for Indian presents, and he also requested that a warship be stationed off the coast of Georgia. Officials at Whitehall apparently shared his sense of urgency—at least to the extent that the Board of Trade and the Treasury processed and approved his requisition of arms and Indian presents before he set sail for America.[3]

If the long list of material deficiencies in the defenses of Georgia distressed Ellis and Knox on the eve of their departure, they must have been even more disturbed by the overwhelming evidence of deteriorating morale among the populace—a result of two years of political dissension under Ellis' predecessor. The methods and manners of Capt. John Reynolds, formerly of His Majesty's fleet and since 1754 the first royal governor of Georgia, had been better suited to the command of a royal ship of the line than the government of a colony.[4] Of course the Georgians' inexperience in self-government had complicated Reynolds' task, but the governor's imperious behavior undoubtedly would have provoked a similar reaction in any of the older colonies. Reynolds had immediately alienated his council by insisting that this body become a rubber stamp for his proposals. And when the council, which included some of the most important men in the colony, had refused to accept the subservient role the governor assigned them, Reynolds had simply ignored them and turned for advice to his private secretary, William Little.

Little had served under Reynolds in the Royal Navy for twenty years. He had accompanied the new governor to Georgia, and soon the authority and favors which Reynolds showered upon him placed him in the middle of the ever-widening breach between the governor and the colonial legislature.

In the best of English traditions, the Georgia council decided to strike at the governor through his favorite. Late in 1755, the council charged Little with malversation in his various offices—specifically with the extortion of exorbitant fees—and also accused him of interfering in constitutional government by withholding from the governor several bills passed by both houses of the legislature. Reynolds forestalled the council's attack on his secretary by personally conducting a hearing on the charges and subsequently removing Little from two of his seven offices.[5]

Thus far the Georgia Commons House of Assembly had not taken an active part in the controversy between the governor and his council. But Reynolds' stubborn determination to protect Little and support his political intrigues drew the lower house into the dispute. Early in 1756, the assembly decided to take up the issue of Little's interference with two bills. This time the governor saved his secretary by adjourning the House, but his action only postponed rather than solved the controversy, which broadened during the interlude. Little subsequently opened a campaign to create a party of his own in the lower house; by using the governor's influence he secured the election of two of his followers to the assembly. But when the House resumed its meetings in February 1756, it raised the whole issue of electoral privilege by refusing to seat Little's two supporters. Reynolds clumsily reacted to this new challenge by declaring that unless the two members were seated he would regard all the proceedings of the House as invalid. The assembly stood firm, however, and finally on February 19 the governor angrily dissolved the legislature.[6]

Reynolds' high-handed treatment of the assembly proved to be a strategic blunder. The council saw an opportunity for an appeal to the British government, and in the spring of 1756 they sent Provost Marshal Alexander Kellett to England to present their case against Reynolds and Little before the Board of Trade. During the months of June and July 1756, the Lords of Trade conducted a thorough investigation of the situation in Georgia, not only hearing Kellett's firsthand account of the controversy but also examining the governor's correspondence, the journals of the council and the assembly, and the private correspondence of the colony's crown agent, Benjamin Martyn.[7] On August 4, the board recommended to His Majesty that Governor Reynolds be recalled to England to defend the conduct of his administration. And on the same day, at the direction of Secretary of State Fox, the board appointed Henry Ellis lieutenant governor of Georgia and commissioned him to act as governor during Reynolds' absence.[8] In Georgia, meanwhile, Reynolds had dismissed Kellett as provost marshal, and Board President

Halifax took advantage of the opportunity to name Ellis' fellow townsman William Knox acting provost marshal of Georgia.[9]

The unmistakably onerous job of rehabilitating the human and physical resources of Georgia under the imminent threat of attack would have presented a forbidding challenge to veteran colonial officials. Henry Ellis was totally inexperienced in government and politics. In fact, during his term in Georgia Ellis, whom one historian has succinctly described as a "gifted dilettante," would exhibit remarkable political acumen and administrative skill.[10] But at the time of his appointment his public reputation rested solely upon his achievements as an explorer and author. Even after Ellis' administration was well established in Georgia, his dispatches to officials in England were punctuated by candid expressions of his persistent fear that inexperience in politics would lead him to commit some disastrous blunder.[11]

The responsibilities which awaited Henry Ellis in America must have seemed particularly awesome as he prepared to sail from England in the company of William Knox—a youth of twenty-four, bright and ambitious, but scarcely more experienced in politics than was the new acting governor himself. Ellis, conscious of the fact that his predecessor had compromised his own position by conspicuous dependence upon his private secretary, chose not to share his burdens with Knox. Instead, from the very beginning the governor adopted a reserved and curt manner toward his young companion. And William, his youthful egotism wounded by Ellis' unaccountable behavior, arrogantly attributed their strained relationship to the novice governor's jealousy of his own previous political experience in Ireland.[12]

According to Knox's account, he sailed with Ellis from Portsmouth on December 8, 1756. After an apparently uneventful voyage, despite the real danger of French privateers, they arrived safely in Charleston, South Carolina, late the following month. Ellis and his company tarried there for almost three weeks to confer with Gov. William Henry Lyttelton. Since Lyttelton was a figure of importance—not only as chief executive of Georgia's powerful neighbor but also as a relative and personal favorite of Secretary of State William Pitt—it is not surprising that Knox was disappointed when Ellis failed to introduce him to Lyttelton.[13] But the ambitious young Irishman showed a precocious aptitude for political maneuver: he struck up an acquaintance with Lyttelton's secretary and thereby wangled an invitation to dine with the governor. On this occasion Lyttelton was, in Knox's words, "particularly civil to me and often attempted to engage me in separate conversation and once in a private one." Knox claimed that he exercised restraint in responding to Lyttelton's notice because he feared giving offense to Ellis. However, William made a sufficient impression upon Lyttelton to establish the basis for what would ultimately become a lifelong friendship.

On February 11, Ellis and Knox left Charleston, and after a four-day trip aboard a South Carolina scout boat they arrived in Savannah. To those familiar with the great cities of Dublin and London, even with the provincial capital of South Carolina, the first sight of Savannah must have been a rude shock. In 1757, Savannah scarcely differed from the desolate little settlement which had greeted Ellis' predecessor three years earlier—a few hundred wooden houses in various stages of decay clung to a river bluff at the edge of a pine forest. Ellis' own initial account of his capital depicted it as ill situated either for general commerce or for communication with the other settlements scattered across the colony.[14] He described the public buildings as "so ruinous as to be in a manner past repair." The church was in such a state of decay that only props prevented its total collapse, while the public prison, a hut only fifteen feet square, was "shocking to humanity," being filled with felons and debtors who were exposed not only to filth and vermin but also "to the scorching Suns of this climate." The new governor's summary recommendation was that the seat of government be moved several miles southward to Hardwick on the Great Ogeechee River.

If the tiny capital Ellis inherited from Reynolds was in a state of physical deterioration, certainly the governmental structure of the colony was in even greater need of reconstruction. During the one-year interval between the dissolution of the legislature (February 1756) and Ellis' arrival in Georgia (February 1757), Reynolds and Little had taken steps to secure a more favorable political climate for their administration.[15] Reynolds removed his critics from official positions and placed the offices at the disposal of Little and his supporters. Consequently, in the election of a new assembly only four members of the House which had defied the governor were returned. Little succeeded in winning seats in the assembly for himself and several of his followers, so that when the lower house met on November 1, 1756, four months before Ellis' arrival in Georgia,

Little was elected Speaker. Reynolds had further insured Little's dominant position in this assembly by placing control of the public funds in the hands of the new Speaker.

Immediately upon his arrival, Governor Ellis found himself thrust into the middle of a partisan tug of war. On one side the anti-Reynolds faction clamored for a clean sweep of Little's followers from public office and called for the election of a new assembly; on the other side Little, who remained behind after Reynolds left for England, was obviously determined to maintain his political position in the colony and had decided to achieve his purpose by using his control of the assembly to embarrass the new governor. And adding insult to injury, Little openly predicted that new elections would only produce the return of a majority of his own supporters to the assembly.[16]

William Knox's first reaction to this political tangle was to recommend that Ellis plunge into the partisan struggle with Speaker Little.[17] He rejected the idea of attempting to do business with the "bad men" who made up Little's party, because any such compromise would taint the new administration with the stigma of Reynolds' regime. Since Knox, along with Ellis, had received a warm reception from the "friends" of the new administration, he was persuaded that Little's real political influence was limited to his handpicked assembly. He urged Ellis to dissolve the assembly and call for new elections immediately.

The governor refused to be rushed into precipitate action by either Knox or his newly found "friends." Although Ellis had little previous experience in politics, he grasped the long-range implications of his position more quickly than his impetuous young countryman. He decided that in the long term a policy of conciliation was more likely to insure the success of his administration than the partisan confrontation Knox recommended. Ellis recognized the essential fact that Little's supporters in the assembly were "placemen" rather than "bad men," and he astutely concluded that by keeping them in office while holding the threat of a dissolution over them, he could eventually win their allegiance away from Little. In this manner he could obtain a tractable assembly for his administration while avoiding the odium of procuring one. Ellis listened with sympathy to those who insisted upon a dissolution, but he only prorogued the assembly in order to avoid immediate conflict with Little while he consolidated his own position.[18]

Knox was not yet convinced by the governor's reasoning, but once his youthful ardor for the charge abated, he characteristically fell back to examine the combatants and the terrain. He took advantage of the prorogation to obtain more information. He studied the journals of the first assembly and was struck by the fact that during its sessions former Carolinians sitting in the Georgia assembly had attempted to introduce the various privileges and practices which prevailed in the lower house of the Carolina legislature. When Knox learned that these Carolinians would probably be returned if Ellis called for new elections to the assembly, he came over to the governor's opinion that Little's placemen were "likelier to join in establishing a British Constitution which was our object, than those that should succeed them."[19]

Knox subsequently played an active part in the governor's plan to undermine Little's control over the assembly. Drawing upon his Irish experiences, he arranged to have petitions for a dissolution inserted in several of the addresses which were being presented to the new governor from different parts of Georgia.[20] The petitions hung like the proverbial sword over the heads of Little's followers. As a threat they inspired good behavior on the part of the assembly, and if necessary they could serve as a popular justification before the Board of Trade as well as the electors of Georgia for the early termination of the assembly.

Governor Ellis delayed reconvening the assembly until May 1757, when Speaker Little left Georgia to join Reynolds before the Board of Trade in England. Little attempted to maintain his political power by proxy in the person of Alexander Mackay. But when the assembly resumed its sessions, the governor immediately demonstrated the effectiveness of his campaign against Little's influence by defeating Mackay's candidacy for Speaker of the lower house. The blow was decisive; hereafter Ellis' administration was never again disturbed by organized political factions.[21]

William Little would no longer trouble Governor Ellis, but the shadow of his turbulent career darkened the whole of William Knox's first year in Georgia. Knox's own account of his early experiences in the colony, although written several years after the fact, provides an invaluable description of his earliest reaction to the subtleties of political relationships.

In his memoir Knox complained especially that Ellis continually subjected him to petty jealousies. Even their common effort against

23

Little and his faction had not brought an improvement in their personal relations. Knox was particularly disgruntled when Ellis rejected his offer to enter the assembly, where he might counter Little's influence. William immediately concluded that the governor's objections were rooted in a jealous fear of his acquaintance with parliamentary affairs. Ellis was admittedly conscious of his own inexperience in politics; nevertheless, what Knox described as petty jealously probably originated in the governor's continuing determination to avoid any suggestion, in either England or America, that his young companion would play the role of favorite in his administration. Knox himself recognized that his arrival with Ellis could jeopardize his own political career in Georgia. In fact, this consideration in part had inspired his desire to enter the assembly rather than the council, where he believed he was likely to be regarded as the "Governor's echo." He could not perceive that the governor's veto of his proposal was probably influenced by the fear that Knox's entry into the lower house would revive memories of Speaker Little's role during Reynold's regime. Instead, the ambitious and egotistical novice chafed at Ellis' apparent disregard of his pretensions.[22]

In any event, on March 1, 1757, William Knox took the prescribed oaths both as councilor and as provost marshal of Georgia. Two days later he took his seat on the council and entered into the deliberations on the business to be presented to Governor Ellis' first assembly.[23]

From the beginning of his administration, Ellis cultivated the confidence and the support of his council. During the spring of 1757, the governor kept its members busy preparing a program to be laid before the legislature once he had crushed Little's faction in the lower house. To Ellis the deliberations of the council were not just a matter of form, for the new governor sincerely desired the advice of those who had extensive experience in the affairs of the colony.

Knox did not share the governor's confidence in the veteran councilors. William was determined to push for a program which would restore to the governor those prerogatives previously forfeited to the popular assembly through Reynolds' abdication of powers to Speaker Little. He suspected that the rest of the council were so sensitive to popular approval that they would never support measures which implied any abridgment of the "Liberties of the People." Knox complained to Ellis that he alone among the council would face the difficulties and the infamy of promoting a true British constitution in Georgia.[24] Ellis generally agreed with Knox's desire to restore initiative to the governor, and to this end he provided him an ally on the council in the person of the newly appointed attorney general, William Clifton. In the subsequent deliberations of the council, Clifton and Knox worked together successfully to promote policies designed to assert the prerogatives of the colonial executive.[25]

Knox's account of the deliberations among Governor Ellis and his council during the spring of 1757 contains an accurate summary of the measures which the new administration submitted to the legislature to deal with the most pressing problems of the struggling colony—problems of finance, local defense, and an inadequate population. Although this account probably presents an exaggerated assessment of Knox's own role in the development of the legislative program, the memoir also contains invaluable insights into the ideas and experiences William derived from his political apprenticeship in Georgia.

Of all the problems the Georgia council took up in the spring of 1757, none was more pressing or more tangled than that of finance.[26] The Reynolds administration had almost ruined public credit, and Reynolds had dissolved his first assembly before any financial provision had been made for the following year. This deficit had been compounded by Speaker Little's manipulation of the public accounts for political purposes. When Governor Ellis balanced his predecessor's accounts up to the date of Reynolds' departure (March 25, 1757), a balance of £630, a sum equal to more than two years' ordinary revenue, remained outstanding. Furthermore, no provision had yet been made by Speaker Little's assembly for the first year of Ellis' government, so that the new administration faced a deficit of three years' revenue.

To William Knox the constitutional implications of the financial situation were more abhorrent than its effect on public credit. During the last years of Reynolds' administration, Speaker Little had been allowed to monopolize the management of public funds. This practice had the effect of establishing a precedent whereby the lower house could challenge the executive's traditional claim to exclusive control over the disbursement of public moneys. Even if the governor and his council were able to reclaim this prerogative power in theory, the assembly would in fact retain control over expenditure if deficit financing were allowed to continue, because the practice of obtaining revenue at the end of the fiscal year meant that the executive depended upon the assembly to fulfill prior public engagements to contractors and officeholders. In either case the executive would be placed at the mercy of the assembly.

Given Knox's conception of a true British constitution, such a relationship between the executive and the popular branch of the legislature was intolerable. Throughout his public life, Knox equated a British constitution with the concept of a balanced or mixed constitution. According to this view, which was a common concept in eighteenth-century Britain, the liberties of the subject, as well as the effectiveness of government, depended upon the maintenance of proper balance among the three essential elements of Parliament: the king, the Lords, and the Commons. Each of these elements represented a basic principle in the body politic: the king represented the hereditary principle; the Lords, the aristocratic principle; and the Commons, the democratic principle. In the colonial legislatures the governor filled the role of the king; the council, that of the Lords; and the assembly, that of the Commons. Any usurpation of powers by one of these elements would result in an unbalanced constitution, eventually leading to a despotism of either one person, an oligarchy, or the mob.[27]

It was in this sense that Knox determined to establish a British constitution in Georgia by restoring a proper initiative in fiscal affairs to the colonial executive. And for all his youthful impetuosity, Knox had become alert to the political realities surrounding the fiscal issue. He was especially sensitive to the fact that in dealing with the financial problem Governor Ellis faced the dilemma of "risquing his popularity by reenstating things in their proper order, or of confirming the innovations and thereby confirming to himself a perpetual fund of discord."[28]

Ellis had no intention of forfeiting the popular acclaim which had greeted his arrival by calling for an additional tax to pay off the debts of Reynolds' administration. He initially proposed to the council that current revenues be devoted exclusively to the payment of current expenses, while the problem of Reynolds' deficit should be left to his friends in the assembly. Knox, however, raised the objection that this plan would undoubtedly provoke an immediate deadlock with the assembly. Ellis then proposed that the whole question of the deficit be postponed until the winter session of the legislature, when an attempt could be made to spread the payment of the debt over several years. But Knox disagreed with this suggestion as well, this time on both constitutional and tactical grounds: a failure to deal with the debt immediately would imply an approval of Little's policy of deficit financing, while at the same time the government would lose the popular advantage of identifying the practice with Little's infamous regime. Obviously Knox wished to deal with the debt in a manner that would restore an independent initiative in fiscal affairs to the executive without provoking the assembly to a defense of Speaker Little's precedents. In fact, he had already worked out a scheme designed to achieve both these goals at one stroke.[29]

Specifically, Knox proposed to call in all outstanding accounts to June 24, 1757, rather than March 25, 1757, so that the whole debt could be dealt with at once instead of drawing a line between Reynolds' and Ellis' administrations. Then the funds on hand, derived from both taxes and Reynolds' paper money issues, should be applied to the debt as far as they would go. Next, Knox proposed that a fund be created for discharging the balance of the debt by issuing bills of credit for Reynolds' devalued currency and adding £2,000 more in new bills of credit. Knox anticipated that the fund would bring in revenue from planters, who would borrow the bills at interest secured by mortgages upon their lands and slaves; the bills themselves were to be kept in circulation without depreciation by virtue of their being accepted in payment for public accounts. Knox calculated that the interest arising from the paper currency would pay off the balance of the debt within three years and that the fund could then be used for current expenses. Finally, Knox proposed that once the assembly had approved the paper currency fund for discharging the debt, it should be called upon to provide revenue in advance for one year beginning June 24, 1757. By this scheme Knox expected to reverse the practice of deficit financing in a way that would neither provoke a controversy over new taxes nor lower the state of public credit.

The essential feature of this ingenious but complicated plan was Knox's proposal to tie the payment of the debt to the solution of another major economic problem plaguing the infant colony of Georgia: the shortage of a medium of exchange. At this time practically all the North American colonies complained of the same economic malady, but in Georgia the usual drain of specie to Britain was compounded by an unfavorable balance of trade with the other colonies, particularly with Georgia's relatively wealthy neighbor, South Carolina. Virtually any measure which promised a remedy for the shortage of specie would certainly win the support of the struggling merchants and planters of the colony. Thus Knox's scheme, by linking payment of the debt to provision of a colonial currency, placed the assembly in the difficult position of choosing between its popularity and its privileges.

At first, Governor Ellis considered Knox's scheme too complicated. According to Knox, Ellis, "being unaccustomed . . . [to] such business," did not immediately understand the proposals fully. But the governor eventually accepted the basic outlines of the plan—Knox, in fact, credited him with improving the details considerably. Knox then drew up a bill incorporating his scheme along with Ellis' improvements. On July 16, 1757, the measure was passed by the assembly, and twelve days later it received the governor's assent.[30]

The next step in implementing Knox's overall scheme was that of persuading the assembly to vote supplies immediately for the first year of Ellis' administration, including the arrears accumulated since his arrival. In the summer of 1757, the assembly balked at laying taxes before the winter session, the usual time for such business. But the imminent threat of a Spanish invasion gave the administration an opportunity to pressure the lower house. When the assembly presented an address to the governor requesting that lookouts be stationed along the coast, Ellis replied that he could not act upon the request since no provision had been made for any contingent expenses. After considerable wrangling, the lower house finally agreed in July 1757 to levy a tax which provided for the entire expenses of government from June 24, 1757, to June 24, 1758, including an increase in the estimates for the defense of the colony. The assembly was able to secure a proviso within the bill stipulating that although the tax was levied in the summer of 1757 collection was to be deferred until the following May.[31] Nevertheless, in Knox's view the administration had won its main point: the assembly had provided in advance for the expenses of government, and the executive had gained the initiative in the fiscal affairs of the colony.

Once the question of finance had been resolved, the Ellis administration turned its attention to the interrelated problems of defense and population.[32] It was obvious that unless Georgia protected the lives and property of its inhabitants from the dangers of Indian and Spanish depredations, new settlers would not be attracted to the tiny colony. In June 1757, under the prodding of the executive, the assembly passed a Fortifications Act providing for the erection of log forts at strategic locations throughout the province, and during the months of August and September the whole colony was set to work erecting the stockades. Knox claimed that he personally drew up the fortifications bill and, in fact, the enabling measure named him a commissioner supervising the construction of the forts in Savannah.[33]

Knox did not believe that the Ellis administration could rely solely upon defensive measures to attract new settlers. By his own account, he personally authored the remarkable Asylum Act of 1757, allowing any debtor who took up residence in Georgia to repudiate all debts except those owed to inhabitants of Great Britain, Ireland, or South Carolina. Obviously by this restriction Knox expected to allay unfavorable reaction among those particular segments of the empire that were politically and economically crucial to Georgia's survival. In the same month that the fortifications bill became law, Governor Ellis assented to Knox's asylum bill. The Asylum Act must be placed, however, on the debit side of Knox's contributions to the Ellis administration, for within two years the Board of Trade disapproved this extraordinary measure. Ellis admirably, but with obvious embarrassment, accepted full responsibility for the abortive law. He pointed out to the board that the act was "extremely popular here"; nevertheless, he admitted that the anticipated advantages had never materialized.[34]

During the remainder of the legislative session of 1757, Knox's primary concern was to expand the foundations of a British Constitution in Georgia. From his study of the records of the colony he learned that the legislature had never passed an act initiated by the upper house. He persuaded the council that they must assert this right immediately. Initially the council obtained leave to bring in the fortifications bill in June 1757, but because it was a money bill they withdrew their measure and allowed the assembly to introduce its own version of the bill. Knox was undaunted. With the assistance of Attorney General Clifton, he prepared a Provisions Bill preventing the carrying of provisions to the enemies of Georgia. Knox guided the measure through the upper house, and when the assembly amended the council's bill, he served on a conference committee. Eventually the young councilor's persistence was rewarded: the Provisions Bill became law on July 19, 1757, and Knox secured his constitutional precedent for the initiation of legislation by the upper house of the Georgia legislature.[35]

Within a year of his arrival in Georgia, Knox had every reason to be satisfied with the beginning of his political apprenticeship. According to his own testimony, he had played a major role in launching Governor Ellis' successful administration; above all, he had laid the foundations for establishing a British constitution in the colony. But in spite of his energetic efforts in behalf of the Ellis administration, his personal relations with the governor had not improved.

Knox's account of his relationship with Henry Ellis is of particular interest because it provides perceptive insights into William's character and temperament at this early stage of manhood. Even by his own testimony, William at first impression projected a personality which could only be described as abrasive. He admitted, indeed boasted, that within a short time of his arrival in Georgia he had managed to antagonize several individuals, including political allies whose cooperation was essential to the success of the administration. Nevertheless, the significant fact is that in most instances this hostility was short-lived; once the initial reaction to William's aggressive precocity wore off, his imaginative intelligence, irrepressible temperament, and candid integrity usually converted antagonists into allies and even into personal friends. In contrast, William's alienation from Ellis was unique in its duration. Clearly the bright young favorite of Thomas Knox and Philip Skelton was distressed by Ellis' apparent disregard for his talents. At first, he had doggedly attempted to win Ellis' approval by fully impressing the governor with his prodigious political skill and sagacity. But when Ellis continued to ignore his pretensions, William, insensitive to the novice governor's own predicament and preoccupation, reacted aggressively—first with private criticism and finally with open defiance.

According to Knox, some time during the spring or summer of 1757 Ellis sent him to Charleston for a conference with Governor Lyttelton. He took advantage of the trip to further cultivate the friendship of the governor of South Carolina, and by the time William left Charleston he was convinced that his relationship with

Lyttelton would be "a foundation for a future notice" and that he would thus be delivered "from an absolute dependence on a selfish man."[36] Returning to Savannah, Knox learned that the reports of his activities in Charleston had only served to deepen Ellis' prejudice against him. Their personal relations deteriorated to such an extent that when Knox was taken with a fever while working on the fortifications of Savannah, Ellis showed no apparent concern for the well-being of his young countryman.

The crisis in their relations finally came in the fall of 1757. Since his arrival in Georgia, Henry Ellis had attempted to arrange a meeting with neighboring Indian tribes, and the appearance of a delegation of Creek chiefs in Savannah on October 29, 1757, provided the tiny capital with one of the most important state occasions in its brief colonial history. The ceremonies greeting the Indians included militia drills, cannon salutes, and dinner at the governor's house.[37] Knox was understandably anxious to take part in the crucial conferences with the chiefs, but at the time of their arrival he was in the country and was unable to find transportation to Savannah. When he sent word of his predicament to Ellis, the governor replied that the situation could not be remedied. Knox eventually arrived in Savannah in time to attend the council's meeting with the Indians, where he signed the November 3 treaty of friendship and alliance.[38] Nevertheless, after this episode William was determined to avenge the public humiliation he had suffered at the hands of the governor. His opportunity came within a short time, when Ellis attempted to give away a lot in Savannah which had been previously granted to Knox.[39] The council consented to the change only if Knox agreed. William saw a chance to embarrass Ellis and simultaneously prove to the council that he was not a "subservient creature" of the governor. He refused to give up his grant and declared his intention of building on the lot.

Whatever the cause of the estrangement between Ellis and Knox —jealousy on the part of the governor, as Knox claimed, or Ellis' excessive zeal in avoiding any implications of favoritism—William's sudden defiance cleared the air. Soon after the dispute over the lot in Savannah, Ellis sent for Knox, and following a frank discussion the two Irishmen reached an understanding. According to Knox, they agreed that Ellis "should treat me with more delicacy for the future and I to follow on my own inclinations." Eventually Ellis and Knox became close personal friends and, in fact, the governor would subsequently play an important role in promoting William's public career.

Knox's personal memoir of his first year in Georgia ends abruptly with what he described as "eclaircissement" between himself and Ellis. The public records nonetheless indicate that William steadily attained increasing stature in the affairs of the colony. With his self-esteem vindicated and his personal independence asserted, he settled into the routine of the council with a characteristically scrupulous attention to the details of business. Eventually Governor Ellis felt secure enough to acknowledge Knox's services, even to officials in London. In February 1759, when Ellis wrote to the Board of Trade objecting to the conduct and character of some of the councilors, he renominated William to a reorganized council, commenting that only Knox and Attorney General Clifton possessed the requisite talents for defending the prerogatives of the upper house against encroachments by the assembly.[40]

In addition to his service on the council, Knox also performed the extensive political and administrative duties of the provost marshal's office. In the tiny colony of Georgia the provost marshal performed for the whole province those functions usually carried out by sheriffs in the counties of the larger and more populous colonies.[41] The provost marshal was the returning officer for elections in every parish and district in the colony; he appointed deputies in the various constituencies who conducted the polls under his writ and instructions. Originally the provost marshal of Georgia had also been responsible for both the selection and the summoning of juries in the province, but Governor Reynolds, in his later attempts to woo the assembly, had allowed jury selection to pass under the control of justices of the peace, who were nominated by the lower house. Governor Ellis was able to recover some of the controls over the legal system which Reynolds had abdicated, but an attempt to restore the power of selecting jurors to the provost marshal was defeated. Ellis was able to retrieve only a partial victory for "Juries agreeable to the British Constitution" by having Provost Marshal Knox appointed to the board of justices of the peace.[42]

One of the most important of Knox's duties as provost marshal was his responsibility for the disposition of unclaimed fugitive slaves. The provost marshal was required to hold runaway slaves eighteen months while advertising for their owners and, then, to sell the slaves at public auction if they remained unclaimed at the end of that period. The proceeds of such a sale were paid to the public treasurer after the provost marshal had deducted the expenses incurred in the proceedings.[43] Of course, long before William had become a Georgian, Philip Skelton had instructed his pupil in the comparative barbarism of "*Hottentots* and some other *African* nations." Now Knox's firsthand encounters with the wretched runaways who came under his charge served to reinforce vividly the racial prejudices learned in youth. And in later years he would summon forth the images and impressions of his experiences as provost marshal to provide evidence supporting his published apologias for black slavery.

Knox's predecessor in the office of provost marshal had complained that in Georgia, on the edge of the American wilderness, the inhabitants expected "at least a temporary Indemnity" from civilized due process. Consequently, they had developed an "implacable Aversion" to the provost marshal and made "an incessant endeavor to render the Execution of that Office Impracticable."[44] Even as late as 1773, a governor of Georgia described the office of provost marshal as "attended with much trouble, fatigue and risque."[45]

Under the circumstances, it is rather surprising that such a tenacious champion of British constitutionalism as Knox enjoyed a relatively uneventful tenure as provost marshal. On the other hand, it is no less surprising that William complained that his office brought him inadequate remuneration. The sole income which Knox derived from his public offices in the colony was the provost marshal's salary of £100 per annum, plus the fees attached to various services which at best brought him £50 annually. He complained that the high cost of imported commodities in Georgia made it impossible for him to live on this income as befitted a member of the council, and he claimed that if it had not been for the financial assistance he received from "Europe" he would certainly have become a scandal to his office.[46]

Despite such complaints about his financial situation, Knox was able to attain the status of a substantial property holder within a few years of his arrival in Georgia. From 1757 to 1760, Knox improved and expanded his real properties in Savannah; he also acquired two lots in nearby Yamacraw and two in the town of Hardwick on the Ogeechee River.[47] In colonial Georgia, however, wealth and position were not measured in terms of town properties, so

Knox quickly took advantage of the liberal land policies of the colony and established a plantation. The official requirements for land grants in Georgia were largely determined by the need to attract productive settlers to the colony. Each head of a household who settled in Georgia was entitled to one hundred acres individually and fifty acres for each dependent, white or black; with the approval of the governor the head of a household could purchase up to one thousand acres at the price of one shilling for every ten acres, subject only to the condition that three out of every fifty acres in the grant be planted.

With financial assistance from Ireland, Knox was able to begin purchasing slaves and establishing claims to landed properties in Georgia, eventually expanding his holdings into a considerable estate. After two abortive efforts to secure suitable land, Knox laid claim in 1759 to seven hundred acres of "River Swamp" on Abercorn Creek, about twelve miles north of Savannah. Within the year, with money advanced by a brother in Ireland, William bought fourteen slaves, thereby securing his claim as head of a household. Although the Abercorn swamp property was potentially quite valuable as a source of lumber, it proved to be entirely unsuitable for rice cultivation. Therefore, in February 1760 Knox applied to the council for an additional grant of five hundred acres on the Savannah River, north of the capital, in order to better employ his slaves. Undoubtedly, Knox's position on the council served at least to expedite the business of his land grants before that body. In any case, the council not only approved his new application but also allowed him to retain his swamp properties on Abercorn Creek, apparently under the original terms of purchase. Furthermore, when the Abercorn grant proved upon survey to be only 610 acres, Knox was allowed an additional 50 acres at nearby Goshen.[48] By March 1760, Knox had acquired fourteen slaves, expected to add six more before the end of the year, and was engaged in establishing a rice plantation on his Savannah River property at a moment when the rice planters of Georgia were entering into a period of rapid trade expansion and sharply increasing prosperity.

Thus, within three years of his arrival in Georgia, Knox had every reason to expect that with some skill and a great deal of luck he would soon become a man of wealth in the colony. Yet, despite his rapid rise to a position of political influence and his improving financial prospects, by 1760 he was determined to quit America.[49]

He complained that his scrupulous attention to the public weal of the colony brought him "all the blame of every unpalatable measure." He expressed concern about the debilitating effects of Georgia's climate on his constitution. His correspondence at this time also betrayed some feeling of homesickness for his family in Ireland. But above all his desire to return to Great Britain was inspired by the hope of finding greater opportunities for the employment of his talents.

Knox was well aware that in Britain talent was not likely to receive its due reward without the benefit of patronage. According to his own estimate of the situation, "a young man without Fortune and connections could not engage in public life with any tolerable prospect of success without stooping to the lowest and even criminal drudgery of office, unless he was so happy to find a patron who would disdain to employ him or any one else in such business." For several years he had cultivated the friendship of Governor Lyttelton of South Carolina, so in 1760, when he learned that Lyttelton, the favorite of Secretary of State Pitt, was leaving his post in America to return to England, Knox planned to offer Lyttelton his services. William's hope was that with Lyttelton as his patron he could obtain an ofice in London, perhaps in the Treasury. These speculations were dashed, however, when Lyttelton was appointed governor of Jamaica; for as Knox candidly admitted to his influential friend, he preferred even a minor appointment in Ireland to any office in America.[50]

Undaunted by this setback, Knox had an alternate plan: he proposed to exchange offices with Benjamin Martyn, Georgia's crown agent in London. Since the appointment was the gift of the crown, he asked Lyttelton's help in securing the post. To Lyttelton, Knox readily acknowledged his motives in seeking the position: "I do not so much want the emolument as the office, for I think in that station I should be able to recommend myself." Lyttelton promised to use his influence in Knox's behalf while he was in London, but he warned Knox not to expect too much from his recommendation.[51] The whole scheme miscarried when Martyn showed no interest in giving up his agency, and officials in Georgia refused to press the issue.

By May 1760, Knox admitted that his hopes of obtaining an office in Britain had proven visionary. Furthermore, during the interval he had received belated news from Ireland that his father and his "dearest" brother had died within a few weeks of each other.[52] The double loss of a revered father and a munificent brother dealt him a considerable emotional blow.

These unhappy circumstances also mark an important turning point in the development of William's personality. Subsequently, his attitudes and actions indicate increasing maturity—particularly as his self-centered impetuosity came to be tempered by considered sensitivity toward the feelings and interests of others. It seems more than coincidental that shortly after his father's death William for the first time admitted and openly acknowledged Governor Ellis' considerable contributions to his success and well-being. At the same time William, although the youngest of his father's children, also willingly accepted personal responsibility for the care and comfort of his widowed mother. Above all, he now fully recognized that his fortunes, as well as the fulfillment of his new responsibilities, depended entirely upon his own judgment and resources. For the present he accepted the fact that he had to forego returning to Britain until he had made adequate provision for his support there. Yet even given these new realities, he was reconciled only to a postponement of his departure from America.

Knox was not alone in his desire to take leave of Georgia. After three very successful years of governing the colony, Henry Ellis requested that the Board of Trade relieve him of his duties. Ellis had every reason to be satisfied with his position in Georgia, for the colony had grown and prospered under his administration. But he too complained that his health was deteriorating in the Georgia climate. With the approval of the board, he left Georgia in November 1760. By this time Knox and Ellis were completely reconciled, and before the governor left Georgia he offered to recommend William as his successor, with the title of lieutenant governor.[53] Knox was forced to decline because he felt that his means would not support the dignity of the office, even with the increased salary due the lieutenant governor.

Instead, Ellis was succeeded by James Wright, a native of South Carolina, formerly attorney general of that colony.[54] Knox, who had earlier been persuaded that the influence and example of South Carolinians posed the greatest danger to a British constitution in Georgia, apparently received Wright's appointment with considerable trepidation. But the new governor had been educated in England and had lived in London for several years while acting as agent for South Carolina; he quickly proved to Knox's satisfaction that he entertained none of those repugnant constitutional principles William had attributed categorically to South Carolinians. Soon after the new governor's arrival, Knox commented that Wright was an honest man who acted with the advice of his council. He was immediately on the best of terms with the governor and continued to take an active part in the affairs of the colony.[55]

Shortly after Wright took office, Knox became deeply embroiled in resisting a substantial challenge to that British constitution which he had helped establish in Georgia. This controversy, which eventually comprehended the full range of constitutional relationships among the governor, the council, and the assembly, centered about the person and activities of Chief Justice William Grover.

Although Grover had been appointed to his position during Ellis' administration to assist in bringing order to the legal and judicial system of the colony, he had demonstrated a singular lack of interest in his duties. Ellis had criticized Grover's indolence, but the chief justice had responded by remaining away from his seat on the council. Even after Ellis left Georgia, Grover refused to resume his councillary duties, and when Governor Wright finally ordered his attendance the chief justice resigned from the council.[56]

While Wright pondered the fate of the chief justice, Grover acted to protect his interests.[57] On May 21, 1761, Grover volunteered to appear before the assembly to give testimony regarding the fiscal program which the governor had submitted to the lower house. The assembly accepted Grover's offer, and the chief justice testified to a committee of the whole that the governor's budgetary estimates for the services of colonial officials were unwarranted because the imperial treasury provided adequately for these expenses. On the basis of this evidence, the assembly struck from the budget specific items of expenses for several officials—including £60 for the provost marshal. Subsequently, Governor Wright, with considerable skill and tact, was able to persuade the lower house that these expenditures had been properly assumed by the province in the past. The assembly agreed to restore all such items to the budget—except for £6 for the expenses of the chief justice and a larger sum of £30 previously allotted to the provost marshal to provide for a jailer.

Undoubtedly Provost Marshal Knox was distressed by the loss of this appropriation, but Councilor Knox was equally disturbed by the threat Grover's actions posed for the continuation of a British constitution in Georgia. From Knox's point of view, the precedent of a chief justice and former councilor appearing before the assembly to repudiate the executive's proper fiscal prerogatives represented a dangerous demagogic threat to the mixed and balanced constitution. Knox immediately assumed the chairmanship of a committee appointed by the council to investigate Grover's behavior.[58]

In the course of its investigation during the spring of 1761, Knox's committee was able somehow to gain access not only to the journals of the lower house but also to extracts of Grover's testimony before the committee of the whole. On the basis of this evidence, the council committee reported that the entire proceedings had "reflected upon the Conduct of the Governor and Council of this Province." Knox's committee tactfully conceded that the assembly had had no cause to distrust the information Grover had laid before them, since they did not seem to be aware that his testimony had been motivated primarily by "private Pique or Resentment" against some of the principal officeholders. On the other hand, the conduct of the chief justice in allowing himself to be examined by the assembly was categorically denounced as a "President [sic] which your Committee apprehend to be of most dangerous Consequences and intirely subversive of the Constitution of the General Assembly of this Province as established by His Majesty's Commission and Royal Instructions to his Governor." The committee explicitly reaffirmed the council's position as an integral but independent branch of the royal government of the province. Finally, the report not only justified the specific budgetary expenditures to which the lower house had taken exception but also repudiated, as "the highest Ingratitude to our Mother Country," Grover's argument that such expenses fell properly to the imperial exchequer.[59]

On June 9, 1761, the full council laid the committee's report before Governor Wright and requested that its findings be sent to the Lords of Trade, along with an address to the governor reaffirming the council's loyalty to a British constitution: "Permit us to assure your Honour of our unalterable Affection to His Majestys Person and Government and of our steady Resolution to support your Honour in asserting and maintaining the just Rights and Prerogative of the Crown in Contempt of the Claims of factions or the malicious suggestions of restless and wicked Men."[60] Wright forwarded the council's report and address to Whitehall as well as his own account, which essentially supported the conclusions of the upper house. Even the Georgia assembly became disenchanted with the chief justice when Grover subsequently launched a libelous campaign of public abuse against the popular governor. Finally, in 1763, the Board of Trade in London upheld the committee's recommendations and had Grover dismissed as chief justice.[61]

Within five years of his arrival in Georgia, William Knox, who was only thirty years of age in 1762, had become in his own right a figure of considerable political influence and promise. No less impressive was his continuing rise to the status of a substantial landholder.[62] Between 1760 and 1762, in five separate transactions, he purchased a total of 450 acres of land near the settlement of Goshen. During the same period he was also awarded sizable grants of land distributed among three parishes: 145 additional acres in Christ Church parish, 1,100 acres in the adjacent St. Matthew's parish, and 315 acres in St. Philip's parish on the Great Ogeechee River. These acquisitions, when added to his previous landholdings, gave him a total of approximately 3,170 acres of land; of this figure, approximately 1,000 acres had been acquired by purchase or headright claim and 2,170 by conditional grant.

In the midst of success and prosperity, however, providence suddenly and dramatically reminded William of the transient and fleeting nature of things of this world. In the summer of 1761, he was struck by lightning.[63] Although he reported to a brother that he had suffered no injury "save the loss of a hatt and the coat I had on which were burned or tore in pieces," the emotional and psychological impact of this trauma was decisive. For a man of William's Calvinistic persuasion, his encounter with divine providence was undoubtedly an occasion for taking stock, especially of the use to which he had put his self-proclaimed talents. In the very letter which recounted his close call with death, William informed his brother that he was making preparations to return to Europe by the following spring. He even qualified this welcome prospect with a note of uncharacteristic but revealing pessimism and introspection: "As the character of my fortune has always been disappointment, in my views tho' not to my disadvantage, I scarce dare flatter myself with the thoughts of returning so soon."

In fact, the opportunity for Knox to return to Britain came rather promptly. In December 1761, the Georgia assembly appointed him to serve as its agent in London.[64] By February 1762, William had completed arrangements for his departure. He had obtained leave of the British government to return to England and had farmed his office of provost marshal to a deputy, who agreed to pay Knox £60 per annum even though Knox retained the salary of £100 per annum. He was also able to lease his plantations and his slaves in Georgia for £130 per annum. The assembly granted him a yearly salary of £50 as colonial agent. Knox was satisfied that the £340 per annum which he would receive from his Georgia offices and properties plus an unspecified income from Irish interests would allow him to live in relative comfort in London.[65]

Before he left Georgia, Knox was disturbed by the news that Lord Halifax had left the Board of Trade in March 1761. He regarded this event as a blow to his ambitions, for he was known to no other officials in the imperial government, and he recognized that such a situation might hamper his effectiveness before the Board of Trade. But even this disappointment could not dampen his enthusiasm for the opportunity of displaying his talents in the imperial capital. On the eve of his departure, Knox wrote Lyttelton of his hope that in London an "upright conduct" would overcome the handicap of having "few friends to depend on."[66]

Knox betrayed little reluctance to leave Georgia. He obviously believed that America offered only limited advantages to a man of his ambitions and abilities. Yet his experiences in America, particularly the fact that he served his political apprenticeship in Georgia, had significant consequences for his future career.

Knox was returning to England at the close of the Seven Years' War, a time when firsthand knowledge of the colonies was at a premium in the councils of British statesmen. His recent experiences in Georgia would give him impressive credentials as a colonial expert and would thus provide him with unusual opportunities for gaining the notice of influential politicians in England—an advantage he would not hesitate to exploit fully. Above all, his Georgia experiences affected his particular outlook on imperial issues. Constitutional relationships in William Knox's Georgia were unique. In most of the older colonies, over many years, the assemblies had extended and consolidated their authority at the expense of that of the royal governors and their councils. By the third quarter of the eighteenth century, colonial assemblies had generally seized the initiative in such areas as finance and public appointments and were even challenging the royal executive in the sphere of policy making.[67] But Knox served his political apprenticeship in a colony which had not yet reached this stage of constitutional and political evolution. Even by the time of William's departure from Georgia, the royal governor still held the initiative in colonial government, while the council retained significant powers as the upper house of the legislature.[68] These circumstances were due in part to the skill and the restraint which marked the administrations of Governors Ellis and Wright. More important was the fact that in Georgia the assembly was unable to secure exclusive control of the purse strings. Since a large part of the public expenses of the young colony, particularly the salaries of civil officials, was borne by the imperial exchequer, the Georgia executive was not at the mercy of the lower house. But whatever the reasons for these unique circumstances, Knox certainly believed that the relationships between the governor, the council, and the assembly of Georgia represented a true British constitution.

During his stay in America, Knox had become fully aware of the growing independence of the assemblies in the other Continental colonies. In fact, several years before he left America—on the occasion of Governor Lyttelton's transfer from South Carolina to Jamaica —Knox had written: "The British Ministry are better judges of merit than the sordid Legislators of Carolina, of whom I think, it may now, without any injustice, be said that no King can govern nor no God can please."[69] William Knox returned to Great Britain convinced that overmighty colonial assemblies posed the greatest potential threat to the imperial connection.

3. "Dancing Attendance upon People in Office": Imperial Problems & the Georgia Agency, 1762–1765

William Knox arrived in Great Britain early in 1762. He returned to the seat of empire at a decisive and opportune moment—during the last phase of the Seven Years' War, when the intoxicating thrill of victory was becoming increasingly dulled by the sobering prospects of expanded imperial responsibilities. By this time Britain, under the great war ministry of William Pitt, had already stripped France of its most important colonial possessions. The British public had been awed and exhilarated by a succession of exotic imperial conquests. After Quebec was taken in 1759, Horace Walpole had been moved to exclaim that like Alexander Britain had no more worlds left to conquer. Municipalities had showered tributes upon Pitt, the architect of victory. Yet within a short time political circles and public opinion were engaged in debate over the feasibility of returning various imperial conquests as the price of peace with France, with Canada and the sugar island of Guadeloupe being the main alternative concessions discussed after 1760.

By the time Knox reached Britain, the Pitt-Newcastle war coalition had disintegrated. The personal animosity which had long existed between Pitt and Newcastle rendered their ministry tenuous even while the tide of victory flowed. Nearing the shores of peace, their joint command was wrecked upon the rocks of cabinet dissension. First Pitt resigned in October 1761; then Newcastle fell from office in May 1762.

George III had no reason to regret the dissolution of the war ministry inherited from his grandfather. Even before his accession to the throne in 1760, the idealistic young king bore personal grudges against both Newcastle and Pitt. Although George III did not instigate the downfall of the two ministers, he obviously withheld his support from them during the separate cabinet crises which led to their resignations. Subsequently, George III and his Scots favorite, the Earl of Bute, undertook the guidance of the affairs of state—the most pressing business being the settlement of peace with the Bourbon powers and the collateral problems involved in managing the fruits of victory which, of course, included sizable slices of colonial territory. These circumstances proved quite propitious for the career of an ambitious colonial official recently returned to the capital from the frontier of the empire.

On April 28, 1762, William Knox was welcomed to England by Henry Ellis. The governor was at the resort town of Bath, where he was still recuperating from the ill-effects of Georgia's climate upon his health. He urged Knox to defer making an appearance before the Board of Trade long enough to pay him a visit and bring him up to date on the affairs of Georgia.[1] But when Knox indicated that he was anxious to enter into the business of his agency, Ellis generously offered to provide him with a letter of introduction to John Pownall, the secretary to the Board of Trade. At the same time, the governor characteristically cautioned Knox against impatience and gave him sound advice: "You must have time to look about you, to survey the ground you stand upon and to know the men you will have to do with and the way to avail yourself of them. You may freely command my assistance in these things, who am now a veteran in soliciting and dancing attendance upon people in office."[2] Ellis' offer of help was no idle boast, for within official circles in London the governor had come to be regarded as chief advisor on imperial affairs to Secretary of State Egremont.[3]

Knox quickly demonstrated that he himself was something of a prodigy in the art of courting favor among British officialdom. Before the end of the year he had become acquainted with Dr. Philip Francis, who was closely attached to the household of Henry Fox.[4] In December 1762, Fox—whom George III and Bute had placed in charge of government forces in the Commons—was engaged in marshaling parliamentary support for the anticipated confrontation with Pitt and Newcastle over the preliminaries of the treaty of peace with France. There was little question that in the debates the colonial provisions of the treaty would be a prime target of Pitt's oratory. Dr. Francis was apparently convinced that Knox's firsthand knowledge of America would be useful to Fox, and he introduced William to his patron and also to the Earl of Shelburne, at that time a rising young protégé of Bute. Shelburne was preparing an address supporting the terms of the French treaty for delivery before the House of Lords, and Knox furnished him with "some materials" for his speech.[5] Although Fox quite typically told William that "it was Numbers and not arg[uments] that he depended upon" to win the day in the House of Commons, he was obliged for Knox's assistance to Shelburne, and as Dr. Francis explained, Fox expected "nobody to do anything for nothing." He offered Knox an office in the newly acquired colonial territories in return for his assistance to Shelburne. Knox declined because he claimed that he "could not endure to be obliged to a man who I heard so ill spoken of everywhere." Undoubtedly, Knox's self-righteous concern about Fox's reputation —notorious even by eighteenth-century standards—was sustained by his distaste for returning to office in America. Moreover, by 1763 he enjoyed several alternative prospects for improving his political connections in England.

At about the same time that Knox was assisting Shelburne with his speech supporting the peace preliminaries, he happened to dine in company with John Huske, Charles Townshend's chief lieutenant.[6] According to Knox, Huske was engaged in collecting information for Townshend concerning the new colonial acquisitions in America, and after hearing William comment upon the "advantages to be derived from the Floridas," Huske introduced Knox to his chief.

At this time Townshend held the post of secretary at war in the Bute ministry, and politicians, including members of the Government, generally regarded this brilliant but fickle *enfant terrible* of contemporary politics with a cautious mixture of admiration and suspicion. Even George III was apprehensive of Townshend's capricious genius, as, for example, when he reported to Bute on November 10, 1762, that in conversation Townshend appeared lukewarm toward the French treaty. In this instance Knox had probably been an unwitting instrument of the king's distress, for according to George III, Townshend in his remarks upon the peace preliminaries had dwelled upon the acquisition of Florida, first discounting its value and then insisting upon his own ability to exploit fully the potential advantages of the new territory.[7]

Knox, political novice as he was, must have been awed by Townshend's nimble but erratic political gyrations during the last two months of 1762 and the first few months of 1763.[8] On November 25, in the Commons debate on the Address from the Throne, Townshend spoke in favor of the peace preliminaries and particularly defended the value of Florida in response to opposition attacks upon the barrenness of the region. Yet on December 8, Townshend summarily resigned from the Bute ministry, the common speculation being that he intended to collaborate with Pitt and Newcastle in opposing parliamentary approval of the preliminaries of peace. The next day in the Commons, however, Townshend joined in support of his recent colleagues on the Government side and delivered a brilliant speech in defense of the settlement with France. Finally, he brought his bewildering gambit full circle when he returned to the Bute government as president of the Board of Trade in March 1763—scarcely a month before Bute himself relinquished power.

If Knox was perhaps confused by the political maneuvers of his mercuric new friend, he was nonetheless impressed with Townshend's penetrating judgment regarding the political behavior of his contemporaries. On March 28, 1763, Townshend and Knox witnessed the debate in the House of Lords on Bute's unpopular Cider Tax. Public opinion was in an uproar; the Commons had passed the bill only after an unusually sharp contest. Now in the Lords' debate, Bute and his administration were subjected to a sound chastisement, with two formal protests being tabled by dissident peers even after the measure passed the House. Townshend came away from the proceedings convinced that Bute had been delivered a "death blow." He invited Knox to accompany him home and at dinner treated his guest to an analysis of the day's events. Knox retained a vivid recollection of the "entertaining" and "eccentrick" scene—Townshend walking about the room, never touching his dinner, while he proclaimed:

> "The Burial is gone by, Knox (says he); Lord Pomfret and Lord Denby the two black staves men. Whose funeral is that? Lord Bute's. Then comes Lord Hillsborough, tolling the great bell —bum bum." Those three [Knox observed] were the only lords that had declared themselves attach'd to Lord Bute in the debate, and their manner of speaking, which [Townshend] took off, made the allusion highly ridiculous. "Do you know (says he again) the meaning of the other speeches you heard? The Duke of Newcastle said, My Lord Bute, you thought it was an easy thing to govern this country thro' the King's favour. Now I can tell you that altho' I had as full possession of the late King as you have of the present, I found it necessary to take the great connexions of the country with me, which you

45

are endeavouring to break and oppose; but, take my word for it, you will find your seat at the Treasury an uneasy one if you dont change your plan, of which what passes here this night is only a specimen. Then Lord Mansfield. My Lord Bute, you gave me reason to think I should be of your Cabinet, but you have neglected me, and paid less attention to my recommendations than you ought. I will now shew you that I can punish you if I chuse to do it, but as I don't mean to break with you, but only to teach you to behave better for the future, I will bring you off now."[9]

For Knox the essential political lesson was obvious: in England, as much as in Ireland and America, the stability of a balanced constitution depended primarily upon the attachment to Government of the "great men" of the body politic.

Indeed, within a month of the Lords' debate on the cider bill, Bute resigned from office. Townshend, who refused to continue in a ministry which was being reconstituted under the lead of George Grenville, left office the day before Bute. Although Knox remained on friendly terms with Townshend, he seems to have abandoned any hopes he may have entertained of attaching his fortunes to the ex-minister's bright but erratic star.

Although Knox's first political associations in England appeared to be more instructive than promising, he continued to enjoy unusual opportunities for displaying his talents and his expertise before imperial officials. The Seven Years' War not only had the effect of stimulating widespread interest in colonies and focusing public attention on imperial economics and politics, but the culmination of the great war for empire in the Treaty of Paris of 1763 also presented the British government with immediate problems of providing for the administration of new colonial possessions. The two officials directly responsible for colonial policy in 1763—Lord Egremont, the Southern secretary, and Lord Shelburne, who had replaced Townshend as president of the Board of Trade—relied heavily upon the advice of colonial "experts."[10] Henry Ellis served as chief adviser to Egremont, while Shelburne was ably assisted by John Pownall, the veteran secretary of the Board of Trade. In turn, both Ellis and Pownall solicited information from William Knox.

Early in 1763, Egremont and Ellis began developing a comprehensive program for North America. The fruits of their joint deliberations emerged officially in Egremont's directive of May 5, 1763, addressed to the Board of Trade. The directive itself only called upon the board to prepare a report on the newly acquired territories in America. Specifically requested were recommendations for obtaining maximum commercial advantages from these acquisitions, for governing the new provinces, for defending the North American continent as a whole, for raising colonial contributions toward imperial expenses, and for regulating Indian affairs. Along with his directive, however, Secretary Egremont submitted definite policy proposals to the Board of Trade in the form of a document entitled "Hints Relative to the Division and Government of the Conquered and Newly Acquired Countries in America."[11] Although Henry Ellis was primarily responsible for drawing up this document, both the general approach and the specific recommendations indicate that the governor's protégé, William Knox, contributed substantially to these "Hints."

Ellis and Knox's "Hints" specifically recommended the erection of a western boundary prohibiting new settlements in the trans-Appalachian regions, the administration of interior territories beyond this line by military authorities, and the creation of four distinct jurisdictions in the newly conquered provinces—East and West Florida and Upper and Lower Canada. The authors justified the western boundary as a means of directing the emigration of surplus population in America toward Nova Scotia and the southern frontier, "where they would be useful to the Mother Country, instead of planting themselves in the Heart of America, out of reach of Government, and where, from the great Difficulty of procuring European Commodities, they would be compelled to commerce Manufacturs to the infinite prejudice of Britain." For a time the projected Canadian provinces, each with French-Canadian majorities, would be best administered by only a governor and a council; however, representative government should be granted to His Majesty's new Canadian subjects "when Circumstances are so much changed as to render it expedient." In contrast, the "Hints" recommended that the two provinces in Florida, which the authors assumed would be settled by British and foreign Protestants, be at once granted self-government—in a form, however, modeled upon the governments of Georgia or Nova Scotia, which were described as "the freest from a Republican Mixture, and the most conformable to the British Constitution of any that obtains amongst our Colonies in North America."

Egremont's directive of May 5, in conjunction with Ellis and Knox's "Hints," established the broad outlines of American policy in 1763. The Board of Trade was left the alternatives of either filling in the details of Egremont's plan or devising a distinct plan of its own. Shelburne resented Secretary Egremont's encroachment upon what he regarded as his own jurisdiction and claimed the same dominant control of colonial affairs which had characterized the Earl of Halifax's presidency during the 1750s. But Shelburne was in no position to make his claims effective. He had entered the board through the influence of Bute, and after Bute's resignation Shelburne's position in the reconstituted Grenville ministry was difficult from the first. Moreover, Shelburne was admittedly ignorant of colonial affairs when he assumed his duties at the Board of Trade. Although unable to remedy the stigma of his attachment to Bute, Shelburne energetically attempted to master the business before the board as quickly as possible. In particular, he sought the expert advice of men who had experience in America, including William Knox, who had recently assisted him with his speech on the peace preliminaries.

Knox found himself in a paradoxical situation. He was aware of the jealousy which existed between Egremont and Shelburne and also of the fact that their rivalry was seconded—indeed, according to Knox it was incited—by their respective chief lieutenants, Henry Ellis and John Pownall.[12] In one sense the situation provided an enviable opportunity for Knox to ingratiate himself with those who held the keys to official favor; on the other hand, the jealousy of the rivals was an obvious pitfall to the ambitious office seeker. Knox decided to steer a middle course: he made his services available to both sides and skillfully, or perhaps fortunately, avoided arousing the resentment of any of the principals in the dispute.

Possibly Knox was bemused by the ironic turn of events when Shelburne sought his comments upon the queries contained in Egremont's directive of May 5. Knox apparently carried out his charge without betraying his double agency. Undoubtedly, he welcomed the opportunity to develop fully his own ideas on imperial affairs without the mediating influence of Henry Ellis. Knox quickly provided Shelburne with a commentary of eight half-folio pages dealing with the specific points raised in Egremont's directive.[13]

The overriding principle of empire which permeated Knox's recommendations to Shelburne was the classic model of mercantilism. Considerations of territorial expansion for its own sake or concern for the sentimental union of common cultures remained subordinate to the balance sheet of commercial advantages for Great Britain. Knox explicitly discounted the heterogeneous motives which had originally inspired colonization in favor of a single postulate: "The British Colonies are to be regarded in no other Light, but as subservient to the Commerce of their Mother Country; the Colonists are merely Factors for the Purposes of Trade, and in all considerations concerning the Colonies, *this* must be always the leading Idea." If the goal of Britain was to establish a territorial empire, or what Knox called a "great Empire in America," then inland settlements should be allowed. Of course, Knox predicted (in agreement with a similar prophecy in his and Ellis' "Hints") that the inland colonists, lacking communication with Europe, would certainly turn their attention to manufactures in competition with those of Britain. If, on the contrary, Britain's commercial advantage rather than its territorial expansion remained the polestar of imperial policy, settlers in America should be restricted as near as possible to the ocean, so that they might continue exporting bulky commodities while importing the products of Britain. Knox not only advised Shelburne to accept the recommended western boundary for America, but he also suggested that British troops be stationed in the former French forts to "restrain the colonies at present as well as formerly." Of course, Knox recognized that such a step might arouse suspicion in America, and so he blatantly commented that "The Pretences for this Regulation, must be the keeping of the Indians in subjection, and making of Roads."

Although Knox's advice to Shelburne regarding the jurisdictions of the new provinces generally paralleled the recommendations of the "Hints," there were some significant additions. Besides the division of both Canada and Florida into two governments, Knox recommended at least one separate jurisdiction for the ceded lands along the Mississippi which had formerly been part of French Louisiana. He also suggested that in all new territories the common law of England should apply with few exceptions and that all future statutes adopted by the respective governments should not be repugnant to either the laws or the commercial interests of Great Britain.

Finally, Knox took up the issue of obtaining colonial contributions for the imperial treasury—a question raised in Egremont's directive to the board but not treated in Ellis and Knox's "Hints." To Shelburne, Knox recommended a tax on colonial exports and imports, excepting goods exported and imported between Great Britain and America or traded between Continental provinces. He reasoned that such levies would not only be the most satisfactory and equitable mode of raising revenue from the point of view of the colonists but would also serve to direct colonial trade toward Great Britain. Since these duties would increase annually in proportion to increases in the trade, wealth, and population of America, they would provide a fair and flexible means of contributing to appropriate civil and military establishments in the colonies. Knox further proposed several fiscal concessions designed to reconcile the colonists to his tax scheme. He argued that any surplus revenue raised by such taxes should go into a fund to provide the colonies with a stable medium of exchange and, also, that quitrents should be abolished, at least near commercial centers, in return for colonial revenue from port duties. Most significant of all, Knox argued that if the projected American port duties proved deficient for the colonial civil and military establishments, the deficit should be made up by Parliament, "because if the Provinces do not carry on any considerable foreign Trade, it is unjust and impolitic to load them with Taxes."

Knox's memorandum to Shelburne was at best a limited, though revealing, commentary on the specific points raised in Egremont's directive. Shelburne's request for information, however, prompted Knox, during the spring of 1763, to draw up several additional papers which encompassed and integrated virtually the full range of his ideas for imperial consolidation and reform.

With respect to the projected colony of East Florida, for example, Knox supplied Shelburne with recommendations for the development of the new colony in a detailed paper entitled "Hints respecting the Settlement and Culture of East Florida."[14] Here Knox advised that the northern boundary of East Florida be set on a line running from the mouth of the St. Marys River to its source and thence west to the Flint River. Next, he speculated that since this boundary would place East Florida in nearly the same latitude as Egypt and since the new province was said to have the same soil and climate as Egypt, East Florida could produce similar commodities. Specifically, he suggested that a bounty be granted for encouraging the cultivation of cotton in Florida. He also recommended that the climate of Florida would be particularly conducive to the production of indigo and silk. In a companion piece, he carried on the analogy between the climate of Florida and that of Mediterranean lands. He suggested that the imperial government promote the transplanting of Christian Greeks to East Florida because the physical constitutions and the economic skills of these people would be particularly suited to the environment of the new province.[15]

The task of synthesizing the mass of data, schemes, and recommendations which Shelburne had collected from various sources into a formal report on American policy for consideration by the Lords of Trade fell primarily to John Pownall, the experienced and efficient secretary to the board. Pownall contributed his own draft proposals, while several people assisted in the revisions.[16] Nevertheless, the final draft report of the Board of Trade, which was completed on June 8, 1763, essentially ratified and elaborated with few changes the specific measures originally suggested in Egremont's directive and Ellis and Knox's "Hints." The outstanding exception was Pownall's rejection of two separate governmental jurisdictions for Canada, with the final proclamation of October 7, 1763, providing only a single province of Quebec. On the other hand, Pownall, who admittedly possessed little knowledge of the region about the Gulf of Mexico, agreed to the division of Florida and also incorporated Knox's proposed boundaries for the province of East Florida into the Proclamation of 1763. Although there is no evidence that Knox's suggestions regarding the potential products and colonists for Florida aroused any immediate interest among colonial officials, subsequently events in East Florida proved that these proposals were far from visionary. In 1768, Dr. Andrew Turnbull established a colony of Greeks, Minorcans, and Italians at New Smyrna in East Florida, and by 1773 the settlement was in flourishing condition. Particularly remarkable was the annual production of indigo, which had reached "respectable proportions."[17]

Such issues as frontier boundaries, colonial economic development, Indian policy, and similar immediate considerations, which were of primary concern to imperial officials, were of only secondary importance to Knox. He had returned from America convinced that the existing colonial constitutions threatened the unity, indeed the very existence, of the empire. Along with his specific responses to the matters raised in Egremont's directive, Knox had also provided Shelburne with a comprehensive scheme for colonial reform.[18] In a lengthy manuscript, Knox not only extended and refined his previous recommendations for restricting colonial expansion and creating and supporting a military establishment in America, but he also provided extensive observations and proposals regarding the "defects in the Constitutions and modes of go[vernment] of the N[orth] A[merican] p[rovinces]."

The basic assumption of Knox's critique of colonial constitutions was that in structure and operation the "civil establishments" in America served to promote divisive tendencies within the imperial connection. In effect, Knox upheld as his ideal the model of a balanced or mixed constitution, just as he had during his years of service on the Georgia council, and he concluded that the common constitutional defect in all colonies was the relative weakness of the royal executive vis-à-vis the popular assemblies. He argued that the pernicious effects of such relationships were at their worst in charter and proprietary colonies, for wherever the executive was responsible to proprietors or to the populace, as was the case in some charter colonies, the particular interests of the localities consistently prevailed over common imperial considerations. Knox insisted that even the sacrosanct principles and policies of mercantilism were thereby undermined: "Where the Governor and all Civil Officers canvass for Votes, and are annually Elected by the People, it will scarcely be expected that the Laws of Trade, will be carried into strict execution; no more is it to be supposed that they will be duly observed, where the riches of the Proprietor consists in the number of Inhabitants, which he can induce to Settle in his Domain." The privileges and immunities which proprietary and charter colonies enjoyed were doubly pernicious because their very existence inspired demands for similar concessions in royal colonies.

In a remarkable passage, Knox characterized the perpetuation of such circumstances as "a policy nearly resembling that of Fathers who carry their Sons to disorderly Houses in order by the excessive licentiousness in those places, to shock the young mind and give it a stronger bias to Virtue." This simile inexorably led Knox to a conclusion which provides an enlightening insight into his essential orientation toward human behavior: "He must surely be very inattentive to what passes within himself, who does not know that Ignorance of Vice is the best preservation of Virtue, and that those are most likely to be contented in a humble sphere who never moved in a higher one." The lessons of Thomas Knox and Philip Skelton loomed large in William's view of human relationships. Even within the compass of an empire, the trustees of benevolent paternalism were obliged to save dependents from themselves.

As a first step in constitutional reform for America, Knox advised that the charters of Rhode Island and Connecticut be revoked and that the proprietary interests in Pennsylvania be purchased. In his opinion, such measures were beyond the competence of the crown in law or in practice and could only be implemented under the aegis of parliamentary sovereignty, "because no other Authority than that of the British Parliament will be regarded by the Colonys, or be able to awe them into acquiescence."

Once such measures had been accomplished, all the colonial constitutions could be reformed along the lines of the royal colonies. But even this model contained defects in structure and practice which hampered the efficacy of the colonial executive and thus undermined imperial authority. In particular, Knox pointed out that the executive in a royal colony possessed neither the human nor the material resources necessary to assert and maintain the prerogatives and interests of the imperial crown, because royal officials from governors down to revenue officials were fiscally dependent to a greater or lesser degree upon the popular branch of the legislature. To remedy this crucial defect Knox recommended that royal officials, especially revenue officers, be made entirely dependent upon the crown for their salaries. He suggested that provincial quitrents might be consolidated into a general fund to defray the cost of such a plan, but he admitted that some other source might be "more eligible" for the purpose. Although he did not offer a specific alternative for supporting the American civil establishment, elsewhere in this document he again advanced his scheme of colonial export and import duties as the best means of providing for a military establishment in America.

Knox argued that the next greatest defect in colonial constitutions was the ambivalent and impotent position of the councils. He pointed out that neither the royal commissions nor the instructions to governors declared clearly whether the colonial councils constituted a distinctly separate branch of the legislature, with independent powers to propose and amend bills, or whether they were only a dependent privy council serving as an advisory body to the governor. The absence of such a definition meant continual contests with the popular assemblies over the legislative role of the councils. Knox insisted that, in fact, the governor's power of suspending councilors without demonstrating cause served equally to undermine the constitutional integrity of the upper house. In combination these factors rendered the provincial councils constitutionally dependent and politically impotent. In Knox's words, "a Seat in his Majesties Council is become a standing Object of Patriotick derision in all the Colonys." Consequently, great men of "influence" and "connection" in the colonies were not attracted to service on provincial councils.

Although Knox did not explicitly draw comparisons between the ideal balanced constitution and royal government as it existed in America, such conclusions would have been unnecesary for a generation steeped in these principles. Obviously the fiscal dependence of colonial executives upon the assemblies, in conjunction with the institutional weakness of the aristocratic or oligarchic element in the provincial constitutions, implied a dangerous imbalance in favor of the popular element in colonial society. Equally apparent was the fact that in such circumstances the colonial executive would be at a distinct disadvantage in any attempt to carry out unpalatable imperial policies in America.

More than a decade later, William Knox's far-reaching proposals for colonial constitutional reform would arouse considerable interest and support within the government. In 1763, however, the attention of politicians and officials was fixed upon the more immediate problems raised by the acquisition of vast new colonial territories. Shelburne does not seem to have paid any attention to the constitutional observations and recommendations Knox addressed to him. In any case, since Shelburne's position in the Grenville government became patently tenuous during the summer of 1763, his opinion ceased to be of great consequence to Knox. In fact, by this time William had been able to attach his fortunes to a more sympathetic and more influential patron in the person of Richard, Baron Grosvenor.

The surviving sources provide no clue regarding Knox's introduction to Grosvenor and only meager information regarding the nature of his relationship with his new patron. Knox himself only commented that some time after he had prepared his paper on the defects of the colonial constitutions for Shelburne, he gave a copy to Grosvenor, who was so impressed with the work that he showed it to Lord Bute.[19] Grosvenor was one of the more influential members of that group of eighteenth-century parliamentarians generally known as independent country gentlemen. He had held a seat in the Commons from 1754 until 1761, when he was raised to the peerage on Pitt's recommendation. In subsequent years he continued to dominate the two parliamentary seats of the corporation of Chester, particularly employing his political influence in support of George Grenville's administration and, later, Lord North's ministry.[20] By June 1763, Grosvenor had not only accepted Knox as his protégé but had also demonstrated the efficacy of his patronage by securing a promise from Secretary Egremont that Knox would be appointed agent for East Florida once the new colony was officially established.[21]

In the same month, Grosvenor and Knox left England for a tour of France. William's firsthand observations of the condition of his country's great rival during the aftermath of the war for empire were to exercise a profound influence upon his imperial thought. Most immediately, he was absorbed in the usual interests of contemporary English tourists: he recorded vividly the thrill he experienced at the sight of the French king riding in procession to a day of shooting, and he was surprised to find that English dogs, horses, clothes, and roast beef were the fashion in France. But during this holiday Knox was above all an interested and acute observer of the political and economic circumstances of the Bourbon kingdom. He left Paris and toured the French countryside, and everywhere he was struck by the potential strength of the nation which had only recently capitulated to Great Britain. In a letter to Charles Townshend, Knox commented particularly upon the flourishing state of French agriculture and the extent of agricultural improvement.[22] He also remarked upon the great amounts of specie circulating in a country which only a year before had been unable to raise new taxes to finance the war. Knox was so impressed that he wrote Townshend, "Do you imagine had Mr. Pitt or yourself been Minister to the Grand Monarque, that England would now have enjoyd the

Treaty of Paris?" For the moment the question was indeed rhetorical, but its implications deeply affected Knox's thought.

Shortly after Knox returned to England, he drew up a manuscript in which he applied the lessons of his French tour to matters of British commercial and colonial policies.[23] He was convinced that France would not "sit down contented under England's superiority" for long but would attempt to overturn the decisions of war—if not by an immediate resort to arms, then certainly by economic rivalry. The entire thrust of his argument betrayed, above all, a deep fear that Britain would not be able to withstand the concerted challenge of France's massive advantages in human and material resources. Only by a comprehensive implementation of the principles and practices of mercantilism could the British empire preserve its foreign trade—the ultimate source of national power—from French encroachment. Under this impetus Knox determined that colonies should be required not only to provide markets and raw materials but also to contribute revenue, because by his reckoning British manufacturers and merchants would be able to compete successfully with France in international trade only if part of their tax burden for imperial defense and administration was redistributed among members of the empire. In this document, Knox omitted any specific suggestions for drawing revenue from the colonies, because he had already done so in "another paper"—undoubtedly a reference to the proposals for colonial import and export duties contained in his plan for reform of the imperial civil and military establishments. On the other hand, he did reveal the comprehensive sweep of his imperial perspective by suggesting that Ireland's contribution to the empire might be increased in exchange for commercial concessions.

While Grosvenor and Knox were in France, Secretary Egremont had died in office before he could fulfill his promise to appoint Knox agent for East Florida. And when Henry Ellis subsequently retired from public life, Knox was deprived of his only intimate connection within the colonial establishment at Whitehall. Nevertheless, William's attachment to Grosvenor more than compensated for the loss of Ellis' influence. In October 1763, Grosvenor wrote directly to George Grenville, reminding him of Egremont's promise to Knox. Grenville's reply contained the usual references to the "multitude of recommendations" and the many commitments which had circumscribed and delayed the appointment, but he was now delighted to report that because of his "great Regard" for Grosvenor, he was able to appoint his lordship's "Friend Mr. Knox" to the post.[24]

Although Knox's new East Florida appointment was substantially more lucrative than his Georgia agency, he continued to prize the latter post as an independent means for recommending himself to the attention of British officials. Certainly during the first two years of his Georgia agency Knox exploited fully and successfully those opportunities which attended the performance of his official duties. By no means, however, did he neglect or even slight the interests of his Georgia constituents for the sake of personal advancement. For over two years, he diligently represented Georgia before the imperial government in a manner which earned the explicit confidence and approbation of the colonial legislature.

Knox's original commission as agent for Georgia required that he act in conjunction with the crown agent, Benjamin Martyn. Martyn had served Georgia faithfully since the days of trustee rule; nevertheless, his primary responsibility was to the crown, which controlled both his tenure and his income. By 1762, the trading interests of Georgia had developed to such an extent that merchants and planters in the colony were no longer satisfied with this arrangement—they wanted an agent in London who would represent their particular interests and would be responsible to the colonial legislature.[25]

In November 1762, the Georgia legislature reviewed the letters and papers dealing with Knox's activities during his first year as assistant agent to Martyn. At the end of these deliberations, early in 1763, Knox was granted sole authority to represent the colonial legislature before the British government. In addition, his annual salary was increased to £100 over and above the expenses incurred on his "Application to the several offices and Boards in Negotiating the Affairs of this Province."[26] Finally, on March 2, 1763, the Georgia legislature approved a series of resolutions listing the measures Knox was to promote before the royal government. These instructions contained four basic recommendations: (1) he should endeavor to acquire for the governor the power of purchasing such Indian lands "as are indispensibly necessary for the immediate Improvement of the Province which [the imperial government has] hitherto opposed our settling"; (2) he should persist in applying for "warlike stores" and for the continuance of royal troops in the colony; (3) he should solicit an extension of the boundaries of Georgia to include St. Augustine if it were ceded to Great Britain in the peace treaty with the Bourbon powers; and (4) he should request a continuance of the bounties on indigo, silk, and hemp.[27]

With these instructions, the Georgia legislature set down the long-range objectives for Knox's agency. In dealing with contingencies he was directed to consult with a committee of correspondence whose members were drawn from both the Georgia council and the assembly. The responsibility for framing the recommendations of this committee fell to the council's secretary, James Habersham, an old friend and colleague of Knox.

Knox's original instructions regarding the continuation and extension of the economic privileges of the colony were explicit. In 1763 and 1764, he persuaded the Board of Trade to recommend a renewal of the British government's subsidy of the silk industry in Georgia.[28] Also in 1764, Knox and Charles Garth, the agent for South Carolina, proposed to the Board of Trade that their two colonies be permitted to export rice directly to Africa and all parts of America. The Lords of Trade refused to extend this privilege immediately, but when they indicated that they would be receptive to more information on the issue, Knox presented them with a formal paper containing further arguments in support of the proposal. Subsequently, he testified before Parliament in behalf of the measure. Later in 1764, Parliament finally passed an act permitting South Carolina and Georgia to export rice to any part of America south of the two colonies, though not to Africa.[29]

On these occasions Knox was able to act in accordance with the explicit instructions of his constituents. But the slowness of communication across the Atlantic and the fact that Knox was in a position to analyze and respond immediately to circumstances in London—not to mention a personal inclination to trust his own abilities—meant that in several instances he had to act, or simply acted, on the basis of his own discretion, even in apparent contradiction to his instructions.

In 1764, for example, Knox was one of several agents summoned before the Board of Trade to hear the commissioners' proposal for a parliamentary bill designed to eliminate colonial issues of paper money. The obvious determination of the board to implement its proposal immediately allowed Knox no time to consult with his constituents. Relying essentially upon his recent experiences with paper currency in Georgia, Knox decided to join the other colonial agents in vigorously opposing the board's recommendations. Within a few days, Knox and Garth submitted counterproposals to the board providing guarantees against colonial abuses of paper currency. Knox personally composed a sixteen-page memorandum from which the other colonial agents drew common arguments against the commissioners' proposals. The outcome of this concerted opposition was the Currency Act of 1764, which permitted colonies to issue paper currency conditionally, a compromise based largely upon Knox and Garth's recommendations.[30]

The controversy between Georgia and South Carolina over the so-called Altamaha lands, which became the most demanding and time-consuming problem of Knox's agency, provides the best single illustration of his difficulties in acting for constituents far removed both in distance and in perspective from the seat of imperial government. This quarrel between Georgia and its powerful neighbor to the north developed out of their rival claims to the lands south of Georgia between the Altamaha River and the St. Johns River of Florida. This region—indeed the territory from which the colony of Georgia itself had been carved—had been included in the lands originally granted to South Carolina. Since the area between the Altamaha and the St. Johns had been claimed by both Britain and Spain, it virtually remained a no man's land until the French and Indian War. Once it became obvious, however, that the Spaniards would be expelled from Florida by the peace settlement, South Carolina began granting the Altamaha lands to its citizens.[31]

Georgia immediately reacted to South Carolina's unilateral action. Governor Wright sent a caveat to Governor Thomas Boone of South Carolina, protesting that province's assumption of jurisdiction over the Altamaha lands. When Boone refused to receive Wright's protest, the joint committee of the Georgia legislature wrote Knox in April 1763 that the colony could expect redress of its grievances only from the British Crown. The committee exhorted its agent to employ his "utmost influence and endeavors" to set aside the South Carolina grants, because upon this issue rested "the future Prosperity and even Existence of this Infant Province."[32]

The Georgia committee of correspondence instructed Knox to base his arguments before the Board of Trade upon the thesis that the de facto rights of Georgia to the lands south of the Altamaha superseded South Carolina's charter claim to the region.[33] Of course, according to the Georgia legislature's original instructions,

Knox was still required to solicit the extension of Georgia's southern boundary even beyond the St. Johns River to include St. Augustine. Thus, if Knox followed to the letter the instructions of both
the legislature and its committee of correspondence, he seemed
bound to assert Georgia's rights to the whole region between the
Altamaha and St. Augustine, including a sizable portion of the
former Spanish claim in Florida. But in the spring of 1763, Knox,
by virtue of his contacts with Ellis, Egremont, and Shelburne,
knew that British officials were interested in creating a new colony
in East Florida. Any assertion of Georgia's tenuous rights to the entire territory from Altamaha to St. Augustine would undoubtedly
have been rejected by the royal government and, furthermore, could
have jeopardized his arguments on behalf of Georgia's basic interest
—the nullification of South Carolina's claim to jurisdiction in the
region between the Altamaha and the St. Johns.

When Knox presented his case before the Board of Trade on
May 27, 1763, he ignored the original instructions of the legislature and modified those of the committee of correspondence. He
laid before the board Governor Wright's protest to Governor Boone,
which simply emphasized the injustice of South Carolina's action in
monopolizing the Altamaha lands and excluding Georgians from a
region essential to the prosperity of the struggling young colony.
Knox himself avoided introducing the question of Georgia's rights
to the Altamaha lands and concentrated on refuting South Carolina's claim to the territory. In this respect he contended that the
lands in question had become part of the empire only by virtue of
the recent treaty.[34] Obviously, if this interpretation were accepted,
the Altamaha lands would be at the disposal of the British Crown.
Knox's plan, though it involved a degree of risk, was nonetheless
better informed and more tactful than the alternatives provided by
his instructions.

On this occasion Knox's independent judgment was justified
by the results. The royal proclamation of October 7, 1763, which
implemented Knox's suggested boundaries for East Florida, also an-
nexed to Georgia the region between the Altamaha and the northern boundary of the new province. In November, the Georgia committee of correspondence approved Knox's handling of the Altamaha dispute. They were still concerned that Governor Boone's land
grants might be upheld even though South Carolina's claim to jur-

isdiction over the region was extinguished, and they instructed Knox on the course of action he should follow if the South Carolina grants were confirmed. But James Habersham, writing on behalf of the committee, admitted that in attending to the business of the colony in London, Knox had to be allowed a large degree of independence: "As this matter now stands both here [Georgia] and at home we cannot pretend to give you any particular directions how to act in behalf of the People of Georgia, [we] only must leave to your prudence to manage their interests."[35]

In January 1764, the Georgia assembly reviewed and approved Knox's work as agent during the preceding year. A month later the assembly not only passed an ordinance reappointing him as agent for another year but also formally commended "the Zeal and Abilities with which William Knox Esquire, the Present Agent, hath hitherto transacted the Affairs of this Province committed to his charge, and his assiduous attention to the welfare thereof." Later in the year, Knox was disturbed by reports that some Georgians considered his agency a sinecure and openly referred to his position as a "job." But Habersham assured him that at a meeting of the committee he had directly confronted the members with this rumor and that "every Person present declared, that they thought you had Acquitted yourself properly and more than deserved your Salary, disclaiming at the same Time ever having considered your appointment as a job."[36]

In February 1765, Knox, apparently enjoying the complete confidence of his constituents, was again reappointed agent by the assembly.[37] Within a few months, however, his independence of mind, which only a year before had brought him success and approbation, provoked the wrath of the whole colony and brought about his dismissal by the assembly. The occasion of this decisive episode in his career was the great watershed in the history of the first British Empire—the Stamp Act crisis.

On March 9, 1764, George Grenville introduced a resolution into the House of Commons providing for the extension of stamp duties to the colonies. This measure, which subsequently assumed such momentous significance for the empire, provoked no unusual response in the Commons that day and was passed in a routine manner. In proposing his resolution, Grenville did not call for the immediate passage of a Stamp Act for the colonies; rather, he postponed its enactment for one year in order to allow time to gather specific information for legislation and also to consult with the colonies on the proposed tax.[38]

If modern historians do not agree in assessing Grenville's motives for postponing the Stamp Act, in 1764 the colonial agents themselves were not certain what he meant by proposing to allow time for consultation with the colonies. But in his speech before the Commons, Grenville had indicated that during the interval between the resolution calling for stamp duties and the actual passage of a Stamp Act he would be receptive to colonial objections to the measure as well as to proposals for an alternative tax from the colonies. The colonial agents sought a clarification of these points from Grenville, and several of them met with him on May 17, 1764.

William Knox was not present at this meeting, but later, in 1765, he published an account of what he had learned from those agents who had attended Grenville.[39] He seems to have drawn most of his information from his close associate, Charles Garth. According to Knox's account, Grenville told the agents that it was only reasonable that the colonies share the financial burden for imperial defense. He considered stamp duties the easiest and most equitable of all tax alternatives, one which ought to be particularly attractive to the colonists since its collection would not require the exercise of any arbitrary powers by revenue officers in America. Apparently Grenville was convinced that if the colonies were informed of these arguments by their agents they would recognize the advantages of stamp duties over other forms of taxation and would accept the measure. By proceeding in this manner, Grenville informed the agents, the colonies would gain the advantage of establishing a precedent for being consulted in "all such cases" in the future. Clearly, it had not occurred to Grenville that the colonies would see little advantage in being consulted on what appeared to them to be a *fait accompli* or that they would so adamantly resist his precedent for taxation of the colonies by Parliament. According to Knox, Grenville did recognize, however, that the colonies might raise specific objections to the Stamp Act, and he therefore informed the agents "that if the colonies thought any other mode of taxation more convenient to them, and made any proposition which should carry the appearance of equal efficacy with a stamp-duty, he would give it all due consideration."

Although Knox was not present at the meeting of May 17, he

claimed later that some time during the postponement he had the opportunity of personally informing Grenville of some of his objections to the stamp duties. He also claimed that on this occasion he and several other agents pointed out to Grenville that if the revenue arising from the stamp duties was applied to defraying the expenses of civil government in the colonies, "the Assemblies would be rendered dependent upon the will of the Governors." Grenville replied that he had no intention of promoting such an arrangement, that his only consideration was imperial defense, and that if the assemblies would provide for their own civil government he would appropriate the revenue arising from the stamp duties to the colonial military establishment only.[40]

Following the May 17 meeting with Grenville, the agents wrote immediately to their respective colonies, informing them of the interview with the minister and requesting instructions on his proposals regarding the stamp duties. According to Knox, some colonial assemblies framed their own petitions "positively and directly questioning the authority and jurisdiction of parliament over the properties of the people in the colonies" and required their agents to present these petitions to the crown and to Parliament, while other assemblies instructed their agents to petition Parliament against the proposed tax "and above all things to insist in their petitions on the right and privilege of the colonies to be exempt from internal taxes imposed by parliament." Some colonies instructed their agents to inform the British government that they were prepared to contribute their proportion of the required revenue, but by methods of their own in lieu of a tax levied by Parliament. Knox claimed, however, that when these agents were asked by their colleagues if they were prepared to commit their constituents to any particular sum, they admitted that they had no authority to do so.[41]

This last colonial proposal evoked much the same response from Grenville during a meeting with a delegation of agents on February 2, 1765. When the agents suggested that the colonies be allowed to raise a revenue by taxing themselves, Grenville asked them if they believed they could agree on the proportions each colony should raise. The agents were forced to reply in the negative. Grenville countered that in such an event the burden for enforcing the obligations undertaken by the colonies would fall upon Britain and that such an arrangement would be more troublesome than a duty directly imposed by Parliament.[42]

Knox's own position during the Stamp Act controversy was paradoxical. On one hand, he admittedly regarded the growing powers of the colonial assemblies as a danger to the empire: he not only argued in private for reforms which would bring greater political independence to colonial executives, but he also publicly asserted the sovereign power of Parliament to legislate for the colonies. On the other hand, true to his ideal of a mixed constitution, Knox openly admitted the existence of certain colonial rights and privileges and specifically advocated concessions to the colonists and their assemblies on the issue of parliamentary taxation—as indeed he would throughout his public career. Thus, in spite of his avowed support of obtaining a contribution from the colonies, Knox in his capacity as colonial agent for Georgia opposed the Stamp Act in 1764 and 1765.

Of course, Knox did not justify his opposition to the Stamp Act on the grounds that parliamentary taxation of the colonies was unconstitutional. In the first place, he believed that Parliament theoretically enjoyed absolute sovereignty over the colonies; furthermore, he also recognized that in practice Parliament would not entertain any objections which questioned the constitutionality of the stamp duties. He recommended to his fellow agents that they petition against the proposed duties in a manner which would in no way question Parliament's right to tax the colonies. The other agents, however, considered themselves bound to submit petitions to Parliament in accordance with the instructions they had received from their constituents.[43] Knox himself, for some unaccountable reason, received no specific instructions from Georgia until almost a month after the Stamp Act had become law.

On February 6, 1765, Parliament resumed its deliberations on Grenville's proposal for a Stamp Act for the colonies and by a large majority refused even to receive any petitions from the colonies which questioned its rights to tax them. The stamp bill passed the Commons on February 15, and on March 22 it received the royal assent.

In a letter dated April 15, 1765, the Georgia committee of correspondence belatedly informed Knox of the colony's sympathies regarding the proposed stamp duties. It is particularly interesting that the committee agreed with Grenville's idea that the stamp duties might be "as equal as any, that could be generally imposed on the colonys." Nevertheless, they protested that whatever the situation in the northern colonies, the expense of the "internal polity" of Georgia was more than its citizens could bear and that, therefore, they were in no condition to be loaded with new financial burdens from the stamp duties. The committee finally informed Knox that although the Massachusetts assembly had called upon the Georgia Commons House to order him to join the other agents in petitioning against the stamp duties, he was to cooperate with the northern agents only as far as Georgia's interests were promoted by their petitions.[44]

Knox subsequently informed the committee of his unsuccessful attempt to have the agents adopt a petition which did not question the authority of Parliament. The committee responded with unqualified approval of his position. It was their opinion that the failure of the other agents to adopt his reasoning had only forestalled a fair hearing before Parliament on the most telling objection against the stamp duties: the hardship they would work on the American colonists. The committee then called upon Knox to petition for the repeal of the Stamp Act when the first opportunity arose. He was free to do so alone or in conjunction with the other agents. But he was warned not to infer that he was required to join in every petition drawn up by agents of other colonies, for the Georgia committee expressed its concern that "it may prove of fatal consequence to some of the Colonys should they go to great lengths in denying the Authority of parliament."[45]

Some time after the passage of the Stamp Act, Knox did in fact draw up a petition against the new levy. Like his earlier proposal to the agents, this petition avoided challenging the right of Parliament to tax the colonies and instead argued for repeal on the basis of Georgia's inability to bear the burden of the duties. In January 1766, Knox's appeal was one of three colonial petitions considered by the House of Commons during the deliberations which led to the repeal of the colonial stamp duties.[46]

Although Knox's activities as agent during the passage of the Stamp Act were explicitly approved by the committee of correspondence, he soon angered the assembly by publicly supporting Parliament's right to tax the colonies. In 1765, immediately after the Stamp Act passed the House of Commons, Knox wrote and published anonymously a pamphlet entitled *The Claim of the Colonies to an Exemption from Internal Taxes Imposed by Authority of Parliament, Examined: In a Letter from a Gentleman in London to his Friend in Amer-*

ica. His avowed purpose in publishing this piece was to justify his refusal to join with those agents who had questioned the authority of Parliament in their petitions against the stamp duties. He specifically stated his own conviction "that the parliament of Great Britain has a full and compleat jurisdiction over the property and person of every inhabitant of a British colony."[47] He then presented a series of arguments designed to prove that the colonists' claims to exemption from taxation by Parliament could not be supported by the common law of England, the provisions of colonial charters, parliamentary precedent, the want of colonial representation in Parliament, or the impracticability or general inconvenience of parliamentary taxation as opposed to other methods of drawing a contribution from the colonies. Particularly significant is the fact that Knox specifically rejected all proposals for colonial quotas and requisitions as well as colonial representation in the British House of Commons—policies he would advocate on numerous occasions in later years.

In spite of his complete indictment of the colonial arguments against taxation by Parliament, in the *Claim of the Colonies* Knox did not entirely abandon his constituents to the arbitrary will of Parliament. He pointed out that in practice there were obvious circumstances which distinguished the situation of the subjects in America from that of Parliament's constituents in Great Britain. He contended that these circumstances provided "cogent reasons for a peculiar tenderness to be observed in laying taxes upon the colonies and that rules and orders which might be proper to be observed with regard to the people of England, should be relaxed of their strictness on behalf of the subjects in America."[48]

The views Knox expressed in this pamphlet were not inconsistent with his actions as agent for Georgia. Throughout the Stamp Act crisis Knox faithfully opposed the stamp duties in accordance with the instructions of his constituents. But his opposition had been based upon the inexpediency of the stamp duties—never upon a denial of the ultimate constitutionality of parliamentary taxation of the colonies or of the obligation of the colonies to contribute to the cost of imperial defense. Apparently, in the *Claim of the Colonies* Knox sought somehow to play the role of mediator between Parliament and the colonies, much as he had done in respect to the agents' petitions against the Stamp Act.[49] On one hand, he refuted the colonies' claims to an exemption from parliamentary taxation, while on the other he questioned the practical equity of arbitrary parliamentary taxation. His one apparent concession to ministerial opinion was his repudiation of quotas and requisitions as an alternative to parliamentary taxes. Grenville had specifically discouraged these alternatives in the meeting with the colonial agents on February 2, 1765, and for the moment Knox accepted his position.[50]

The *Claim of the Colonies* clearly indicated that the Stamp Act riots in America had excited Knox's deepest fears of the dangers of demagoguery in the colonies. He asserted that his views represented those of many "cool thinking" Americans, who were prevented from speaking out because of their fear of the giddy multitude. And, finally, he criticized the colonial assemblies for insisting upon petitions which raised the theoretical issues of parliamentary authority, thereby forfeiting an opportunity for a fair hearing on specific objections against the Stamp Act. Nevertheless, he hoped that in the future the colonies would again be allowed to express their sentiments on the best means for raising imperial contributions from America.

Knox apparently had little notion of the stormy reaction his pamphlet would arouse in Georgia. Indeed, the views he expressed in the *Claim of the Colonies* seemed to mark no great departure from his previous position regarding the Stamp Act, a position which had received the approbation of his colonial constituents. From his vantage point in London, however, Knox misgauged the intense resentment which the Stamp Act had excited in America even among the most intimate of his recent neighbors and colleagues in Georgia.

In July 1765, Governor Wright received a copy of the pamphlet, and at the insistence of Knox's friend Habersham he withheld its circulation. By the time the legislature convened in October, however, the contents of Knox's pamphlet were known throughout the colony.[51] On October 28, Habersham wrote to Knox that the *Claim of the Colonies* "has given the greatest Umbrage, and . . . has not left you a single person, who will open their mouths for you in the Assembly." Habersham, moreover, made it quite clear that he personally rejected Knox's refutation of the colonial claims against parliamentary taxation. Habersham, a substantial merchant and planter, concluded his remarks with a concise but able summary of the colonial arguments against the stamp tax—arguments based upon the rights of the colonies to an exemption from taxation by Parliament as well as those based upon the inability of the colonies to pay the tax.[52]

The Georgia Commons House of Assembly lost little time in dealing with Knox's public apostasy. On November 15, the assembly passed a resolution instructing the committee of correspondence to "acquaint Mr. Knox that this Province hath no further Occasion for his Service as Agent." Governor Wright, who had no sympathy for Knox's public declarations, did nothing to defend him and in fact recommended a successor to the lower house. But when the assembly decided to replace Knox with Charles Garth, agent for South Carolina, Wright objected that Garth could not simultaneously represent two colonies whose dispute over the Altamaha land grants had not been finally resolved by the British government.[53]

The assembly's unilateral action in dismissing Knox and appointing Garth also provoked a constitutional controversy with the council. The upper house, guided by its president, James Habersham, sought to win repeal of the Stamp Act by peacefully petitioning the king and Parliament. The councilors opposed such coercive measures as obstructing the execution of the act or even placing an embargo on British trade. Above all, they feared the effect of public disturbances upon law and order. In this respect they lent credence to Knox's claim that his sentiments generally represented those of a significant element in America. When violence did in fact break out in the colony, Habersham was one of those singled out for intimidation by the radicals. On January 29, 1766, he wrote Knox that he had been "waylaid in the night" and threatened with having his house pulled down. Habersham, who had firmly defended the liberties of the colonies to Knox only a few months before, now wrote pathetically to his friend in London, "How dreadful it is to have one's person and property under the Dominion of a Mob? O Liberty whither art tho' fled?"[54]

Undoubtedly the violent course of the Stamp Act crisis in Georgia served to rally the council to Knox's defense. In March 1766, the council informed Governor Wright that it refused to concur with the assembly's action in dismissing Knox as agent. The upper house defiantly passed a resolution commending Knox for the "faithful services" he had rendered the province. The assembly, however, ignored the council and continued to deal with Garth as colonial agent. The whole affair reached the proportions of a major constitutional crisis in March 1767, when the assembly sent the upper house a tax bill which included an article providing £100 as salary for "Charles Garth Esqr Agent for this Province." The council issued a formal protest against the inclusion of this article in the tax bill, passed a resolution that the assembly had no right to appoint an agent for the province without the concurrence of the whole legislature, and finally named a committee, which included Habersham, to correspond with Knox for the purpose of securing his assistance in defending the rights and privileges of the council before the government of Great Britain.[55]

The deadlock between the upper and lower houses of the Georgia legislature over Knox's dismissal and Garth's appointment remained unresolved until early in 1768. But on March 15 the assembly finally admitted that there was "an absolute necessity to appoint an agent to Solicit the affairs of this Province in Great Britain," and it offered a compromise candidate for the position in the person of Benjamin Franklin. The council accepted, confirming Franklin's appointment the following month.[56] Apparently as part of the compromise, the lower house in December 1768 provided a token payment of £16.2.6 to William Knox "for monies by him Distributed in Consequence of his being Agent for this Pro[vin]ce."

Knox, in fact, had already derived a full sense of satisfaction and vindication from the council's tenacious defense of his agency. In May 1766, after receiving the council's resolution of thanks for his services, Knox replied that it was "the highest Satisfaction to have the Approbation of those whose Opinion is to be influenced neither by the Frowns of Power nor by the more despicable Menacies of a deluded and artfully instigated Populace." In gratitude he pledged himself to support the council in any future contests with the assembly:

> I beg you will also on my Behalf assure the honourable Gentlemen of that House that whenever thro' any Attempts to usurp on their Rights they may find themselves engaged in any Contest with the Commons House of Assembly they shall Always find me ready to do them any Service here they may desire of me without looking for any Gratification, other than the Thanks of Gentlemen who act with Consistency and Honour.[57]

During his term as colonial agent for Georgia, William Knox had certainly achieved his primary goal: he had gained admission to the highest councils of imperial administration and had commended his talents to political figures who held the keys to public office. Equally important, he had reshaped and tempered his theories of imperial relations in the political crucible at Westminister. Above all, the experiences of his agency had reinforced his conviction that the empire could be maintained against the increasingly disruptive forces of provincialism and separatism only through the consistent assertion of a firm, though benevolently paternalistic, authority on the part of the imperial government.

4. "An Offer . . . Advantageous & Honourable to You": Pamphleteering & the Pursuit of Office, 1765–1770

In 1765, at the time of his dismissal from the Georgia agency, Knox was thirty-three years old. The surviving contemporary references to his physical appearance indicate only that as he reached middle age he became noticeably corpulent. Even as early as Knox's twenty-seventh year, at a time when he was complaining of the detrimental effects of Georgia's climate upon his health, Lyttelton had teasingly reprimanded him for remaining "so fat" while his friends were "so lean."[1] The only extant portrait of Knox, painted when he was seventy-one,[2] indicates that he retained this corpulence throughout his mature years. Yet his face, in contrast, remained surprisingly gaunt. Even in old age, he conveyed a strong image of intelligence and resolution: angular features, a tautly pursed mouth and a cleft chin, were sharply etched beneath a broad forehead, with deep-set eyes fixed in a distant and detached gaze. In overall effect, the distinguishing firmness of Knox's face suggested an essentially intense and choleric temperament, yet his corpulent torso seemed to betray a susceptibility to compromise and indulgence.

As he reached middle age, William might have regarded himself as a modest success in terms of income and property. His office of provost marshal of Georgia brought him about £250 annually, and as crown agent for East Florida he received £200 per annum from the imperial exchequer.[3] With a fixed income of £450 per annum, he could maintain a comfortable if modest bachelor existence within official circles in London. During the same period, James Boswell managed to scrape along in London's society of authors and dilettantes on an allowance which was less than half Knox's income.[4]

In addition to salaries derived from his colonial offices, Knox also received a fluctuating return from his properties in Georgia. Of course, as an absentee planter he was never able to exploit fully the economic potential of his rice plantations. During the colonial period, rice cultivation was a particularly intricate and demanding enterprise: in addition to the usual hazards of climate and weather, rice planting was complicated by the problems of tide-flow irrigation. The construction and maintenance of irrigation banks and flood gates and the proper regulation of flooding—all carried out of course by unfree labor—required the constant supervision of an experienced and attentive manager. Even if the frequent droughts and storms were avoided, incorrect flooding could destroy an entire season's rice crop.[5]

Such in fact was the fate of Knoxborough, William's Savannah River rice plantation, during the first two years after he returned to Britain. After 1764, however, Knox's plantation affairs improved steadily, due mainly to the assistance of several friends in the colony. James Habersham, himself an experienced rice planter, in particular took up the responsibility of supervising the activities of Knoxborough's resident overseers. For his part, Knox returned these favors by attending to his American friends' business and private interests in London.[6]

The immediate improvement of Knox's plantation affairs was due largely to the diversification of enterprise at Knoxborough. A sizable portion of the plantation consisted of swampland covered with cypress trees, highly valued for lumber and shingles. Indeed, since lumbering and shingle making required less managerial skill and attention than rice cultivation, Knox went, in Governor Wright's words, "more upon Lumber than planting," a considerable number of his black bondsmen being employed in shingle making, which became the "chief profit" of Knoxborough plantation.[7]

In July 1765, Habersham, acting as Knox's attorney, informed his client that he had credited £267 to Knox's account but that after expenses there remained a balance of only £67. Later in the year, however, Knox's affairs were so improved that Habersham was able to send £230 due him from his Georgia properties.[8]

Of course, the relatively meager sums Habersham posted to Knox's account in no way reflected the value of his real property in America. As the population and economy of Georgia expanded during the 1760s and 1770s, the value of land, particularly the limited acreage for rice plantation properties, rose sharply. Under these circumstances it is hardly surprising that in 1765 Knox took advantage of his influence at the Board of Trade to obtain a grant for an additional five thousand acres of land on the Crooked River in Georgia—his only cost being a gratuity of £50 paid to a deputy surveyor of the province for "information."[9]

Considering Knox's substantial properties and his favorable prospects as an officeholder, it is not unusual that he was regarded as an eligible candidate for a marriage alliance. In fact, some time before he left Georgia, he had courted and won the affections of a daughter of Governor Wright. After two years, the young woman sailed for England in 1764, accompanied by her mother and a sister. In March, Habersham wrote Knox that he was charging him with a commission in London which would require consultation with the bearer of his letter, "whose company and Presence must make you . . . happy." Habersham playfully insisted that Knox must thank him for this assignment since he was certain that "you will think it an honour to take the trouble of trotting the Streets of [London in] her Hands."[10] Whatever the young woman's personal qualities might have been, the prospect of an alliance with her family was most attractive, for Governor Wright was one of the wealthiest rice planters in Georgia.

Habersham's charming letter, designed as the harbinger of a happy reunion between Knox and his bride-to-be, was destined to become instead a cruel memorial to tragedy. The ship carrying Governor Wright's daughter to England foundered, and all aboard were lost at sea. Although Knox left no personal account of this sorrowful episode, the depth of his grief distressed Governor Lyttelton, who mustered an admirable but understandably feeble attempt to console his friend "upon the melancholy event which has been so just a cause of affliction to you."[11]

Knox put his tragedy behind him and in 1765 married Letitia Ford, the daughter of a fellow Irishman, James Ford.[12] Their marriage would be long and fruitful: the couple were blessed with several children, and Knox's subsequent correspondence was filled with references to a contented family life. Yet it is curious that Letitia Knox—much like William's mother—is scarcely mentioned in her husband's numerous letters, memoirs, and publications. Although William composed a relatively complete record of his children—the personalities and activities of both daughters and sons—his personal documents provide no substantial clues to his wife's individual personality and only the barest outline of their private life together. Within the surviving evidence, Letitia Knox can be seen only in mirrored images: as a dutiful wife and mother as well as a gracious hostess, whose generous hospitality enhanced William's social and professional status by no small measure.

Not the least of Letitia Knox's documented assets was the substantial dowry she contributed to her husband's estate. Indeed, Philip Skelton congratulated his former pupil for choosing such an "excellent wife, who brought you a large fortune." Of course, the bachelor parson also assured the young groom that his marriage must properly rest upon a greater calling: "Although you are yet in love, a time will come when you will only love, and that upon an higher and nobler basis than passion."[13]

By the fall of 1765, the Knoxes seemed to be well established in their "own house" on Marlborough Street. Within a year, however, they abandoned their first home for a more pretentious and fashionable residence on New Street, Hanover Square.[14] From its completion in 1721, Hanover Square had been a favorite residential quarter of the aristocracy. By mid-century, even with the development of rivals at Grosvenor and Berkeley squares, Hanover Square remained a center for the social elite of the capital. The tall baroque houses, constructed in the so-called German style with bright cheerful exteriors and elaborate interiors, provided an elegant backdrop for the social and political life of the oligarchy, into which the Knoxes eagerly and energetically sought admission.[15]

Philip Skelton grew alarmed at the apparently extravagant turn of Knox's domestic life—especially in view of his recent dismissal from the Georgia agency. In the fall of 1766, he wrote William from Ireland that he had been disturbed, "in the same manner it would do, if I were your father," by rumors that his finances were in a "shattered condition." William was immediately able to assure Skelton that he remained as prudent as ever and that his financial condition was sound. He undoubtedly did much to reconcile the old man to his new affluence by generously helping to replace Skelton's precious personal library, which he had sold earlier to feed his famine-stricken parishioners.[16]

Knox might confidently assure his friends that he would scarcely notice the loss of the £150 salary he had received as Georgia's agent, for he had never valued this agency as a source of income. He had always admitted that the principal advantage of the office was the opportunity it afforded for promoting his public career. And in this respect Knox's East Florida agency did not provide a satisfactory alternative to his Georgia office. As crown agent for Florida, Knox was primarily responsible for administering the annual grant by which Parliament financed the government of the new colony. In addition, he regularly supplied the Board of Trade with information and recommendations on such matters as land grants, the construction of churches, the appointment of schoolmasters, and the distribution of presents to Indians within the province.[17] Since East Florida was not sufficiently developed to support representative institutions, however, Knox found himself categorically excluded from the crucial deliberations at Westminster between imperial officials and representatives of colonial assemblies.

On one occasion, Knox himself provided a cynically humorous, yet typically candid, accounting of the long-term "profit and loss" from that public support of Grenville's Stamp Act which had cost him his Georgia agency:

[The *Claim of the Colonies*] being the first Pamphlet publish'd on the side of Government in this Controversy the Printer Printed it at his own risk and it cost the author nothing for Publishing———[balance] 0:0:0 . . . the author [was] then Provincial Agent for Georgia from which he was dismissed by the Assembly the same year in consequence of writing this Pamphlet. He might otherways have held this appointment 'till the year 1775 . . . which is 10 years at £150 p. a.; his loss therefore by this Pamphlet amounts to———1500:0:0. All that he gained by it was the honor of being hung & burn'd in Effigy with Lord Bute and Mr. Grenville at Boston and Savannah, the Pleasure of being examined at the Bar of the House of Commons against the Repeal of the Stamp Act which procured him great commendations from the Duke of Bedford's Friends communicated to him by Lord Frederick Campbell, the notice and applause of Mr. Rigby which continud untill that Gentleman became Paymaster when the business of that Office shoved him out of his memory, all which he values at——— 0:5:0. From which must be deducted the hire of a hackney coach one morning to attend of the opposition in 1765 at Mr. Rigby's———0:2:0. Also six small Basons of Soup the six days he was in attendance at the House of Commons waiting to be examined———0:3:0.[18]

Thus the immediate balance sheet arising from the *Claim of the Col-*

onies produced a deficit of £1,500 by Knox's reckoning. He readily admitted, however, that the account was satisfied in full because his public defense of the Stamp Act eventually won him "the real Honor and Pleasure of Mr. Grenville's Confidence and Friendship."

Of course, as Knox knew by experience, in contemporary politics talent, knowledge, and enterprise were not sufficient to obtain tangible advantages without the recommendation of influence. It was Lord Grosvenor's patronage which sustained Knox's pursuit of office after his dismissal from the Georgia agency.

Following his elevation to the peerage, Grosvenor continued to exercise considerable political influence from his base in the parliamentary borough of Chester. From 1755 to 1795, Grosvenor's brother Thomas represented the constituency in the Commons without a break, while his lordship's nominee Richard Wilbraham-Bootle succeeded in winning the other seat at Chester without opposition in every election from 1761 to 1784. In Parliament the Grosvenor brothers and Wilbraham-Bootle were noted for their independence. Thomas Grosvenor and Wilbraham-Bootle voted, for example, against the Grenville government twice in the critical divisions in the Commons over general warrants (February 15 and 18, 1764)—apparently in contradiction to Lord Grosvenor's personal wishes. Nevertheless, the Grosvenor influence in Parliament was generally considered friendly to the Grenville administration. Grenville, who courted the independents in Parliament because his personal following was never large, maintained a cordial and solicitous relationship with Lord Grosvenor while in power, and after Grenville was dismissed from office in 1765, Grosvenor and his political allies joined the expremier in opposing the Rockingham ministry. Thomas Grosvenor and Wilbraham-Bootle voted in the Commons against the repeal of the Stamp Act, while Baron Grosvenor signed the Lords' Protest against both the second and the third readings of the repeal bill.[19]

With Lord Grosvenor's consent, Knox tendered his services to Grenville. As early as November 1764, while Grenville was still in power, Knox had sent the minister a copy of his paper on the comparative economic circumstances of Britain and France. Then, several months after Grenville had been dismissed from office and one month after Knox had been fired from his Georgia agency, Knox for the first time informed Grenville of his authorship of the *Claim of the Colonies* and asked if he would favor a second edition of the pamphlet. Subsequently, Knox testified before the Commons against the Rockingham government's proposal to repeal the Stamp Act—ironically, at about the same time, the House finally agreed to consider his original petition against the stamp duties.[20]

On the morning after "the Resolution had passed in the House of Commons, to repeal the stamp act and to bring in the declaratory bill," Knox was summoned to a meeting of the parliamentary opposition to Rockingham's government: ". . . when I came there, Mr. Grenville and Mr. Rigby came out to me and told me, the Duke of Bedford and several others desired to know my opinion of the effects which those Resolutions would produce in America. My answer was in a few words—*addresses of thanks and measures of rebellion*. Mr. Grenville smiled and shook his head, and Mr. Rigby swore by G-d he thought so, and both wished me good morning."[21] With this near-ritualistic interrogation, Knox was initiated into the inner circle of George Grenville's adherents.

The prospect of entering office under Grenville was certainly encouraging to such an ambitious office seeker as Knox. Following his dismissal from office, Grenville continued to command a large political following, and his return to power seemed inevitable.[22] Although he did not possess the personal wealth usually asssociated with party leadership, the connections and obligations he had acquired as First Lord of the Treasury enabled him to take many politicians into opposition. And his political following was swollen temporarily by the accession of officeholders who had been dismissed by the Rockingham government. When it became obvious that the Rockingham ministry did not enjoy the full confidence of George III, many of the so-called king's friends also attached themselves to Grenville for a time. In fact, the parliamentary strength of Grenville's party was more apparent than real, and after the fall of Rockingham in 1766 a large number of Grenville's followers entered office under Chatham. Yet as late as 1767, Grenville's personal following in Parliament numbered about twenty-five members, and he was generally regarded as the key figure among the opposition leaders.

In 1767, the factions opposing Lord Chatham's administration seemed formidable indeed. Besides Grenville's party, the main groups in opposition were the Bedfordites and the Rockingham Whigs. For some time the Bedford party had been closely associated with Grenville. The Bedfordites generally shared his views on America; they had supported Grenville in office, and after his fall they followed his lead in opposition. Rockingham and Grenville, on the other hand, were irreconcilable. Their differences over American policy had become personal, and—even more important—the two expremiers were obvious competitors for the leadership in any government coalition. The chief lieutenants of the parties in opposition—Richard Rigby of the Bedford party, Thomas Whately of the Grenvillites, and William Dowdeswell and Edmund Burke of the Rockingham Whigs—attempted to construct a working alliance, but the undisguised antipathy between Rockingham and Grenville made such arrangements tenuous at best.

Actually, the question of Grenville's position in any projected ministry was a moot issue. During his term in office, Grenville had made himself personally obnoxious to George III, and the king subsequently placed an absolute veto on Grenville's return to office. Apparently Grenville was not aware of his exclusion until July 1767. By this time, the Chatham administration seemed on the verge of collapse, and the various groups in opposition conducted negotiations for a coalition government. Grenville, however, indicated to the Bedfordites that he would not press his claims to office. Although the negotiations miscarried because of differences over the allocation of offices in a coalition government, the Rockingham Whigs and the Bedfordites attempted to preserve at least the façade of united opposition in Parliament. But in November 1767, Grenville toppled the entire edifice when he delivered a wholesale indictment of Rockingham's American policy before Parliament. The Rockingham Whigs were furious. Bedford, recognizing that effective opposition was hopeless, permitted his followers to come to terms for office with Chatham's successor, Lord Grafton.[23]

After learning of his exclusion from office, Grenville lost interest in partisan politics and, although he was only in his middle fifties, assumed an attitude of detached statesmanship in public affairs. He subsequently allowed his party to disintegrate, and among his supporters only the efforts of his lieutenant, Whately, preserved the fiction that Grenville was actively engaged in the struggle for power. First-rate politicians, such as Alexander Wedderburn and Lord George Sackville, severed their connections with Grenville and sought preferment elsewhere.

For some time, however, Knox did not perceive—or perhaps could not accept the fact—that Grenville had completely abandoned the pursuit of office. In September 1767, Knox accompanied Thomas Grosvenor on a visit to Grenville's country estate at Wotton.[24] Grenville spoke at length with his two guests about the opposition's July negotiations for a coalition, but in the course of his conversation he gave no hint that he had personally given up his own pretensions to office. This visit only reassured Knox that his connection with Grenville was most promising.[25]

Knox in fact had developed a strong personal attachment to Grenville. Grenville's historical image has generally suffered from the accounts left by such Whig wits as Edmund Burke, who caricatured the narrow pedestrian features of his personality. But Grenville's honesty, his capacity for work, his competence in matters of trade and finance, and even his tedious speeches on the details of government business were fully appreciated by large numbers of parliamentarians. The independent country gentlemen, greatly agitated by the increased tax burden following the great war for empire, especially preferred the sound dullness of Grenville's fiscal lectures to the lofty brilliance of Burke's orations.[26] Many politicians were attracted to Grenville by his reputation for loyalty to his supporters. On one occasion, Edward Thurlow, whose own record for political loyalty was inconsistent, to say the least, testified to this singular feature of Grenville's personality. While serving as attorney general in Lord North's government, Thurlow complained to Knox that he was called upon to bear full responsibility for the coercive measures against Massachusetts. He insisted that one would be foolish to risk oneself for the likes of North's cabinet and commented, "Now if it was George Grenville who was so damned obstinate that he would go to hell with you before he would desert you there would be some sense in it."[27]

Obviously Grenville inspired either constant devotion or persistent aversion among his contemporaries. In later years, Knox himself described Grenville in a passage which certainly provides as great an insight into Knox's personality and his attraction to Grenville as it does an analysis of Grenville's character:

> Under a manner rather austere and forbidding, he covered a heart as feeling and tender as any man ever possessed. He liked office as well for its emoluments as its power; but in his attention to himself he never failed to pay regard to the situations and circumstances of his friends, though to neither would he

79

warp the public interest or service in the smallest degree; rigid in his opinions of public justice and integrity, and firm to inflexibility in the instruction of his mind, he reprobated every suggestion of the political expediency of overlooking frauds or evasions in the payment or collection of revenue, or of waste or extravagance in its expenditure. But although he would not bend any measure out of the strict line of rectitude to gain popularity, he was far from being indifferent to the good or ill opinion of the public.[28]

For Knox, the appeal of Grenville's character was essentially a matter of like attracting like. The "austere" and "forbidding" manner which Knox observed in Grenville had been consciously cultivated, largely as a defense against the arrogance and imperiousness he had endured over the years from Lord Temple and William Pitt, his elder brother and brother-in-law respectively.[29] Similarly, Knox had responded to scrupulous training at the hands of his father and Philip Skelton by developing a disposition toward priggish egotism, which served mainly as a defense mechanism for a hypersensitive personality.

In the privacy of Grenville's country estate at Wotton, Knox was treated with warm hospitality. And he replied in kind with manifestations of gratitude and expressions of affection which, like exotic hothouse plants, seem momentarily to burst into bloom in the normally "austere" and "forbidding" ground of his own correspondence.[30] Nor do these sentiments appear to be only trite incantations, drawn for the proper occasion from the office seeker's formulary. Even after Grenville's death in 1770, the memory of his rigid but benevolent character held a position of esteem and respect in William's affections, shared only by Thomas Knox and Philip Skelton.

During the brief years of their association, Grenville, in his new role of elder statesman, found Knox's expert knowledge and literary talents of considerable use. In the course of the Stamp Act controversy, Grenville had been stung by the unfavorable reaction to his policy among the British public. He was persuaded that the advocates of imperial reform had not received a fair public hearing in the press because their opponents, as he informed Knox, "have bought those Channels of Public Intelligence, that the People of

Great Brittain may be continued in Ignorance of the State of things in America, a Conduct which I fear will finally turn out a great Misfortune both to this Country & to that."[31] Grenville obviously hoped that his new protégé would be a useful instrument in countering the propaganda advantage his rivals enjoyed. Knox, for his part, found in Grenville a demanding yet appreciative master. And under this stimulus, William published two major treatises, which were to establish his reputation as a significant political and imperial theorist.

In 1768, Knox began work on a definitive reply to the British and American critics of Grenville's policies. In gathering materials for this treatise, he demonstrated a unique interest in exploiting official records for historical precedents and statistical evidence. Particularly remarkable is the fact that he claimed that he studied the papers and correspondence of the Board of Trade—a source which would provide a wealth of material for the so-called imperial school of American historians centuries later.[32] Grenville personally provided Knox with materials from his own records, and he also read and criticized the manuscript at various stages.

In June 1768, Grenville drew up a comprehensive critique of one of Knox's earlier drafts.[33] He especially approved Knox's argument that Britain should always import available raw materials from the colonies even though the colonial products cost more than those of foreign countries. On the other hand, he took exception to a proposal that the colonies be allowed to export directly to other countries those commodities not essential to the British economy. He commented that although such concessions had been allowed in certain instances, "to do it universally might be dangerous, if not fatal to Great Brittain." The former finance minister and chief architect of the colonial stamp duties also objected to every one of Knox's specific alternatives for raising a revenue in America. For example, Grenville rejected Knox's suggestion that quitrents and the 4.5 percent West Indian export duties be extended and applied to imperial expenses; according to Grenville, under existing fiscal practice both revenues were at the disposal of the crown and technically could not be considered part of "the Colony Funds for Public Service." His most vehement criticism, however, was directed against Knox's recommendation of a system of colonial quotas and requisitions in lieu of direct taxation by Parliament. Grenville insisted that such a proposal was completely unacceptable: "If Great Britain under any conditions gives up her Right of Taxation she gives up her Right of Sovereignty which is inseparable in all ages and in all countries."

Grenville's pointed comments came as a traumatic shock to his sensitive young protégé. Never before had Knox's imperial theories been subjected to such meticulous scrutiny and critical comment. It seems that the criticism affected William physically as well as emotionally, for more than a week after Grenville penned his letter, Knox replied, "I have had a disorder in my head which affected my Eyes so much since I had the favour of your letter from the Grove that I have not ventur'd to look into the places you have remarket upon and to alter them."

Knox's claim of illness in this instance was neither the first nor the last occasion when setbacks to his professional interests or private fortunes were accompanied by complaints of physical infirmity. On the other hand, he also proved consistently that he was temperamentally incapable of more than a temporary retreat to maintain his personal, intellectual, or professional integrity. Even as he informed Grenville of his recent incapacity, Knox forwarded a lengthy defense of his colonial theories and proposals.[34]

In response to Grenville's criticism of his revenue proposals, Knox gave up entirely his suggestions concerning quitrents and the 4.5 percent duties—his only defense being a lame taunt about "Mr. Townshend's having told me the King had desired him to make any use he pleased of those Revenues." Knox was more assertive, however, in upholding his proposal for colonial requisitions, and he explained his reasoning in detail. Although he conceded that in terms of commercial considerations only, colonial internal taxes were preferable to trade duties, he insisted, on the basis of his own experience with Americans, that it was "impracticable" to raise a revenue in the colonies "by Parliamentary Taxes of any kind." In contrast, he argued that his requisition scheme would at one stroke obtain all the advantages, while avoiding the disadvantages, of the alternative forms of taxation. Thus, he speculated, should the colonies accept the requisition scheme, whatever sum they granted would certainly be raised by self-assessed internal taxes. But should they instead "fall out upon the proper contingent to be contributed by each," as they had during the last war, then the imperial government would obtain justification and sympathy, in America as well as Britain, for the assertion of its sovereign powers in the form of parliamentary taxation or, at least, requisitions assessed by authority of the crown or Parliament.

On several subsequent occasions, Knox was to draw up sophisticated and persuasive arguments in support of requisitions and quotas as practical alternatives to parliamentary taxation of the colonies. In contrast, the exegesis on requisitions which he pressed upon Grenville in this letter smacks of a schoolboy's sophomoric exercise, designed primarily to impress and assuage a biased and pedantic master. The impertinent undertones of William's argument became patent when he remarked to Grenville that—by adopting the requisition scheme—the former minister might allay the current opinion that were Grenville in power he would "carry matters to extremity" in order to assert Parliament's sovereign right to tax the colonies.

Paradoxically in this document, so filled with clever and facile expedients, Knox also indicated that his essential conception of empire was nonetheless perceptive and realistic. Most important of all, he admitted without qualification that the preservation of an advantageous imperial connection depended entirely upon consent rather than force:

> The British Colonies I conceive require a different System for their Government from those of other Countries. We cannot exercise the same power over them that other nations can over theirs, and besides they now make and still more will they do so hereafter, a much greater share of our Empire than do the Colonies of other nations. *The only means of taking from them the power of casting us off is to take from them the Inclination so to do, for whenever they wish to get rid of us it will be our wisest measure to get rid of them.*[35]

In subsequent years Knox would expend considerable energy, mental and physical, in the effort to peacefully reconcile the principles of authority and consent within the imperial system. Ultimately, the riddle would prove insoluble, and Knox, in contradiction to these sentiments, would be drawn into the attempt to maintain the imperial connection by coercion.

For the moment, the deeper implications of Knox's concept of imperial relations escaped George Grenville. He generally seized upon the clever superficialities of Knox's apology for his original manuscript. And although Grenville persuasively countered some of Knox's more facile arguments in behalf of colonial quotas and requisitions, he was conspicuously less concerned with their expediency and relative prospects of success than with their implications for the principle of parliamentary supremacy. Grenville insisted that if Parliament explicitly accepted colonial contributions in lieu of direct taxation, the actual exercise of Parliament's sovereign power over America would be abandoned, because "no man would think it worth a Quarrel with the Colonies for a sum of money when the Right of Taxation and that of Sovereignty from which it has ever been inseparable has in effect and in reality been surrendered." On this basis, Grenville commented that Knox's requisition plan would, in effect, deprive Great Britain of one-fourth of its subjects and would thus constitute the "highest Species of Treason against the Constitution and Sovereign Authority of this Kingdom."[36]

In later years, Knox would comment that this issue represented a fundamental divergence between his approach to imperial relations and Grenville's—"The single point upon which we differed, was the omnipotence of Parliament in its jurisdiction over the Colonies. I thought it ought to be limited, in the case of taxation at least, but he would consent to no stipulation of restraint."[37] And Knox, even as he defended Grenville's memory against contemporary caricatures, admitted that his former chief's conception of the imperial connection was restricted by his partiality toward England vis-à-vis the other members of the empire:

> . . . for he not only considered England as the head and heart of the whole, as it certainly is, but he wished to render every other part the mere instrument or conduit of conveying nourishment and vigor to it. He was not well acquainted with the internal State of Ireland, and he knew still less of the circumstances of the American Colonies, and every encouragement that he thought either ought to receive, had no other reference than the increase of the trade or revenue of this country [England].[38]

During the summer of 1768, as Knox revised and rewrote his manuscript, he realized that his materials were too extensive and too varied for a single comprehensive volume. He decided to publish his work in the form of two separate pamphlets: one dealing in a general fashion with the problems of the empire as a whole, the other focusing on the specific issues involved in the controversy over American taxation.[39] By early fall, the first pamphlet was ready for publication, and Knox's correspondence began to betray an author's characteristic last-minute vacillation between enthusiasm and trepidation. On September 8, the manuscript was ready for the compositor, but Knox could not agree to begin printing because he wanted to check "the deficiencies of the malt tax during the last peace." By late September, the publication of new papers on colonial administration prompted him to insist upon additional revisions. On October 4, the first impression was struck; still, Knox insisted that he could not release his work for publication until he had Grenville's approval. Even as Knox hedged about submitting his work to public scrutiny, he was unable to restrain his enthusiasm for the promotional campaign projected by his publisher, John Almon.[40] Almon, whom Knox described as "an excellent fellow at circulating a work, and understands all the mystery of raising its character and exciting purchasers," planned to hold back distribution until the fortnight's interval between the races at Newmarket. Then he would send copies of the pamphlet to the numerous members of Parliament who had standing orders for such works. Obviously, the politically wily publisher sensed—with unerring instinct as events proved—that Knox's pamphlet would stimulate considerable interest, comment, and sales among those politicians who made the rounds of the social and political meetings held at the country seats of the great aristocrats during the racing season. By October 15, Knox could scarcely keep his excitement from turning to melodrama, as he wrote to Grenville: "This night the circulation begins. Almon tells me there have been many enquiries about it, particularly from Administration. I imagine they got notice of it thro' the Post Office, but this night they will be gratified."[41]

Knox's treatise, *The Present State of the Nation*, provides, in fact, the best and most comprehensive expression of his imperial theories. As such, it merits extensive treatment and analysis in any study of his life and thought.[42]

The major premise of the *Present State of the Nation* is familiar: although the Seven Years' War had ended gloriously for Great Britain, the war and the succeeding years of peace had brought the nation to the brink of economic catastrophe. This of course had been the gist of the manuscript Knox had composed after his return from France—the manuscript Grosvenor had persuaded him to submit to Grenville four years earlier. In the *Present State of the Nation*, Knox supplied a most impressive array of statistics to support his original contention. He calculated that at the end of the war the total national debt stood at £148,377,618. This sum burdened the public with an annual interest charge of £4,993,144. Of the total debt, he estimated that the obligations undertaken during the war amounted to £75,087,945, more than double the prewar funded debt. He calculated the annual interest charge on this war debt at £2,614,892. With the acquisition of new territories as a result of the war, the cost of imperial defense had also increased considerably since 1764. Knox claimed that the annual "charge of the military guard then settled, as the permanent peace establishment," exceeded the prewar charge by nearly £1,500,000. On this basis he argued that the increased interest on the national debt plus the additional cost of imperial defense produced an annual figure of £4,114,892, "which may properly enough be called, a rent charge laid upon the people of Great Britain by the late war."[43]

In addition, Knox contended that because the current cost of the imperial "peace establishment" exceeded the current unappropriated revenue, it had become necessary to make up the deficit from the sinking fund, which should have been applied to the discharge of the debt. In the last two year, 1767 and 1768, the deficiency of the unappropriated revenue had increased because of the repeal of "American taxes" and the reduction of the land taxes at home, and therefore larger sums from the sinking fund had been applied to current expenses rather than to debt payments.

Thus Knox painted with detailed strokes a dark image of public finance. Yet even more depressing was the chaotic outline he sketched for national economy as a whole. Given the constant burdens of the debt and the cost of the imperial establishment, there seemed little hope that Parliament could redeem any of the taxes which had been imposed upon British manufacturers, artificers, and and mariners. Knox claimed that the effects of heavy taxes could already be seen in the increased prices of labor and the necessities of life, and he predicted that soon British merchants and manufacturers would have to raise wages and prices to such a level that exports would fall, the balance of trade would become unfavorable, and circulating specie would be drained from the country. The alternatives to this calamitous course seemed equally disastrous to Knox: the continuation of high taxes and low wages would drive manufacturers from Britain to a "cheaper country," perhaps to its perennial Bourbon rival; on the other hand, a reduction of taxes would alarm public creditors and, thereby, aggravate the basic difficulties of the state. Economizing in the appropriations for imperial defense was out of the question because such a policy would only invite national disaster at the hands of Britain's enemies.

This last point, the question of imperial defense, was truly the keystone in the logical structure of Knox's *Present State of the Nation*. Knox was still haunted by the specter of a rejuvenated France—in combination with its Bourbon ally, Spain—bent on exploiting the first opportunity to reverse the disasters of the Seven Years' War. In this pamphlet, Knox developed fully the basic theme of his earlier manuscript: after a seemingly ruinous war, France ironically enjoyed distinct advantages over Britain. He argued that during the latter stages of the war France's distress had prohibited the raising of loans and that, therefore, it had been compelled to finance campaigns through onerous taxes. This burden, however, was only temporary. In contrast, Britain had mortgaged its people in perpetuity for the sake of victory, while the rewards of that victory had, in fact, compounded Britain's disadvantages by increasing the cost of imperial defense. Knox tersely summarized Britain's fiscal dilemma: "Present safety cannot be had without an expensive peace establishment, and an expensive peace establishment prevents relief from taxes or reduction of debt."[44]

For Knox the solution to this fiscal and economic paradox was obvious—the burdens of imperial expense ought to be more equally distributed among the members of the empire. He estimated that the peace establishment could be reduced by £3,300,000 per annum. Of this total, the American colonies—the islands as well as the Continental colonies—could assume an annual contribution of £200,000, while Ireland should provide £100,000 yearly. Knox insisted without reservation that the fiscal circumstances of the American colonies enabled them to bear their share of imperial expenses more easily than the British taxpayers. Nor did he doubt the equity of calling upon the colonies to assume such a burden:

> Whilst 8,000,000 of subjects, inhabiting Great Britain, are made to pay four millions, as the consequences of the late war, one great object of which was the safety and prosperity of the colonies, it surely is not too much to require of the 2,000,000 of subjects residing there, to contribute 200,000 for the general service, especially as the expense of the troops and ships

87

stationed among them for their immediate protection amounts to near double that sum. Nor ought the sovereign authority, which rules the whole empire, and is bound to do equal justice to every part, to admit of any pleas for exempting the subjects in the colonies from sharing in the common burdens, and contributing to the necessities of the state; a sum so much within their abilities, and so much below their proportion of the sums levied from their fellow-subjects in Great Britain.[45]

Although Knox insisted that the colonies were obliged to contribute to imperial defense, in the *Present State of the Nation* he openly declared his willingness to make concessions in their favor. He specifically ignored Grenville's objections to a system of quotas and requisitions and suggested that the most expedient method of raising a contribution from the colonies was for "parliament to assess each colony a specific sum, and leave the mode of raising it to the respective assemblies."[46] And despite Grenville's objections, Knox also recommended that Parliament grant trade concessions to the colonies in recognition of their assumption of imperial fiscal obligations. The navigation system should be maintained, but it should be revised to allow the colonists "to carry directly to foreign markets almost every production of their several climates, which [Britain] has no occasion for." Certainly the following passage indicated that Knox's advocacy of mutual and equitable obligations within the empire was not mere cant:

> It surely is not equal conduct to our colonies, nor politic in respect to Great Britain, that, whilst bounties are given to facilitate the export of British grain, the products of the colonies should be restrained to come and enter a British port, before they can be carried to market, and thereby loaded with the expences of a double freight, port-charges, and all the inconveniences of a prolonged voyage merely to benefit a few individuals in Great Britain.[47]

Knox also argued that the colonists should be granted representation in Parliament, not as a prerequisite to parliamentary taxation of the colonies—in his view, Parliament already possessed this sovereign right—but rather as a just recognition of the status the colonies had attained within the empire.

In the *Present State of the Nation*, Knox firmly fixed the scope of his imperial vision by recommending that Ireland be admitted to full partnership with Great Britain and the American colonies. He estimated that Ireland could provide an additional revenue of £100,000 for the imperial peace establishment. In return, Ireland should be allowed to export to the colonies those commodities they could not conveniently obtain from Great Britain. Knox argued that such a concession would more than compensate Ireland for its increased fiscal contribution, while the trade of Great Britain would in no way be diminished. Above all, Ireland would thus become a great counterbalance to the centrifugal forces threatening the unity of the empire: "The people of Ireland would then find it to be their interest, equally with the people of Great Britain, to continue the colonies in their dependence, and to protect them from foreign attacks."[48]

Although the imperial concepts Knox expounded in the *Present State of the Nation* were not originally inspired by party considerations, in purpose and intent the pamphlet was a partisan tract. Knox admitted explicitly that his plan for "extricating the nation out of its difficulties" was really an extension of the program commenced by the "administration of 1764"—George Grenville's ministry. The *Present State of the Nation* is liberally sprinkled with direct attacks on the policies enacted by subsequent ministries, particularly the Rockingham government's repeal of the Stamp Act. However, Knox went beyond specific issues and individual personalities and drew up a general indictment of the political system which, he believed, had evolved in recent years. He argued that at one time parties had represented great principles of public interest, but recently they had become factions solely pursuing selfish gain and personal interests. The measures advanced by those in power were "proposed only to serve a turn, to prevent clamour against themselves, or to throw blame upon their adversaries."[49] With the disappearance of principles from public affairs, political leaders had "lost their influence over the lower order of the people; even parliament has lost much of its reverence with the subjects of the realm, and the voice of the multitude is set up against the sense of the legislature."[50] In this respect, Knox was obviously alluding not only to the Rockingham administration's repeal of the Stamp Act in response to public clamor but also to the Chatham ministry's difficulties during the Wilkes riots. In Knox's opinion, the evils besetting the state could be remedied only if the king chose his coun-

selors from men of virtue and ability rather than from those syco-
phants and demagogs who banded together for survival in factious
parties:

> Very different must the conduct and characters of those minis-
> ters be, from whom we are to hope the restoration of energy
> to government, and of vigor to the state. Men to whom the
> King shall give his confidence, and the people shall think
> worthy to possess it; who will not sacrifice the interests of the
> state for gaining popularity to themselves, nor seek to make
> their court to the prince by narrowing the liberties of the
> people.[51]

Above all, the circumstances of Great Britain demanded, according
to Knox, the services of a wise and upright finance minister who
would save the nation from disaster much as the great minister Sully had saved France during the reign of Henry IV. Needless to say,
Knox's candidate for the British Sully was obvious.

George Grenville, who had received an advance copy of the *Present State of the Nation*, responded with uncharacteristic enthusiasm.
He complimented Knox upon the "Temper and Force . . . Knowledge and Precision" of his arguments, and he expressly approved
Knox's defense of his own opinions and public measures. Grenville's
praise was qualified, however, by additional objections to Knox's
proposal for colonial quotas and requisitions, and he recommended
that Knox take these points into account when he prepared subsequent editions of the pamphlet.[52]

If Knox was pleased by Grenville's predictable reaction to the
Present State of the Nation, he was more noticeably affected by the
public success of his treatise. The *Gentleman's Magazine* for November 1768 carried a four-page summary of the pamphlet, which it
described as being written with "great force and perspicuity" and
containing matters which deserved "the serious attention of every
subject of Great Britain, as well abroad as at home."[53]

Within two months, the *Present State of the Nation* had run
through three printings. Knox's financial profit from this publication would finally total £200, a high figure for a work of this nature
and, in fact, the only clear profit he received from the sale of any of
his numerous published works. More immediately, the enthusiastic
public reaction provided him with grist for an understandably in-

flated sense of importance. Within a month after publication, he wrote Grenville that his pamphlet had apparently persuaded the king to give up the remnants of Chatham's "unconnected independent Administration" and to declare Grafton "first Minister, with full confidence and ample powers." And Knox even ventured to write that he was afraid to sign this letter because he had become concerned that his correspondence with Grenville might be opened and inspected by the administration.[54]

Knox's *Present State of the Nation* did in fact provoke an immediate political stir. John Almon had been especially prompt in providing Rockingham and Burke with copies. Although the Rockingham Whigs did not wish to alienate Grenville's supporters irrevocably, they could not ignore the public denunciation of their party and its policies in the *Present State of the Nation*. There was some speculation about the individual authorship of the pamphlet—Grenville and his chief lieutenant, Whately, as well as Knox, were suspected—but it was obvious that the piece emanated directly from the Grenvillites and that Grenville himself had a hand in its preparation.[55] Burke began a rejoinder immediately.

Burke's pamphlet, *Observations on a Late State of the Nation*, appeared in February 1769.[56] Although the *Observations* contained embryonic expositions of the author's later masterpieces on political parties and imperial relations, this piece was not generally representative of Burke's best literary efforts. His great rhetorical talents were restricted by the nature of his task—refuting the specifics of Knox's attack on the Rockingham Whigs. This is especially evident in the first part of the *Observations*, where Burke addressed himself to the statistical analysis in the *Present State of the Nation*. He summarily challenged Knox's figures on the decline of British trade, on the increase in the debt arising from the Seven Years' War, and on the cost of the peace establishment. The thrust of his argument was that the author of the *Present State of the Nation* had consciously distorted statistics not only to exaggerate the economic difficulties of Britain but also to discredit the policies of the Rockingham Whigs.

Actually the discrepancies between Knox's figures and those of Burke were largely based upon semantic differences, each author employing statistics according to his own definition of "navigation" or "carrying trade," "peace establishment" or "military guard." And despite these distinctions, Burke ultimately agreed with

Knox's general conclusion that the national debt and the cost of defending the empire had increased enormously since the Seven Years' War.[57]

Burke presented a more positive and convincing argument when he challenged Knox's evaluation of the comparative economic circumstances of France and Britain. Quite correctly, he argued that the high wages and high prices prevailing in Britain were not the harbingers of economic disaster, as Knox depicted them, but were instead signs of a prosperous and expanding economy. Burke's analysis of the fiscal problems which plagued the French monarchy was certainly more realistic than the advantageous circumstances which the *Present State of the Nation* allowed Britain's great rival. However, the supporting evidence advanced by either author was tenuous, to say the least. On the other hand, Knox had not missed the mark entirely, for by the time of the American Revolution, French finances had recovered sufficiently to support a war of revenge against Britain. The consequences, of course, were ultimately disastrous for the Bourbon monarchy; nevertheless, Knox's fears of *revanche* were justified by the event.

In the course of his *Observations*, Burke rejected all Knox's proposed remedies for Britain's fiscal maladies—the economies in defense estimates, the quota and requisition system for America, and the increased contribution from Ireland. Yet he offered no specific alternatives to Knox's proposals. Actually, it was not the individual remedies which Burke found repugnant but rather the systematic and speculative nature of Knox's solutions, which ran counter to Burke's pragmatic view of political relations. Regarding Knox's general scheme for fiscal salvation, Burke wrote:

> This is his perpetual manner. One of his projects depends for success upon another project, and this upon a third, all of them equally visionary. His finance is like the Indian philosophy; his earth is poised on the horns of a bull, his bull stands upon an elephant, his elephant is supported by a tortoise; and so on for ever.[58]

Burke was particularly critical of Knox's approach to imperial problems. He argued that the British Empire was such a unique phenomenon that imperial policies could be successful only if predicated upon actual circumstances rather than upon abstract principles of government, ancient or modern authorities, or even "our own ancient constitution." Burke insisted that this approach was the essential feature of the Rockingham ministry's American policy.

Burke finally ended his *Observations* with a rejoinder to Knox's call for an administration composed of men of "ability" and "virtue." Such a description, he said, was vague and indefinite, since all politicians laid claim to these attributes. Burke argued that the ideal arrangement would be one in which government was in the hands of those who shared mutual trust and fidelity as well as public confidence. In this respect, he anticipated the classical defense of party politics, which he later developed fully in his *Thoughts on the Cause of the Present Discontents* (1770). In the *Observations*, however, Burke was no less vague and indefinite than Knox, for Burke described a party as a group united by its devotion to right and uniform principles rather than its own ambition and profit. Certainly Knox might have protested that all politicians pretended to these virtues.

Burke's *Observations* did not succeed in driving the *Present State of the Nation* from the forum of opinion, although it did provide a challenge to Knox's arguments in the public market. Both works were recognized as important commentaries on public affairs. The *Gentleman's Magazine* insisted that the two publications should be bound together, "for whoever reads one pamphlet, should read both; and they cannot in the same compass, meet with as much political knowledge in any other performance."[59] The same journal also published a delightfully perceptive summary of the difficulties which beset anyone who attempted a synthesis of the two points of view:

> France and England may be considered as two persons dangerously ill; these two writers; as two doctors of physic; the first tells John Bull that his case is very deplorable, much worse than that of his mortal enemy, Louis Baboon; However, he offers John a remedy, which he says will save his life; the second doctor says the first is an ignorant quack, and his remedy not worth a farthing; he does not, however, prescribe at all for poor John, but tells him for his comfort that Louis is certainly worse than he, and without a miracle must die first.[60]

The author of these lines provided a cogent analysis of one of the major disorders afflicting British leadership prior to the American Revolution. Although Knox and Burke were recognized as representing the alternative policies of major political factions, their differences were superficial. In their basic attitudes toward fiscal policy, they shared the common limitations of contemporary mercantilist principle. Knox advocated colonial contributions to the imperial exchequer because he could not reconcile the alternative sources of revenue with his mercantilist concepts. He predicted that increases in either of the traditional sources of revenue—the land tax or trade duties—would lead to higher prices and wages, thereby destroying Britain's competitive economic position, upsetting the balance of trade, and bringing about national catastrophe. Burke's criticism of these arguments was mainly concerned with matters of degree and expediency. He did not challenge the basic assumptions of Knox's economic principles, and consequently the *Observations* provided no alternative solutions for the nation's fiscal difficulties. Although Burke argued that the nation was much more prosperous than Knox allowed, he did not come to grips with the essential fact that after the Seven Years' War the British state remained in financial distress while the nation as a whole grew increasingly prosperous. The traditional sources of revenue were not successfully tapping the wealth which accrued to the nation during this incipient period of Britain's industrial revolution. For several decades after the Seven Years' War, successive ministries searched for new taxes. But it was not until after the American disaster, not until the long ministry of the Younger Pitt, that the government freed itself of antiquated fiscal concepts and succeeded in diverting an equitable portion of the increasing national wealth into the exchequer. Then, for almost a century following the American Revolution, Britain's economic supremacy allowed it to avoid the sensitive issue of colonial contributions to imperial defense.

During the two decades preceding the American Revolution, the specific issue of colonial taxation steadily developed into a general conflict over constitutional relationships within the empire. William Knox's colonial writings reflected this evolutionary pattern. In both the *Claim of the Colonies* and the *Present State of the Nation*, Knox had recommended concessions to the colonial point of view even while he asserted the ultimate sovereignty of Parliament over the colonies. In 1769, however, he published an unqualified defense of the absolute supremacy of Parliament "in all cases whatsoever" in *The Controversy Between Great Britain and her Colonies Reviewed*.

Originally, Knox had planned to treat specific issues of American policy as part of his broader study of imperial relations. During the summer of 1768, however, he decided to "keep the American controversy for a separate work" from his *Present State of the Nation*. This decision did not simply represent an author's grudging admission that his manuscript had grown too large for one publication; it reflected instead a fundamental transformation in his perception of the conflict between Britain and the Continental colonies. In the *Present State of the Nation*, Knox had essentially maintained the integrity of his own long-term conceptions of imperial relations—a synthesis derived from his firsthand experiences as well as from contemporary theories of politics and economics. In contrast, his *Controversy Reviewed* was a tract of the moment, polemical in its origins, purpose, substance, and form.

During the summer and fall of 1768, as Knox was gathering material and developing arguments for the American part of his imperial treatise, the issue of colonial taxation had provoked another confrontation between Britain and the Continental colonies. As reports of American resistance to Townshend's duties circulated through London, political circles were set abuzz with facts and rumors of mounting colonial defiance and projected countermeasures on the part of Government. John Dickinson's *Farmer's Letters*, with its unqualified repudiation of the distinction between internal and external taxes and its sophisticated reaffirmation of colonial immunity from parliamentary taxation, became a prominent topic of discussion. Simultaneously, the Government manifested an apparent determination to uphold parliamentary supremacy when Lord Hillsborough, the American secretary, dispatched a circular suspending the defiant Massachusetts General Court and threatening other colonial assemblies with a like fate should they collaborate with the Massachusetts Bay colony.

Events would prove that the determined policy of the government was more apparent than real: Hillsborough's actions were essentially a matter of individual initiative rather than concerted ministerial policy. Similarly, in historical perspective Dickinson's *Farmer's Letters* would eventually be recognized as a relatively restrained challenge to unlimited parliamentary authority, one designed to conserve rather than destroy the imperial connection. From the perspective of London during the summer and fall of 1768, however, William Knox's perception of the situation was quite different. The business of his Florida agency, as well as his research into colonial records, took him frequently to the Colonial Office, and after several interviews with Hillsborough and his undersecretary, John Pownall, William came away convinced that the Townshend duties would be enforced in America.[61] Furthermore, within the official and private circles which Knox frequented, Dickinson's *Farmer's Letters* was uniformly regarded as another step in the long-range campaign of American radicals to undermine British authority in America and lay the foundation for colonial independence. The immediate fear among such groups was that the renewed threat of American economic boycott would produce a sequence of events in Britain similar to the Stamp Act crisis: under economic duress, aggravated by agitation and propaganda on the part of American sympathizers and opportunistic political factions in Britain, the British public and particularly the merchant community would be lulled by subtle legalities, such as those Dickinson employed, and would again call for an expedient retreat in the face of increasing colonial defiance of parliamentary sovereignty.[62]

In such a charged environment, Knox—already flinching under the prod of Grenville's unflagging criticism—could scarcely persevere in recommending a conciliatory colonial policy with specific concessions for America. Given William's admitted ambition for office, it is not surprising that during the crisis of 1768 and 1769 he became a public advocate of Grenville's and (possibly more significant) Secretary Hillsborough's policy of enforcing parliamentary supremacy in America.

Knox's "research" for the *Contoversy Reviewed* was largely determined by the specific requirements of answering the *Farmer's Letters*. In his study of official records, for example, he consciously sought precedents which could be used to repudiate Dickinson's claim of colonial immunity from parliamentary taxation.[63] Knox also leaned heavily upon George Grenville for general arguments and specific facts in rebuttal to the Pennsylvania "farmer." Grenville, obviously pleased with his protégé's total capitulation, responded with almost overwhelming generosity, stipulating only that Knox incorporate as his own any information which Grenville supplied and in no way indicate publicly the elder statesman's contribution to the pamphlet.[64]

To a limited extent, Knox's *Controversy Reviewed* presented an expanded and refined version of imperial concepts contained in his earlier manuscripts and publications.[65] According to Knox, the empire was not, as the colonists implied, a loose collection of self-governing communities joined together by common economic advantages and a common allegiance to the British monarch. In his view, the empire was a single community in which all members shared obligations as well as privileges. Constitutionally, the advantages and responsibilities of the imperial connection were all derived ultimately from a single source—the sovereign authority of the king in Parliament. In practice this authority alone could insure an equitable distribution of the burdens and privileges of the empire.

In the *Controversy Reviewed*, however, those practical considerations of reciprocal advantages and obligations which had underpinned Knox's previous writings on imperial relations were purged in favor of dogmatic proclamations of parliamentary supremacy "in all cases whatsoever." Indeed, in this pamphlet Knox not only asserted the theory of unlimited parliamentary sovereignty, but he also explicitly repudiated his previous support of such specific concessions to American sensibilities as requisitions and colonial representation in Parliament.

In its logical structure the *Controversy Reviewed* resembles a legal brief. Knox, for example, employed the evidence he had gleaned from official documents to rebut, point by point, the various colonial claims to exemptions from parliamentary taxation. He also marshaled an imposing array of constitutional precedents to prove the absolute sovereignty of Parliament over all members of the empire. In several places, particularly in his treatment of taxation and representation, he reproduced *in toto* the lengthy legalistic refutations of colonial claims which Grenville had provided in abundance. Eventually, the logic of Knox's argument led him to an uncompromising summation worthy of his master:

> Whatever impeaches the jurisdiction of parliament over the Colonies, however insignificant in itself, becomes of importance from its consequences; for if the authority of the legislative be not in one instance equally supreme over the colonies as it is over the people of England, then . . . the Colonies [are not] of the same community with the people of England. All distinctions destroy this union; and if it can be shown in any particular to be dissolved, it must be so in all instances whatever. There is no alternative: either the Colonies are a part of the community of Great Britain, or they are in a state of nature

with respect to her, and in no case can be subject to the jurisdiction of that legislative power which represents her community, which is the British Parliament.[66]

Knox's arguments in the *Controversy Reviewed* were theoretically
consistent and legally sound. Perhaps the abstract logic of his rhetoric was ultimately inescapable. Many years after the American
Revolution, he would indeed claim that his experiences in the colonies had convinced him of the Americans' tendency toward independence and had enabled him in the *Controversy Reviewed* to "tear
off the masque from all their professions of loyalty to the King and
attachment to Great Britain."[67] This claim, however, was largely
a statement of retrospective wisdom. In fact, during the decade before the outbreak of war with the Continental colonies, Knox would
vacillate between alerting Britons to the American propensity toward independence and seeking compromises which would, in effect, void the inevitable logic of his theories.

The year 1768 was undeniably a vintage season for Knox's labors
in the vineyard of pamphleteering. Some time during this year, in
addition to publishing the *Present State of the Nation* and writing the
major part of the *Controversy Reviewed*, he also published a comprehensive apologia for Christian slaveholding. Shortly after he had
returned from America, the Church of England's Society for the
Propagation of the Gospel had enlisted his services as an expert adviser on colonial affairs, particularly in the management of the society's experiment in Christian slaveholding at the Codrington
plantation on Barbados. At the behest of Thomas Secker, archbishop of Canterbury, Knox in 1768 published a pamphlet in response
to attacks upon the society's proslavery sentiments and activities.[68]

Knox's *Three Tracts Respecting the Conversion and Instruction of the
Free Indians and Negroe Slaves* is a unique piece of British proslavery
literature, a defense of Negro bondage based upon the principles of
Anglican evangelicalism.[69] Ultimately, his whole argument rested
upon a negative estimate of the character and intellect of African
slaves—an assessment of racial inferiority which undoubtedly owed
as much to Philip Skelton's early *ad hominem* strictures upon the
barbarism of "*Hottentots* and some other *African* nations" as it did to
William's own experience with the wretched blacks who had come
under his command in Georgia, when he was both provost marshal
and slaveowner. In his *Three Tracts*, Knox wrote:

The dull stupidity of the Negroe leaves him without any desire for instruction. Whether the Creator originally formed these black people a little lower than other men, or that they have lost their intellectual powers through disuse, I will not assume the province of determining; but certain it is that a *new Negroe* (as those lately imported from Africa are called) is a complete definition of indolent stupidity, nor could a more forcible means be employed for the conversion of a deist, than setting one of these creatures before him, as an example of man in a state of nature *unbiassed* by revelation or education.[70]

From this essential premise Knox proceeded inexorably to the conclusion that slaveholding was a positive moral good because it provided the only means in that day to bestow the blessings of Christian salvation upon black Africans. This argument is of course typical of the well-known circular logic of the slaveholder's apologia, but it is more than just typical. Knox's *Three Tracts* contains one of the earliest efforts in print to justify slavery in terms of evangelical Christianity. Nowhere is the tortuous attempt to reconcile the doctrines of evangelicalism and the expedients of slaveholding better exemplified than in the message and the method Knox recommended for conversion of African slaves:

I would confine them to a short summary of religion. That there is one God in heaven who never dies, and who sees and knows every thing. That he made all people, both whites and blacks. That he punishes all roguery, mischief, and lying, either before death or after it. That he punishes them for it before they die, by putting it into their masters hearts to correct them, and after death by giving them to the devil to burn in his own place. That he will put it into their masters hearts to be kind to those who do their work without knavery or murmuring. To take care of them in old age and sickness, and not to plague them with too much work, or to chastise them when they are not able to do it. That in the other world, after they die, he will give all good Negroes rest from all labour, and plenty of all good things. That it was God almighty who put it into their masters heads to give them Sunday for a holiday, and for that reason they ought to say prayers to him, and sing songs to him on that day. That the missionary was come to them to tell them what God Almighty would have them to do, that they might deserve his kindness for them, and that they would anger him if they did not mind what he told them.[71]

The techniques of slave control which permeated this "catechism" are too obvious to belabor; nevertheless, the fact remains that for Knox slave conversion was more than a slaveholder's expedient.

In a concluding passage, Knox, true to his evangelical tenets, charged owners, public officials, and clerics with awesome responsibility for the eternal and temporal well-being of black slaves: "To those therefore who have the power or influence to redress the grievances of these poor wretches, is their case committed, and from those, who through indolence, or by feigning ignorance, or pretending an abhorrence of their condition, turn away from considering it, will the impartial Judge of all the earth one day require an account of the misery of these their fellow creatures."[72] In fact, Knox would himself expend an unusual amount of attention and effort, albeit futile, in behalf of implementing on his own plantations those principles espoused in his *Three Tracts*.

Three Tracts, *Present State of the Nation*, and *Controversy Reviewed* certainly established beyond question Knox's reputation as an expert in colonial affairs. Of course, all three pamphlets were published anonymously, but Knox privately acknowledged his authorship to such friends as Lyttelton and Skelton.[73] Undoubtedly, he also enlightened those acquaintances who were in a position to advance his candidacy for office.

Despite his attachment to George Grenville, Knox continued to court the attention of prominent politicians who enjoyed the distinct advantage of being in office. He was particularly successful in gaining favor with Lord Hillsborough and Lord Clare, two former Grenvillites who had successively presided over the Board of Trade during Chatham's administration. At first, it seemed that the incumbent president, Lord Clare, who was on friendly terms with Lord Grosvenor and Henry Ellis as well as Grenville, would provide the surest route to office. Late in 1767, on the eve of Hillsborough's appointment as secretary of state for America, Clare had told Henry Ellis that if Hillsborough enlisted the board's secretary, John Pownall, for the Colonial Office, he would appoint Knox to Pownall's post.[74] This arrangement miscarried when Clare left the Board of Trade a few weeks later to become vice-treasurer of Ireland. Knox nevertheless continued to cultivate his relationship with Clare, even prevailing upon his lordship to stand as godfather to a daughter born in 1768.

Simultaneously, Knox pursued his acquaintance with Hillsborough. During the crisis over the Townshend duties, Knox became convinced that Hillsborough's political star was in the ascendancy. William's regular appearances at the offices of the American secretary, on business for the Florida agency or in search of materials for his pamphlets, allowed him frequent opportunities to engage Hillsborough in lengthy discussions of American affairs and colonial policy. Knox consistently informed Grenville of his conversations with Hillsborough and confided to his chief that the American secretary obviously expected him to convey information to Grenville. Knox, however, seemed moved by sentiments other than loyalty and candor when he reported to Grenville that "Lord Hillsborough told me he wished the public would avail itself of your abilities but that he saw no likelihood of it at present."[75]

By 1769, Knox was aware that Grenville had withdrawn from party politics and the pursuit of office, even though he continued to maintain the outward appearance of partisan leadership. After Chatham resigned from Government late in 1768, Grenville joined with the Chathamites and the Rockingham Whigs in opposing Grafton's administration. This heterogeneous coalition was particularly active during the Middlesex election controversy, when John Wilkes provoked the new government into an embarrassing constitution conflict with the electorate. Yet despite the apparent solidarity of the opposition, astute politicians recognized that a durable alliance among Chatham, Rockingham, and Grenville was hopeless. And once it became obvious that Grenville had given up the pursuit of office, his supporters, particularly the Bedfordites, steadily crossed over to the administration.[76]

Knox became impatient with Grenville's apathy toward the obvious disintegration of his party and decided to prod his chief into action. In October 1769, on his own initiative, Knox published Grenville's speech to Parliament denouncing the administration's expulsion of John Wilkes from the House of Commons. Grenville, however, wanted no part of Knox's forwardness. He immediately demanded that Knox stop the publication of his speech, insisting that it would only subject him to public abuse. Since the speech was already in circulation, Knox could only issue a statement that Grenville had not consented to its publication. But Knox did not repent his precipitate action. He wrote Grenville that in his opinion publication of the speech would restore Grenville's reputation with the king, the public, and especially "the Bedford people," who "would be rather pleased with the speech." Knox was obviously disappointed with Grenville's reaction to the entire episode.[77]

By 1770, officeholding was no longer just a matter of personal ambition to Knox. Increasing family responsibilities were pressing upon his financial resources. In 1767, during the second year of their marriage, William and Letitia had celebrated the birth of their first child, a boy. Governor Lyttelton, recently appointed ambassador to Portugal, was delighted by Knox's request that he stand as godfather and wrote from Lisbon in December 1767: "I rejoice that my little Man and his Fairy Mama are well. Give her a kiss for me, and a Sugar Plumb [sic] to the boy." Within a few months, however, the child was dead. Lyttelton, once again burdened with the impossible task of consoling his friend in deepest grief, expressed the hope that "what has happen'd is rather to be considered as an interruption of your present happiness rather than as a lasting misfortune."[78]

William sought refuge in his work. Immediately after the death of his first-born, Knox launched himself into the sustained effort which resulted in the publication of the three treatises between 1768 and 1769. And within a short time, Lyttelton's earlier prayer was realized. In August 1768, Knox wrote Grenville that he was unable to attend him at Wotton to discuss a manuscript because the moment was "so critical to my wife that I dare not go from home." Finally on August 20, with obvious relief, he reported to Grenville that his wife had been safely delivered of a daughter. The parents named her Henrietta, and William secured an eminent patron for the child when Lord Clare agreed to serve as her godfather.[79] Lyttelton was a bit disappointed that he had been denied a godson, but hardly a year had passed before William and Letitia were able to make amends by asking him to serve as godfather to infant Thomas, born November 15, 1769.[80]

Besides these additions to his own family, Knox found himself increasingly burdened with his Irish relatives. Some time after the Knoxes had established their residence in Hanover Square, William's brother Bob joined their household. Subsequently, William found it necessary to expend his limited political influence in abortive efforts to obtain official employment for his brother.[81] Then

William's familial obligations were further compounded when, in response to Philip Skelton's persistent and reproachful pleas, he assumed responsibility for the family of a bankrupt brother in Ireland. Finally, in 1769, Tom, the eldest offspring of this fraternal line, a penniless half-educated youth, arrived in London to seek his fortune under the protection of his uncle. In these difficult circumstances, Skelton could only recommend that William turn to divine providence to "wind your way out of that labyrinth, wherein you are at present [intricated]."[82]

It must have seemed instead that providence had completely abandoned Knox, for during the winter of 1769–70 he was taken seriously ill. Certainly the persistence of this illness heightened his concern for the precarious nature of his financial resources. He particularly realized that in the event of his death, his family would be deprived of the income from his Georgia and Florida offices. In February 1770, he applied to Hillsborough for the reversion of his provost marshal office to his infant son. Within a week Hillsborough's undersecretary, John Pownall, replied that he had forwarded Knox's petition to his chief and that Hillsborough wanted to see Knox as soon as he was well.[83]

Knox described the upshot of his subsequent interview with Hillsborough in a concise if laconic manner: "The Earl of Hillsborough sent to me and offered me the joint under secretaryship with Mr. Pownall."[84] Although Knox's account of this meeting and subsequent events was written several years after the fact, his narrative provides an intimate insight into the subtle art of contemporary office seeking. Knox immediately responded to Hillsborough's offer with expressions of delight at the prospect of serving under his lordship, whose principles so nearly corresponded to his own views. But he insisted that he could not think of accepting any engagement without first obtaining the approval of George Grenville. Hillsborough was pleased with Knox's reply and indicated that he would have been disappointed if Knox had answered him in any other manner. Knox therefore waited upon Grenville at Wotton, where he decided to broach the delicate subject of his interview in this fashion:

I did not . . . think it right to acquaint him immediately with the particular occasion of my coming, but waited first to learn from him what were his own purposes or views respecting public matters, and especially with regard to his expectations of coming into office, for I considered that by informing him of the offer made to me, and asking his opinion whether I should accept or refuse it, I should lay him under the difficulty of either allowing me to quit him, though he might be desirous that I should continue with him, or give me a stronger claim to service from him, by preventing me from taking what had been offered me by Lord Hillsborough.[85]

In the course of their conversation, Grenville revealed to Knox that he had given up all thoughts of office. His health was declining, he disliked being in opposition, and he realized that he could not force his way into office. Knox then told Grenville of Hillsborough's offer and, according to William's account, Grenville graciously approved his taking office:

He said that he was very glad; for . . . he had thought it would never be in his power to be of any use to me, in return for all attention I had shewn him; that it was his wish that all his friends should accept situations which they thought honorable and proper for them, without any attention to him, and as he thought me very fit for office, he would advise me to accept it if I felt no objections in my own mind.[86]

When Knox accepted Hillsborough's offer, at least one contemporary did not entirely believe the account of Grenville's approbation which Knox circulated. On July 3, 1770, Charles Lloyd wrote to Grenville:

If (between ourselves) my opinion is asked of what you did say to [Knox], I own I do not believe it was exactly as . . . stated by him. I *conjecture* that you might tell him, if he thought his acceptance of the office fitting for him in every other respect, that you begged him not to decline it from any personal considerations relating to yourself. This conveyed in the language of good will and good humour, which is natural to you, will be easily metamorphosed, by a partial relator, into what is construed as a request from you to him that he would take it. Am I a good guesser or is this mere chimera?[87]

Lloyd undoubtedly spoke with authority, for three years earlier he too had left Grenville's service to accept a government office.[88]

Knox was neither the first nor the last Grenvillite to abandon his connection for the fruits of office. According to the practical rules of eighteenth-century politics, Grenville had in fact forfeited his claims to Knox's services. Many of Grenville's "friends"—Lord Suffolk, Lord Halifax, and Thomas Whately—remained aloof from administration until after Grenville's death in 1770, but these were men of considerable political reputation and influence. Minor party figures such as Knox could not afford the virtue of loyal indifference to political opportunity.

As a veteran politician, Grenville was well aware of these political realities. Shortly after Knox accepted office, Grenville wrote him a note of congratulations. He assured Knox that he "should have been truly sorry if any Consideration relative to me alone had prevented you from accepting an Offer which you thought advantageous and honourable to you and which I am persuaded no man is more able or more willing to discharge with Industry and Fidelity towards the King and his People in the present distracted state of Affairs in America."[89] Possibly Grenville's pedantic style obscured his true sentiments, as was so often the case. Probably the elder statesman resented desertions, even as he accepted them as inevitable. Certainly Grenville must have known that Knox considered an undersecretaryship in the American Department both "honourable" and "advantageous."

5. "The Dye Is Cast & More Mischief Will Follow": Conflicts of Interest & the Coming of the American Revolution, 1770–1775

With an appointment as undersecretary in the Colonial Office, William Knox certainly realized to the fullest those ambitions which had inspired the talented but unconnected young Georgia councilor to return to England. No one could more fully appreciate Knox's success and satisfaction than Henry Ellis, who conveyed his warmest congratulations immediately upon learning of his former protégé's good fortune.[1] Ellis could not resist a gratuitous reference to his own recent efforts on Knox's behalf with his friend Lord Hillsborough; nevertheless, he admitted that his recommendations were probably of limited consequence, since Hillsborough's senior undersecretary, John Pownall, still bore a grudge against Ellis dating from their postwar rivalry over American policy. Ellis now took vicarious pleasure in the perverse speculation that Knox's appointment was "not very favorable" to Pownall. Although Knox, in fact, avoided his former patron's immediate legacy, becoming instead a close partner and personal friend of Pownall, Ellis' observations nonetheless anticipated a predominant condition of Knox's tenure in office. The American Department, from its creation to its dissolution, was the center of exceptionally strong and treacherous political crosscurrents.

This secretariat was a recent innovation in the administrative structure at Whitehall. Over the years, a variety of departments, boards, councils, and committees had exercised authority over colonial policy and administration. By the middle of the eighteenth century, these functions were generally divided between the offices of the secretary of state for the Southern Department and the president of the Board of Trade. For more than a century, the decentralized and often chaotic nature of colonial administration had been a perennial object of criticism among imperial officials and theorists, yet the creation of a separate Colonial Office in 1768 had been a direct result of domestic political considerations rather than a movement toward improved imperial efficiency.[2]

Following the Earl of Chatham's collapse and virtual abdication of ministerial leadership in 1767, his nominal successor, the Duke of Grafton, desperately sought an alliance which would bolster Chatham's crumbling administration. The Bedford party, always anxious for office and recently disillusioned with the opposition after Grenville's attack on Rockingham, agreed to join the administration late in 1767. But the Bedfordites placed a condition on their accession: the removal of Chatham's main ally in office, the Earl of Shelburne, secretary of state for the Southern Division. Grafton decided to force Shelburne's resignation by proposing to establish a new colonial department, which would be assigned much of the work now performed by Shelburne's office. Apparently Grafton believed that Shelburne would retire rather than accept this humiliation, but the secretary surprisingly agreed to the arrangement and remained in office for almost a year. The unexpected issue of this intrigue was brought about in January 1768, when Hillsborough became the first secretary of state for America, bringing the long-anticipated Colonial Office grudgingly into being.

This unfortunate provenance would persistently dog the American Department from the beginning of its brief span. Hillsborough soon discovered that cabinet colleagues were not at all inclined to grant the new secretary equal status in the deliberations of the administration.[3] Throughout Hillsborough's term, his fellow secretaries of state, particularly the incumbent Southern secretaries, treated the American Department as an inferior office and a temporary encroachment on their proper jurisdictions. Hillsborough's personal arrogance and rashness made him a difficult partner at best. But under the circumstances his irascible temperament served him well, for it was mainly by the force of his personality that the new secretary firmly established his control over colonial policy and administration—for better or worse.

Only a few months after he entered office, Hillsborough asserted his independence in matters of colonial policy by a decisive rejoinder to the Massachusetts assembly's circular repudiating the Townshend duties. Grafton, already distressed by the Wilkes' riots at home, had balked at the prospect of provoking further disturbances in America. But Hillsborough, an outspoken advocate of parliamentary supremacy over the colonies, discounted such fears, and in the spring of 1768 he dispatched an uncompromising warning to the colonial governors to dissociate their colonies from the Massachusetts circular. Hillsborough's action produced an immediate furor in America. One historian of the American Revolution has written, "Lord Hillsborough's Circular Letter deserved to rank not far below the Stamp Act and Townshend duties among the contributions of British ministers to the formation of the American Union."[4] Grafton and Lord Chancellor Camden, both supporters of a moderate American policy, openly repudiated Hillsborough's letter to the colonial governors. But Grafton's cabinet was strongly divided over America, and Hillsborough successfully weathered the storm aroused by his unilateral action. When Grafton resigned in January 1770 and the ministry was reorganized under the leadership of Lord North, Hillsborough retained the seals of the American Department in the new administration.

Although Knox was not yet a member of the American Department, he had readily approved Hillsborough's response to the Massachusetts assembly. By this time Knox, still in the midst of composing his *Present State of the Nation* and *Controversy Reviewed*, was beginning to succumb to Grenville's inflexible American policy, and in May 1768 he wrote Grenville that in his opinion Hillsborough's firm measures would make the colonists "peaceable subjects in the future."[5] But when Hillsborough's dispatch served only to revive nonimportation agreements in the colonies, provoking British merchants in turn to join the Americans in a petition campaign against the obnoxious duties, Knox began to entertain second thoughts about the efficacy of a hard line toward America. Late in 1769, on the eve of his appointment to office, he expressed qualified approval of the government's decision to remove all Townshend's colonial levies except that on tea: "I like the idea of letting the colonies alone, but I do not approve of starting new divisions, or giving fresh occasions for altercation."[6]

By the time Knox entered the American Department in 1770, the organization and routine of Hillsborough's office at Whitehall were as fixed as the secretary's attitudes toward colonial policy.[7] Since Hillsborough served simultaneously as president of the Board of Trade, most of the day-to-day activities of administering a far-flung empire were concentrated in the old Plantation Office, located on the second floor of the Treasury building. There a staff—consisting of two undersecretaries, one first clerk, two senior clerks, four ordinary clerks, and one or more messengers—conducted business in four large but crowded rooms. The physical appointments were generally typical of government offices of the period, with white plastered walls enclosing a clutter of chairs and green baize–covered desks surrounded and interdicted by the contrasting woodwork of well-filled presses, drawers, bookcases, and cupboards. The exotic maps of imperial and plantation geography hanging from the walls must have provided a unique visual orientation for permanent occupants as well as visitors.[8]

The undersecretaries, particularly the senior incumbent, were responsible for the general supervision of departmental correspondence. They usually handled routine dispatches without troubling the head of the department. Important items requiring the secretary's personal attention were laid before him or, if he were absent from the capital, were forwarded to him. The undersecretaries might even volunteer suggestions to their chief, but in Hillsborough's office all correspondence was conducted under the explicit or implicit guidance of the secretary. The same rule applied to the various other duties performed by the undersecretaries, especially to the preparation of colonial business for cabinet meetings or for the defense of colonial policies before Parliament.

Even within the limited sphere of responsibility which fell to the undersecretaries in the American Department, Knox performed only routine duties during Hillsborough's tenure. His senior colleague, John Pownall, was an efficient administrator with long experience in colonial affairs.[9] Since 1741, Pownall had served on the Board of Trade, first as clerk and later as chief secretary. When Hillsborough assumed the dual roles of American secretary and president of the Board of Trade, he retained Pownall's services at the board in addition to appointing him undersecretary in the American Department and assigning him the task of organizing the new office. The departmental archives leave no doubt that during Hillsborough's tenure Pownall overshadowed Knox in the daily business of the Colonial Office: Pownall's signature adorns a large number and wide variety of departmental documents, while Knox's signature, or even his distinctive handwriting, can be found on only two minor pieces of correspondence.

Knox admittedly undermined his own effectiveness under Hillsborough by contradicting his chief in a matter of American policy. In 1770, the North government, despite the repeal of the Townshend duties, sought to put an end to Massachusetts Bay's consistent defiance of parliamentary supremacy. In June, a committee of the Privy Council opened an inquiry into the affairs of Massachusetts, while the American Department began preparing recommendations for reforming the constitution of the colony. According to Knox's own account, Sir Francis Bernard, a former governor of the colony and a close friend of Pownall, appeared at the Colonial Office with papers calling for major alterations in the Massachusetts charter. Knox of course had advocated the reform of colonial constitutions since his return from America. Yet on this occasion, the new undersecretary, apparently persevering in his recent conversion to the belief that the time was not ripe for a "fresh altercation" with America, took a moderate stand and opposed "any alteration but that of the Council." Hillsborough and Pownall, however, supported Bernard's proposal. Knox claimed that because of his dissent over the Massachusetts reforms, he was "ever after excluded by Lord Hillsborough from all consultations whilst he staid in office."[10] Certainly for the first time he was brought face to face with the reality that even in high office unguarded opposition to one's superiors could be a futile and emasculating exercise.

Even as Knox was sensibly distressed by this momentary ostracism within the Colonial Office, a succession of disasters to his private fortune drove him to the point of physical collapse. In 1770, he had decided to divert most of the enterprise on his Knoxborough plantation from lumbering to rice cultivation in order to take full advantage of a decade-long rise in the price of rice. By fall, however, Habersham, who had advised Knox against such expansion, began warning his client that the fields at Knoxborough had not been adequately banked to protect them from the usual tides and freshets.[11] Habersham's letters succeeded only in making Knox painfully aware of the impossibility of directing the intricate affairs of a rice plantation across thousands of miles.

In his anxiety, Knox untypically replied with artless recriminations. He reproached Habersham for not having kept him adequately informed of the details of his plantation affairs. He even charged his friend with holding back considerable sums due him from Habersham's Savannah commercial house of Harris and Habersham. For a while, Habersham bore Knox's reproaches with only mild rejoinders, but finally the benevolent old man's patience was exhausted.[12] On the first day of December 1770, Habersham candidly replied that he would no longer bear the blame for the failure of a planting scheme which Knox had initiated under the direct supervision of others. He insisted that conditions at Knoxborough had reached such a state that he could not provide Knox with firsthand accounts, "unless you expected that I was to wade through your Rice Field, (where you had no Banks) up to my middle in mire and Water to the manifest Hazard of my Life." Rather than persevere in providing only "unthankfull Advise," Habersham informed Knox, "I came to [the] resolution to have no further concern in your affairs."

The worst was yet to come for the absentee planter. During the spring and early summer of 1771, torrential rains brought the worst floods in memory to tidewater Georgia. As swollen streams overflowed their banks, all plantations from four to five miles above Savannah came under water. Rice fields, including those which had been well banked, were severely damaged—even harvested rice stored at plantations was destroyed by the floods. Habersham reported to a friend that at Knox's plantation "there is 7 feet [of] water, and I dont expect he will raise a grain of rice in his Swamp."[13]

It is not surprising that Knox's health, always tenuous at best, collapsed during the winter of 1771–72 under the strain of personal economic misfortune in America. Skelton received reports that Knox was an "invalid," while Habersham's son Joseph, recently returned to Georgia from London, reported firsthand to his father that Knox was hardly recognizable, "being so much emaciated."[14]

James Habersham's genuinely charitable nature would not allow him to ignore the desperate plight of his old friend. He immediately offered to resume the management of Knox's Georgia estates, assisted by a mutual friend, John Graham. For his part, Knox had the good sense to allow these two resident "attorneys" full powers over his plantation affairs. By late 1771, they had carried out improvements at Knoxborough, and Habersham predicted that Knox would have "a tolerable Crop of Rice next year." Habersham's deeds matched his dedication: in February 1772 he shipped forty-two barrels of Knox's rice, valued at £125, and in July he wrote that Knox had about 140 acres of rice in a "very flourishing condition" and that his plantation affairs were daily growing better. Habersham also invested some of Knox's available funds in rice shipping, reporting in February, for example, that he had purchased fifty barrels

of rice carrying an insured value of £160, which he would ship in
Knox's account to the London merchant house of John Nutt.[15]

Although these figures reflect a considerably inflated market
price for rice in 1772, due largely to the shortages of the previous
year, Habersham's reports gave Knox every reason to regain confidence in the prospects of his American plantation investments. His
health improved steadily, and with renewed optimism he energetically resumed the expansion and improvement of his Georgia properties. In 1772, Graham completed purchase, in Knox's behalf, of
one thousand acres of land at Goshen.[16] A year later, Habersham
wrote that Graham had bought thirty-two slaves for Knox at a cost
of £772.17.0. Apparently this expenditure was owing to the expansion of enterprise upon Knox's estates rather than the need to
replace labor, because Habersham particularly remarked that Knox
had been "fortunate in having your People preserved, and if I mis-
take not have lately had two or three children born."[17]

The extent of Knox's accentuated regard for his American plantations is especially evidenced by his substantial investments in enter-
prises which did not promise immediate economic returns. For example, he had a "sick house" erected for the care of slaves on his
Knoxborough estates. And with Habersham's assistance he also
tried to implement his program for Christian conversion of slaves
upon his own estates. As early as 1770, Habersham and Knox had
attempted to promote the cause of slave conversion by recommending to the Society for the Propagation of the Gospel the ordination
of one Cornelius Winter, a lay preacher successful in spreading
Christianity among slaves on plantations about Savannah. Despite
Habersham and Knox's energetic lobbying among influencial lay
members of the church in England, however, the SPG denied holy
orders to this erstwhile Anglican missionary. Habersham, whose
long friendship with George Whitefield had earned him the reputation of a crypto-Methodist, bitterly denounced the church hierarchy for its "prejudice" toward the lay preacher. Knox, on the
other hand, vented his own frustrated evangelicalism, as well as his
disillusionment with the Anglican hierarchy, by direct means. In
1774, once his plantation affairs were again flourishing, Knox sent
out to Georgia two Moravian lay missionaries, who were given employment as carpenters at Knoxborough and were charged with
teaching Christianity to the slaves on Knox's plantation and those
of interested planters in the vicinity. Within a short time, Haber-

sham was reporting enthusiastically on the progress and prospects of the two evangelists. Unfortunately, this dedicated attempt at slave conversion was terminated prematurely. Habersham's death in 1775 deprived Knox of the on-the-spot assistance of a planter sympathetic to the cause, while the outbreak of the American Revolution soon rendered the point moot anyway.[18]

Two years before Habersham's death, declining health had forced him to give up direct supervision of Knox's estates. Although Graham agreed to continue acting as Knox's attorney, Habersham advised Knox that his "considerable planting Interest" required the continuous attention of someone who understood accounts, and he recommended that Nathaniel Hall, a neighboring planter, be employed as joint attorney with Graham.[19] From 1773, Knox's plantation affairs continued to prosper under the careful management of Graham and Hall. By the outbreak of the American war, the two Savannah River plantations, known as Knoxborough, totaled 2,585 acres worked by 122 slaves; in 1776 the entire estate—including land, slaves, livestock, crops, structures, and equipment—would be appraised for the revolutionary government of Georgia at a total value of £15,025. By Knox's estimation, this figure was considerably under the real market value of his plantation. He particularly noted that although only part of his rice lands had been brought under cultivation, during the years immediately preceding the war Knoxborough had provided him an income of £1,500 to £2,000 a year.[20] Of course, in evaluating his total property interests in Georgia, the potential market value of over 5,000 acres of unimproved land acquired over the years must be added to any assessment of Knoxborough.

The economic value of Knox's Georgia investments, in annual returns as well as long-term capital worth, is especially significant compared with the income he derived from his various imperial offices. As undersecretary in the American Department, Knox received a salary of £500 per annum. His senior colleague, Pownall, enjoyed a similar salary, but in addition he collected all the fees which accrued to the undersecretaries in the performance of various departmental services. Although Knox, after he entered the American Office, was allowed to retain the post of provost marshal of Georgia, from which he derived a total income of about £160 per annum, Hillsborough apparently required to him to resign his East Florida agency in favor of another office seeker.[21] This loss of a £200 per annum income came, of course, at the very moment of Knox's financial embarrassment over his planting scheme in Georgia. Apparently this distress prompted him to ask Hillsborough for a share of the undersecretary's fees, which Pownall monopolized, but his lordship promised instead to compensate Knox with the first office that fell vacant. Consequently, in 1772, William was allowed to purchase the reversion to the secretaryship of New York for £3,000; he subsequently transferred the duties of the office to a resident deputy, Samuel Bayard, who agreed to pay him £1,000 per annum plus specified fees.[22]

From this mélange of offices and sinecures—an arrangement quite typical of the eighteenth-century civil service—Knox derived a substantial income of over £1,500 per annum. But the most significant fact is that more than £1,000 of Knox's income from his officeholding was drawn directly from American sources in New York and Georgia. When his private economic interests in Georgia —annual income as well as capital investments—are added to this figure, it becomes obvious that the nature and extent of the undersecretary's concern for American affairs were more complex than his ideological commitments and official responsibilities alone might indicate. Nor had the implications of potential conflict between his official responsibilities and private interests escaped his attention —a conflict most candidly acknowledged in his own flattering recreation of a supposed conversation between John Dickinson and Benjamin Franklin:

> There is another Fellow says Dickinson who mauled [Franklin] & me cursedly & who we got turned out of the Agency of Georgia. He has been much in the way of our Friends in England altho' we hung him in Effigy in America. He got thro' means of that Devil Hillsborough the Reversion of the Secretary & Clerk of the Council's office in New York and he has lately given £3000 to the present occupant for his Interest in those offices taking it for granted that the Fees which have been allowed to be taken for Fifty years past would still be continued and that he would receive a proper recompense for his money paid down. Let us then prevail on the Board of Trade to represent the Fees in New York as enormous and altho the representation be made under the same roof & drawn up by his Colleague in office, let him be kept ignorant of what is in-

tended untill it is carried into execution. By this maneuvre let us have the emoluments of the offices he has purchased reduced above three fourths and provoke him to set up his Patent and the Ordinance of the Colony against this arbitrary act of the Crown and so force him out of the Secretary office and into our party.[23]

Although Knox himself was able for many years to avoid the fate he conjured up in this parody, in 1772 he was witness to a more substantial combination of conflicting interests and political intrigue, which succeeded in bringing down Hillsborough. Throughout North's long ministry, his colleagues persistently plotted against his leadership. The Bedfordite faction and the so-called king's friends—those figures who claimed political allegiance to no one but George III—were particularly active in periodic attempts to oust North from power. In 1772, the Bedfordites, whose jealous animosity toward Hillsborough had never abated, decided to strike at North by humiliating the American secretary. Their opportunity came when Hillsborough, as president of the Board of Trade, advised against American land grants sought by the Grand Ohio Company. The English and American promoters of this land scheme had taken the precaution of winning the support of powerful political allies. According to Knox's account, the Bedfordite ministers Rochford and Gower, as well as two secretaries of the Treasury, had been granted shares in the projected company and had used their influence in the Privy Council to overturn Hillsborough's veto of the land grants.[24]

Hillsborough, finding himself ensnared by the Bedfordite trap, threatened to resign. North was shaken by the controversy, but he skillfully blunted the main thrust of the assault by accepting Hillsborough's resignation and placating him with an English peerage. Subsequently, North ignored the Bedfordites' demand for the dissolution of the American Department, and in August 1772 he arranged the appointment of his own half brother, the Earl of Dartmouth, to the American secretaryship.

The temperament and attitudes of the new secretary could scarcely have contrasted more sharply with those of his imperious predecessor. Personally amiable and congenial, Dartmouth had earned the reputation of a friend of America in both Britain and the colonies by his opposition to the Stamp Act.[25] It is hardly surprising then that shortly after his appointment one correspondent, who identified himself only as a "Londoner," entreated Dartmouth to be "Ever watchful and jealous of your two Secretarys, for they carry with them into office, all the injurious and illiberal Ideas and *Enmity's, publick* and *personal*, of their late Lord, and will insidiously labor to possess your Lordship, with their private Prejudices and Resentments."[26] Although the new secretary sincerely desired to conciliate and pacify America, such well-wishers as the Londoner mistakenly disregarded the fact that Dartmouth, even as he had voted to repeal the stamp duties, had voted in favor of the Declaratory Act. Dartmouth in fact generally shared William Knox's dedication to the principle of parliamentary supremacy over the colonies, qualified only by the promptings of imperial expediency.

At the beginning of Dartmouth's tenure, Knox feared that hostile counsels, such as those of the Londoner, might persuade the new secretary to require his resignation.[27] But these trepidations were quickly proven ill founded. The new secretary was pathetically conscious of his own lack of knowledge in the details of imperial affairs and welcomed Knox's expertise in such business. In addition, Dartmouth, a pious evangelical, was undoubtedly reassured by his new lieutenant's devout but latitudinarian profession of the doctrines and practice of Anglican Christianity. Under Dartmouth, Knox rapidly secured a greater degree of confidence than had ever been granted by Hillsborough.

Although Pownall retained primary responsibility for the execution of departmental business, Knox's role was expanded in degree and kind. Throughout Dartmouth's tenure, Knox frequently drew up routine dispatches to governors and other officials in the colonies, and in the secretary's absence he even took the liberty of sending out such documents under his own signature. And when Pownall was away from the office for any extended period, Knox took over his substantial responsibilities. Indeed, Knox so succeeded in winning Pownall's confidence that he was increasingly entrusted with more important assignments—providing relevant departmental papers for the cabinet and Parliament and conducting visiting colonial officials through the maze of protocol at Whitehall and the court—duties previously a special preserve of the senior undersecretary.

As Knox extended his purview in departmental business, he began to proffer advice to the secretary on matters of American policy. In September 1773, he advised Dartmouth to avoid embroiling His Majesty's government in the controversy between Gov. Thomas Hutchinson and the assembly of Massachusetts over the so-called Hutchinson-Oliver correspondence. In these private letters, written to various figures in Britain, Hutchinson and Lt. Gov. Andrew Oliver had defended British policies and supported parliamentary supremacy. Somehow Benjamin Franklin had obtained the correspondence and sent it to Massachusetts, where it was published by provincial patriots. When the ensuing public uproar in the colony, accompanied by a sharp exchange between Hutchinson and the assembly, seriously discredited his administration, the governor begged the American secretary for some expression of His Majesty's displeasure over the publication of the correspondence. Although Knox sympathized fully with the sentiments expressed in the Hutchinson-Oliver letters and agreed that their publication had been "base and unworthy," he nevertheless insisted to Dartmouth that since the documents had not been addressed to the British government it would be impolitic to "transfer the Assembly's enmity from these gentlemen to the Secretary of State."[28] Dartmouth apparently accepted Knox's view, for although the Privy Council castigated Franklin severely for having transmitted the letters to America, the North administration avoided any direct controversy with the Massachusetts legislature over the issue.

It is most significant that Knox's advice in this instance, although *politique*, completely contradicted his previous pleas in behalf of supporting and strengthening friends of British policy in America. Nor does it seem that this lapse into cold-blooded expediency was only a momentary aberration. Within a few months of the Hutchinson controversy, Knox took a similar stand against a more ominous request for assistance from royal officials in New York.

This incident involved a long-standing conflict between New York and New Hampshire over land claims along their ill-defined boundary. In 1773, the smoldering controversy erupted in violence when about two hundred armed men claiming land under New Hampshire grants burned buildings belonging to persons claiming the same land under grants from New York. As late as the preceding December, Dartmouth had instructed Gov. William Tryon of New York to settle the land dispute in a manner satisfactory to all parties and above all to avoid the use of military force, except "in cases of absolute necessity."[29]

Dartmouth was absent from the capital on October 6, 1773, when Knox received a dispatch from Governor Tryon requesting a detachment of royal troops to put down a "mob" rioting on the New Hampshire border. Recognizing the serious implications of the governor's request, Knox consulted with Pownall, and together they agreed to detain the New York packet for Dartmouth's reply. Pownall immediately forwarded Tryon's dispatch to Dartmouth, enclosing his own recommendations against granting the governor's request for troops.[30] In Pownall's opinion, the provincial militia would be adequate to restore order; while, in any event, caution was warranted, since the rioters' claims might eventually be upheld in law. In a separate letter, Knox seconded Pownall's advice to Dartmouth, adding his own argument that compliance with Tryon's request would be unprecedented and unwarranted:

> . . . exclusive of the violence & inhumanity of employing the Soldiery upon such occasions I always understood from Lord Hillsborough that the King was particularly averse to the detaching his Troops for such purposes as it seems to make the Army odious to the public. . . . I really suspect that an occasion is sought by the Governor & Council of New York to employ the Kings Troops in this business; not because they are necessary, but as a manifestation of the King's authority being on their side.[31]

On this occasion, as in the case of the Hutchinson-Oliver letters, Knox gave advice in keeping with his recent conversion to avoiding "new divisions" between the colonies and the imperial government. Yet this apparently sensible middle-of-the-road course plotted by officials at Whitehall would turn out to be a treacherous two-way path. Within a short period of time, Knox and Pownall would find cause to complain of an inexplicable lack of firmness and initiative on the part of Governor Tryon and his council in dealing with radical disruptions in the pivotal colony of New York.

By 1773, Knox found himself fully restored to the councils of his department. But the fact was that under Dartmouth the Colonial Office generally exerted minimal influence on imperial policy and administration. Lords Rochford and Suffolk, respectively secretaries of the Southern and Northern departments, aggressively assumed functions exercised by the American Department during Hillsborough's tenure. According to Knox, Rochford simply wished to engross his powers by reclaiming the jurisdiction his office had lost to the new secretaryship; Suffolk, on the other hand, had his eyes fixed upon a greater prize: "Proud and ambitious, he looked up to the chief command, and considered that no way was so likely to obtain it as by frequent changes and disagreements among his colleagues."[32] Finally, Dartmouth's ministerial colleagues, in addition to their ambitions and their long-standing jealousy of the American Department, felt little sympathy for the Colonial secretary's personal dedication to the conciliation of America. Dartmouth, whose amiable and congenial personality stood in sharp contrast to Hillsborough's pugnacious temperament, failed to defend the prerogatives inherited from his predecessor. While his fellow ministers steadily encroached upon the jurisdiction of the American Department, Dartmouth chose to avoid the whole issue by indulging in frequent and lengthy absences from his office at Whitehall.[33]

Undersecretary Pownall made a determined effort to maintain the authority and integrity of his department. On his own initiative, he assumed increasing responsibility for colonial correspondence and interdepartmental liaison relating to America—even to the point of invading the proper jurisdiction of his chief.[34] But within a year of Dartmouth's accession, Pownall was forced to admit to Knox that in the absence of their superior he was unable to resist the "unwarrantable encroachments" upon their office.[35] Nor can Pownall's complaints be casually dismissed as signifying only the self-serving anguish of a wounded bureaucratic ego. During the winter of 1772–73, the overlapping authority and the administrative confusion which the veteran civil servant decried became, in fact, a source of considerable public embarrassment for the North government.

Late in 1772, rumors circulated throughout London that a military expedition against the native Caribs on St. Vincent Island was in a desperate state, with ill-equipped troops being decimated in an unseasonable campaign. The North ministry was persuaded that imminent disaster could be averted only if Gov. William Leyborne of Grenada, who claimed jurisdiction over the recently conquered island, was restrained from interfering in military operations on St. Vincent.[36] Since Dartmouth was away in the country, Pownall was given charge of the delicate business of coordinating orders issued to military and civil authorities in the colony; however, he immediately encountered considerable jurisdictional obstacles within White-hall itself. From Secretary at War Barrington, he learned that ex-tensive redeployments of troops in the West Indies had been ar-ranged by the other secretaries of state without any effort to inform the American Department. Pownall attempted to restore regular channels of authority, but he met only limited success in persuad-ing Rochford and Suffolk to issue orders to colonial officials under the auspices of the American Department.[37]

When persistent rumors of disasters on St. Vincent circulated through Westminster, the opposition sensed an opportunity for a successful attack upon the government. On December 9, 1772, Thomas Townshend, a leading whip of the Rockingham party, raised the issue before the Commons as the House sat in committee on the army estimates. Two days later, Townshend forced North to accept a motion calling for all papers relative to the expedition.[38]

With Pownall away at Bath recuperating from the strain of his recent jurisdictional encounters at Whitehall, the overall responsi-bility for researching and supplying relevant Colonial Office papers for the Commons fell to Knox. Between December 23 and January 25, he forwarded to Parliament more than fifty papers relating to St. Vincent, some dating from the seventeenth century, including translations of French documents.[39]

By the time Parliament reassembled following the Christmas holiday, the Whig opposition under Townshend's leadership had a well-organized plan of attack. On February 10, 1773, when the St. Vincent papers were officially laid before the Commons, Townshend castigated the administration for supplying only outdated docu-ments and produced his own intelligence detailing the deplorable state of the expedition, dated from the island as recently as Novem-ber 1772. In the subsequent exchange, Townshend drew from North a most embarrassed admission: "To be certain, I sent be-fore I came here to the Secretary of State's office, and I received this note: 'There is not a scrap of paper in this office of a later date from St. Vincent's, than the 9th October, and which was received here the 17th November.'" Two days later, North was able to lay "fresh papers" before the House—possibly items obtained from the Northern and Southern secretaries. Townshend and his allies, never-theless, took advantage of the patent mismanagement on the part of the government to table three motions censuring the entire cam-paign against the Caribs. Although all three efforts were defeated, the government majorities in a full House were disturbingly narrow.[40]

The obvious embarrassment of North's administration over the St. Vincent expedition certainly demonstrated, among other things, that Pownall's criticism of jurisdictional confusion was both substantial and ominous. Admittedly, this particular episode took place early in Dartmouth's administration, before he was entirely settled in office; nevertheless, almost a year after Pownall's original outburst, and six months after the St. Vincent fiasco had erupted in Parliament, Pownall again wrote Knox: "Our business had been hitherto as light as you could wish, and I think it is likely to continue so, for what can Lord Dartmouth have to do whilst Bamber Gascoigne is minister for America at the Board of Trade and Lord Suffolk at the Council Office, where they will not let us have anything to say."[41] Under these circumstances, Pownall feared that the department, and ultimately North's government, was doomed to "ruin and disgrace."

Although Knox sympathized with Pownall's frustration, the fact is that during Dartmouth's administration the junior undersecretary offered only sporadic assistance to his colleague's energetic activities. Ill health periodically prevented Knox's attendance at the Colonial Office. After his return from America, he was chronically debilitated by physical illness (probably recurrences of the fever he had contracted in Georgia), usually accompanied by symptoms of emotional stress. There is evidence, however, that his lethargy during this period was not entirely due to pathological causes. Once, when Pownall was particularly demoralized by the inactivity and inconsequence of his department, he wrote Knox that he was beginning to feel "as much contempt as my betters for that solicitude for the public Welfare you have so often laughed at me for cherishing."[42] On several occasions Pownall himself was indisposed by illness, and Knox took charge of departmental affairs. More frequently, however, it was Knox who withdrew altogether from the business of Whitehall and with his family sought convalescence in the congenial society of such resort towns as Bath, Tunbridge Wells, and Spa on the Continent.

It seems rather remarkable that Pownall spared Knox the lash of his stinging thrusts against official inertia and incompetence. In fact, by 1773 the increasingly testy civil servant had not only begun to confide his deepest feelings to Knox but had also come to accept him as a qualified peer in the conduct of colonial business. Pownall explicitly admitted as much late in 1773, when he asked Knox to return to Whitehall as soon as possible, because after years of neglect the government wanted to settle the "business of Quebec" in a hurry. With an obvious note of self-satisfaction, Pownall commented: "Lord North has begg'd that he may have from us a Précis of the Affairs of Quebec from the establishment of it, so far as regards the claims and complaints of the New Subjects & what has passed thereupon, &c., &c." But Pownall also confessed to Knox, "You know how little able I am to sit down to such a work, and you know that nobody but you or I can do it."[43]

Certainly Pownall and Knox were singularly qualified to carry out the Quebec business. Both men had made substantial contributions to the Canadian provisions of the Proclamation of 1763, and both were intimately acquainted with the continuous but unsuccessful attempts of successive ministries to deal with the complicated problems of Canadian government and western lands. Although many minds contributed to the final shaping of the Quebec Act, Pownall and Knox provided the initial conceptions and basic outlines of the measure, which Parliament would eventually pass into law in June 1774.

Between the initiation of the Quebec business and the final passage of the act, however, Knox and Pownall's deliberations upon Canadian affairs were unexpectedly interrupted once again by a compelling social diversion—this time a tea party in Boston harbor, which abruptly restored the entire American Department to the center of imperial controversy.

The North administration had anticipated no serious disturbances in the colonies when, in 1773, it obtained parliamentary approval for the direct export of tea to America. The measure was inspired primarily by the government's desire to relieve the financial difficulties which beset the East India Company, while considerations of American policy were secondary at best. Knox claimed that the American Department had not even been notified when the tea was sent out.[44] The violent reception the colonists accorded the tea shipments in America immediately produced an equally violent reaction among Britons of all varieties of opinion. The explosive issue of parliamentary sovereignty over the colonies was reopened in an atmosphere charged with emotion on both sides of the Atlantic. Even Dartmouth, avowedly a "strong friend to America," was alienated by the events at Boston. With uncharacteristic abruptness he wrote:

> The supreme legislature of the whole British Empire has laid a duty (no matter for the present whether it has or has not a right so to do, it is sufficient that we conceive it has) on a certain commodity on its importation into America; the people of America, at Boston particularly, resist that authority and oppose execution of the law in a manner clearly treasonable upon the principles of every government upon earth.[45]

According to Knox's account of subsequent events, Dartmouth was so provoked by the destruction of the tea that he immediately took the lead in cabinet deliberations on restoring order and punishing the culprits in Boston. During one of the most crucial sessions, on February 4, 1774, Dartmouth recommended that the seat of government in Massachusetts be removed beyond the influence of the radicals in Boston; he also persuaded his colleagues to accept Pownall's proposal for closing the port of Boston. In addition, the cabinet decided to issue orders for the arrest of radical leaders John Hancock, John Adams, and John Cushing—Speaker of the Massachusetts assembly—on charges of high treason.[46]

Originally, the cabinet intended to execute these measures by royal decree rather than parliamentary legislation. Dartmouth particularly supported this procedure, because he wanted only limited punitive measures directed by the British executive against the lawbreakers of Boston. Unlike several of his colleagues, Dartmouth was not anxious for a general confrontation between Parliament and the American colonies. But when the law officers of the crown reversed their previous approval of proceeding by royal decrees, the government decided to lay its proposals before Parliament.[47] Knox provided a vivid account of the atmosphere and attitudes of the February 19 cabinet meeting at Dartmouth's office in Whitehall, when this decision was reached:

> Mr. Pownall & myself were sitting in the outer room waiting the result when the Attorney and Solicitor came out. "Well," cried Pownall, "is it done?" "No," answered Thurlow, "nothing is done. Don't you see," added he, "that they want to throw the whole responsibility of the business upon the Solicitor General and me; and who would be such damned fools as to risk themselves for such—fellows as these."[48]

Given the contentious and mutinous record of North's cabinet, it is not surprising that the government found it necessary to draw Parliament into its deliberations on the fate of Boston. It is remarkable, if no less surprising, that under such circumstances the cabinet also decided to expand the scope of its recommendations by reviving the long-postponed issue of altering the charter of Massachusetts Bay.

Knox claimed that he again counseled restraint in reforming the constitution of Massachusetts. He hoped that the radicals in Boston could be brought to heel without extending the controversy to other colonies, and therefore he advised only an "alteration in the council."[49] On this occasion Knox's proposal was taken up by his chief. When the cabinet discussed proposals to be submitted to Parliament for the reform of government in Massachusetts, Dartmouth recommended a single alteration in the charter—a measure granting the crown exclusive control over appointments to the council. North was inclined to support the moderate course proposed by the American secretary. Within the cabinet, however, Lord Chief Justice Mansfield delivered a stinging denunciation of the ministry's previous irresolution in American affairs; Suffolk, an ex-Grenvillite, and the Bedfordites Gower and Sandwich were all persuaded that the day of reckoning was long overdue for Massachusetts Bay.[50] Most important of all, the demands for an aggressive policy were consistently seconded by the king, who was determined upon a comprehensive reform of the recalcitrant colony.

The balance in favor of constitutional confrontation with Massachusetts was finally tipped by a chance event. At the end of February 1774, North suffered an unexpected defeat in Parliament when the Commons voted to perpetuate the controverted elections laws. This measure was entirely extraneous to the American issue and did not even involve a question of confidence in the government. But North was personally unnerved, and, according to Knox's account, when exgovernor Bernard unluckily appeared on the scene with his proposals for a drastic revision of the charter of Massachusetts, North yielded.[51] Bernard's recommendations—calling for the suspension of town meetings in the colony and the selection of juries by summons rather than by election—were incorporated in the measures the cabinet submitted to Parliament early in 1774.

The so-called Coercive Acts which Parliament passed during the spring of 1774 went far beyond the policy of limited sanctions against Massachusetts advised by Dartmouth and Knox. In addition to legislation aiming at a comprehensive reform of the Bay colony—the Boston Port Act, the Regulating Act, and the Impartial Administration of Justice Act—the government also secured an extension of the Quartering Act of 1765, which applied to all the colonies. Collectively these measures, which came to be known as the Intolerable Acts in America, represented an extreme departure in British policy. The North administration had decided to force the recognition of parliamentary sovereignty in America by making an example of Massachusetts Bay. The possibility of provoking open resistance in other colonies was consciously accepted as a calculated risk, and steps were immediately taken to increase royal forces in America.

The adoption of a coercive policy created a dilemma for the Earl of Dartmouth. A pacific man by nature, Dartmouth dreaded the prospect of civil war. Yet he was equally devoted to upholding parliamentary sovereignty over America and defended the actions of the government:

> The mother country very unwilling to proceed to extremities passes laws (indisputably within its power) for the punishment of the most flagrant offenders, for the reformation of abuses, and for the prevention of the like enormities for the future. The question, then is, whether these laws are to be submitted to: if the people of America say no, they say in effect that they will no longer be a part of the British Empire; they change the whole ground of the controversy, they no longer contend that Parliament has not a right to exact a particular provision, they say that it has no right to consider them at all as within its jurisdiction.[52]

Like a mariner clinging to the mast of a foundering vessel, Dartmouth seemed to clutch desperately at the principle of parliamentary supremacy. He feared the consequences of the coercive measure, but he enigmatically accepted the task of executing His Majesty's business in America.

For William Knox the comprehensive policy of coercion involved much more than a test of abstract principles. Considering the extent of his investments in plantation properties and offices in Georgia and New York, it is hardly surprising that he was alarmed by the prospect of extending the controversy to colonies other-than Massachusetts. Thus it was with pathetic irony that on June 1, 1774, Dartmouth's circular to all colonial governors announcing the sweeping coercive measures directed against Massachusetts Bay went out from Whitehall under Knox's signature.[53] Moreover, during the last half of 1774, the North government found the talented Knox especially useful in defending the administration's aggressive American policies.

Knox's first literary effort in 1774 came in reply to criticism of the Quebec Act. Although this measure had been initiated by Knox and Pownall late in 1773, its passage had been delayed by the tea crisis until June 1774. In its final form, the Quebec Act provided a comprehensive constitutional settlement for the Canadian province. Political power in the colony was vested in the military governor and an appointive legislative council until the inhabitants, particularly the French majority, were deemed ready for representative institutions. The English system of criminal law was established in Quebec, but French civil law was retained, and the French-speaking subjects were allowed full legal rights. Roman Catholics were granted toleration, and the tithes of the church were given legal status. Finally, the boundaries of Canada were extended southward to the Ohio River and westward to the Mississippi.

The saints of Massachusetts Bay immediately denounced the popish provisions of the Quebec Act, and the other colonists soon joined them in opposing the measure as part of a conscious scheme to punish and coerce the older American colonies. In Britain members of the opposition, particularly Edmund Burke, attacked the Quebec Act as cruel and oppressive, not only to the older colonies but also to the subjects in the Canadian province itself.[54]

Many supporters of the North administration were concerned that such criticism of the Quebec Act would have inimical effects upon the impending elections for a new Parliament. The "Court members for Counties and Popular Burroughs," according to Knox, were especially afraid of opposition attacks upon their support of the Quebec bill, "as had been done in the case of the Tea Bill, which might prejudice them at the approaching General Election." Knox's pamphlet defense of the Quebec Act was ready for publication less than a month after the measure became law, and it was immediately printed and circulated at government expense.[55]

Knox opened his pamphlet, *The Justice and Policy of the Late Act of Parliament for . . . the Province of Quebec*, with a lengthy history of the evolution of the Quebec legislation.[56] In this fashion he effectively countered the argument that the Quebec Act was essentially a reactionary response to recent developments in America. Once he had neutralized the main thrust of the opposition attack, he proceeded to a comprehensive defense of the individual provisions of the act. He persuasively depicted the Quebec Act as a piece of enlightened statesmanship which provided an equitable settlement of long-standing problems and grievances in America. Finally, he took the offensive against the opposition, especially the Rockingham Whigs, castigating them as "railers" whose attacks on the Quebec Act had been compounded of "misrepresentation of facts, and unfounded imputation of motives."

In fact, the opposition attacks on various aspects of the administration's American policy proved to be vocal but unsuccessful. In parliamentary divisions during the passage of the coercive measures and the Quebec Act, the opposition had been consistently beaten by wide margins. And their extraparliamentary campaign aroused no significant response among former allies, particularly the British merchants who had answered similar appeals in 1765 with a deluge of petitions calling for repeal of the Stamp Act. Finally, the parliamentary campaign of summer 1774 failed to arouse more than a trace of sympathy for the American cause.[57]

Apparently the merchants and many other former friends of America were alienated by the violence of the American response to the East India Company's tea shipments and adopted an attitude of watchful waiting toward the government's policies. The North administration pursued a similar course. During the summer, the ministry awaited developments in the colonies, while Gen. Thomas Gage, governor of Massachusetts and commander in chief of British troops in America, attempted to execute the acts of Parliament. Parliament was prorogued at the end of June, and the members withdrew from the heat of London. Throughout the summer, Whitehall received unofficials reports that Massachusetts was resisting the coercive measures and that the other colonies were rallying to its support. There were even rumors of a general assembly of the colonies in a congress at Philadelphia.[58] Yet by the middle of August, most of the members of the cabinet had abandoned London and followed their parliamentary colleagues into the country.

During this summer lull, Thomas Hutchinson arrived in London. Within a short period of time the controversial exgovernor of Massachusetts became a frequent guest at the haunts of political and commercial figures whose interests centered in America. Hutchinson recorded in his diary that Undersecretary Knox had been among the first to call and welcome him to England, and on several occasions during the summer of 1774, Hutchinson encountered Knox at social gatherings—the most memorable occasion for the governor being a dinner at North's country estate at Bushy Park outside London, where the company conversed at length upon how Franklin had come by the Hutchinson-Oliver letters.[59]

Despite the pleasant diversion of Hutchinson's company, during the late summer Knox followed the example of his superiors and departed with his family for a long holiday on the Continent. In southern France, he joined his old friend Henry Ellis in taking the waters at the fashionable resort town of Spa. Then, traveling to Bonn, he easily made a fast friend of George Cressner, who pleasantly distracted the undersecretary from affairs across the Atlantic with the latest gossip of Continental courts.[60] These pleasant diversions were only occasionally interrupted by letters from Pownall, who forwarded the most recent Whitehall rumors about the American Congress and as usual complained equally about the dearth of official information and the general inertia which pervaded all ranks of the administration.[61]

Knox confidently believed that the intercolonial meeting which assembled at Philadelphia in September represented no serious threat to British rule in the colonies. This smug complacency was soon laid bare by the course of events. Hutchinson, who encountered Knox with increasing frequency after the latter's return from the Continent in October, left an intimate account of the progressive deterioration of the undersecretary's sanguine views.[62] Shortly after he returned to Whitehall, Knox predicted to Hutchinson that the deliberations of Congress would only reveal the impracticability of any alternative to parliamentary supremacy: "The issue will be an acquiescence in the supreme controuling power of Parliament, as necessary, not only for their protection from foreign enemies but from irreconcilable disputes and quarrels within themselves, as no other umpire can be so fit."[63] By the end of October, however, disturbing reports of the proceedings at Philadelphia began to arrive in London. During September and October, the American Congress had adopted a series of resolutions which not only called for defiance of the Coercive Acts and the Quebec Act but also asserted the exclusive legislative jurisdiction of colonial assemblies in internal affairs. Knox was able to derive only feeble consolation from the fact that Congress had not specifically repudiated those acts of Parliament which were, as he said, "bona fide for the regulation of Trade."[64]

On the last Sunday in October, Hutchinson journeyed through a gloomy and rainy late autumn day to Whitehall, where he was surprised to find Knox—usually a strict observer of the Sabbath—in attendance at the American Office. The governor recorded that the undersecretary was "much altered" by news of the resolutions from Philadelphia: "The first thing, he says, will be to let America know, that Britain will support its authority; and then concede what shall be thought fit." The next day, Hutchinson found Dartmouth and Pownall similarly "thunderstruck" by the news; both, he noted, "at present seem to suppose it impossible to give way." By the end of the week, however, these initial alarms had so abated that thoughts turned to lighter diversions, and on Saturday evening, at Letitia Knox's invitation, Hutchinson and his daughter Peggy accompanied the Knoxes to Covent Garden, where they witnessed what the critical Bostonian described as a "wretched" performance of Shakespeare's *Much Ado About Nothing*.[65]

Throughout the fall and winter of 1774, the intelligence from America was uniformly ominous. General Gage reported that he was unable to restore order in Massachusetts Bay, and his subsequent dispatches vacillated between requests for reinforcements and pleas for permission to suspend the coercive measures. For the moment the British cabinet seemed determined to uphold parliamentary authority in America by military force, regardless of the consequences. In the face of growing intransigence on both sides of the Atlantic, even Knox momentarily abandoned the frustrations of moderate counsels for the decisiveness of a belligerent reckoning with America. One year earlier, Knox had explicitly opposed the use of royal troops against the colonists in New York, but in November 1774, he told Hutchinson that he welcomed the prospect of colonial resistance to His Majesty's forces, because "we shall then be at no loss how to proceed."[66]

Some time early in November, while the cabinet debated methods of enforcing the Coercive Acts in America, North personally asked Knox to prepare a defense of the administration's American policy, addressed to the merchants of Britain.[67] Although the merchants had given no evidence of abandoning their passive acceptance of the government's policies, North was nonetheless disturbed by news that the American Congress had adopted resolutions designed to enforce nonintercourse against Great Britain. On two separate occasions during the 1760s, similar tactics had provoked economic distress in Britain, inciting mob riots and prompting British merchants to petition Parliament for the repeal of the unpopular colonial measures. In November 1774, North must have been haunted by the specter of those unheavals in public opinion which had preceded the fall of Grenville in 1765 and the resignation of Grafton in 1770.

Knox responded energetically to the prime minister's request. Before the end of the year he published a pamphlet, *The Interest of the Merchants and Manufacturers of Great Britain in the Present Contest with the Colonies Stated and Considered*. To a great extent, Knox simply applied the basic imperial concepts contained in his earlier writings to a defense of the navigation system. He argued, for example, that in its economic aspects the imperial relationship depended upon an equitable distribution of burdens and advantages between Britain and the colonies. Although much had been said in this respect about the restraints imposed upon the colonial economy, little notice had been taken of the burdens borne by Britons. Knox specifically referred to the high prices Britons paid for sugar, tobacco, indigo, and coffee because the colonies were allowed a monopoly of the home market for these commodities. He also noted that although the colonies were legally restrained from certain manufactures, Britons would be surprised at the variety and extent of the colonial export trade in native manufactures, even to the point of "rivalling the people of England in several of their most valuable manufactures."

The *Interest of the Merchants* was not primarily an academic treatise upon the commercial aspects of the imperial connection. Instead, Knox's arguments were essentially directed toward one immediate goal—persuading the merchants and manufacturers of Britain that their interests would be best served by supporting the policies of the North administration. He argued that the public resolutions and the private pamphlets emanating from the colonies proved that their objections to parliamentary authority were not restricted to the right or expediency of taxing America. The colonists now openly impeached "the authority of the Legislature to bind them in any case whatsoever." Knox insisted that the Americans were too shrewd to give up the advantages of the imperial connection by calling for complete separation from Great Britain, but neither would they abide by the economic obligations levied upon them by Parliament. He predicted catastrophe for the British business community if parliamentary sovereignty were not upheld on this occasion:

> The continuance of [the British merchants'] trade in the Colonies clearly and entirely depends upon the laws of England having authority there. It is their operation which binds the commerce of the colonies to this country. It is their operation which gives security to the property of the trader sent thither. Give up the authority of Parliament and there is an end to your trade, and a total loss of your property.[68]

Knox also warned that in the long run the American denial of parliamentary supremacy represented a positive economic threat to all Britons, for he speculated that if the colonial economy were allowed to develop in a manner rivaling rather than complementing that of Britain, the Americans would ultimately destroy the commerce and agriculture of Great Britain.

With respect to this last point, Knox may be justly charged with employing an illiberal argument for polemical purposes. But he can hardly be impeached for invidious malice toward colonial prosperity, since a large part of his private fortune was derived from properties in America. In fact, even in the *Interest of the Merchants* Knox's perspective, if not his purpose, remained consistently imperial rather than parochial. And the illiberality of his polemical argument in no way diminishes the essential perceptiveness of his prophecy of eventual economic competition from America. Significantly, his sentiments seem to have been shared, at least momentarily, by large numbers of the English business community. Although in subsequent months the merchants of London generally rallied behind the American position, the ministry was able to mobilize substantial counterdemonstrations from provincial trading towns and from various manufacturing centers which were only beginning to experience the potential of industrial expansion.[69]

Under such circumstances, the North administration anxiously prepared to meet the recently elected Parliament. Even as Knox was composing his pamphlet addressed to the merchants, he assisted Pownall in drawing up the American clauses for the king's address at the opening session of the new Parliament. On December 30,

1774, William and Letitia, accompanied by Governor Hutchinson, Peggy Hutchinson, and Governor Bernard, crowded into the Lords' gallery to hear George III denounce the violence and illegality of recent acts in America and announce his government's determination to maintain order in the colonies.[70]

Although Knox claimed that the substantial majorities in the Commons supporting the king's address raised the spirits of the administration, the fact was that his own chief at the Colonial Office had begun to experience doubts about the policy of coercion. Originally, Dartmouth had agreed to the use of force against Massachusetts Bay because he hoped that firm action would avoid bloodshed. But he became increasingly distressed with the realization that his policy of punishing offenders in Massachusetts had in fact developed into a general confrontation with the Continental colonies. During the last months of 1774, while ministerial advocates of coercion, such as Rochford, Suffolk, and Sandwich, insisted that the American secretary order Gage to take aggressive action in Massachusetts, Dartmouth only procrastinated as he sought alternative policies through both official and unofficial channels.[71]

According to Knox, some time after the opening of the new Parliament, the American secretary consulted with the members of his department on possible concessions to the colonial position.[72] Everyone remained convinced that the principle of parliamentary sovereignty had to be upheld and that the radicals of Massachusetts had to be punished. Yet two basic proposals for conciliating the colonies emerged from these deliberations. First, Pownall recommended that commissioners be sent to America to negotiate with "deputies" of the colonies. And second, the Colonial staff agreed that "taxation ought to be given up in practice and that the Colonies should be invited to make some proposition as an equivalent" —a proposal corresponding in principle with the quota and requisition plan Knox had advocated privately and publicly for a decade. Throughout these discussions, Knox argued that in any negotiations mutual benefits had to be balanced against mutual burdens, and by his own account he particularly recommended, as he had to Grenville years earlier, that some of the more burdensome commercial restraints on the colonies be removed and that Ireland be comprehended within the reformed navigation system by extending similar concessions to the island kingdom. But apparently his colleagues felt that such concessions were premature and too extensive.

For the moment, Knox's suggestions for liberalizing the imperial economy were shelved.

Throughout the months of December 1774 and January 1775, the American secretary attempted to persuade the cabinet to adopt the conciliatory proposals of his department.[73] Rochford, Sandwich, and Suffolk—supported by the king—persistently objected to concessions and insisted on a consistent policy of coercion. But Dartmouth received unexpected support from Secretary at War Barrington, who argued that the military repression of Massachusetts was impossible and advised a naval blockade accompanied by negotiations for an honorable settlement of outstanding grievances. North characteristically vacillated between coercion and concession. The upshot of this conflict was that in January 1775 the cabinet decided to pursue both courses simultaneously. Pownall's proposal for sending commissioners to America was dropped because the cabinet did not wish to place Britain in the position of supplicating a settlement before an "American Parliament." But the cabinet agreed to lay before Parliament a resolution promising that Britain would give up the exercise of taxation, except for commercial purposes, whenever the colonies should provide adequate contributions for their own civil and military expenses. At the same time, however, the cabinet decided to send reinforcements to General Gage and to exert additional pressure on Massachusetts and the rest of New England by restricting the commerce of the northern provinces.

In February 1775, Knox found himself in the remarkable position of contributing simultaneously to the coercion and conciliation of America. He and Pownall drew up the government bill restricting the trade of New England to Great Britain, Ireland, and the British West Indies and barring the New Englanders from engaging in the Newfoundland fishery.[74] North presented the measure to Parliament on February 10. The administration delayed, however, in introducing its conciliatory resolution allowing colonial contributions in lieu of parliamentary taxation. And so Knox, either from despair or in anticipation of government action, decided to initiate the policy of appeasement by extraofficial means.

On February 15, Knox communicated his own compromise scheme for colonial contributions to John Blackburn, a London merchant with extensive trading interests in America.[75] He specifically gave Blackburn permission to forward these recommendations to his associates and friends in New York and predicted that if the people of New York adopted his proposals, the British government would immediately implement the scheme.

Knox was well aware that the mutual distrust which prevailed on either side of the Atlantic would militate against the Americans' accepting any concessions at face value. Therefore, his proposals were designed to provide integral guarantees that Britain would abide by the provisions of his scheme. Specifically, he recommended that the colonies provide financially for their own civil government "in order to secure the importance and frequent meetings of their Assemblies." Each colony should also contribute its fair quota to the common defense by means of export and import duties to be levied by the colonial assemblies. The colonial legislation imposing these duties should include an enacting clause declaring that they would commence "whenever the Acts [of Parliament] imposing Duties on Tea and Wines imported into the colonies should be repealed, and continue in force for so long as Parliament desisted from imposing Taxes and Duties in the Colonies for any other than commercial purposes." Knox argued that by this arrangement the privileges of the colonies would be protected by the most constant of all sanctions—political expediency: "For what Minister would ever think of exposing himself to the resentment of all the Colonies and every good man in this Country, and sacrificing a handsome revenue into the bargain, for the sake of an uncertain income from a New Tax." Knox also pointed out that disputes over the ultimate purpose of any parliamentary tax could be eliminated by providing that any revenue accrued from such a levy should go to the colonies rather than Britain.

Undoubtedly Knox's considerable personal investment in the secretaryship of New York had prompted him to pay special attention to developments within that colony. Late in 1774, he had informed North and Dartmouth—much to their satisfaction—that according to intelligence shown him in confidence, the New York delegates to the Continental Congress had put up considerable resistance to the nonimportation resolutions. Knox also brought to their attention Gov. Cadwallader Colden's accounts of successful resistance on the part of New York merchants against mob attempts to halt shipments of goods to General Gage. According to Knox, Colden predicted "that even if a non-importation resolution should be taken at the Congress that the people of New York will not come into it as the Farmers and Merchants are all disposed to remain quiet and the lower people in the town are only turbulent."[76] Such predictions of predominant Loyalism in New York were proven visionary in the subsequent course of events. Nevertheless, in February 1775 both private interests and official considerations provided ample inspiration for Knox's unofficial efforts to initiate a specific plan for imperial accommodation with this pivotal province.

Although there is no conclusive proof that the conciliatory scheme contained in Knox's letter to Blackburn enjoyed official sanction, it is probable that Knox's superiors in the ministry were aware of his activities. Knox readily informed Hutchinson of the letter and its contents. It seems likely that Dartmouth and even North were similarly enlightened. Throughout the winter of 1774–75, Dartmouth himself employed several intermediaries to conduct unofficial negotiations with Franklin; the final meeting of these abortive efforts at compromise took place on February 16, only one day after Knox composed his New York proposals.[77] Certainly the North government had compelling reasons for encouraging any efforts which might reconcile New York to the imperial connection. Geographically and economically, the province was of preeminent strategic importance to Britain, whether the government's policy were one of coercing or conciliating the Continental colonies. Royal government in New York exercised considerable political influence through an extensive system of patronage, which more closely approximated the circumstances of Knox's ideal constitution than any other colony. In addition, the strong commercial and financial ties of New York merchants with business interests in Britain led the North government to anticipate considerable support for the imperial union among the wealthier classes in the province.[78]

These considerations notwithstanding, in the early part of 1775 the North government was unable to follow such initiatives with anything more than a hollow gesture toward peaceful resolution of the dispute with the colonies. North introduced the ministry's conciliatory resolution into the Commons on February 20, five days after Knox wrote his letter to Blackburn. After years of recommending quotas and requisitions, Knox had the satisfaction of seeing the imperial government enact in principle his panacea for colonial grievances. But in contrast to the proposals in Knox's letter to Blackburn, the propitiating motion offered no specific concessions

to colonial susceptibilities and suspicions. The resolution was only
a general declaration of intent; specific proposals for alternatives
to parliamentary taxation would have to come from individual colonies. Yet even this cautious measure provoked considerable opposition in the Commons from those who usually supported the administration.[79] During the course of a lengthy debate, the proposals
were denounced as a shameful sacrifice of the principle of parliamentary supremacy and a contradiction to the policy of firmness
previously announced in the king's Address from the Throne.
North's conciliatory motion passed the House only after government spokesmen, supported by known friends of the king, insisted
that the resolution was an integral part of the government's enlightened policy of combining firmness with openness to peaceful
alternatives for restoring imperial authority in America.[80]

Burke subsequently attempted to persuade Parliament to take
the initiative by offering definite concessions to America.[81] On
March 22, 1775, with the approval of Chatham and Rockingham,
he introduced his plan for conciliating America. His scheme contained several recommendations, including the repeal of the coercive legislation, but the essential point of his argument was that
Parliament should adopt specific proposals for colonial grants in lieu
of parliamentary taxation as the most practical approach to peace
with America. Five years earlier, in his *Observations on a Late State
of the Nation*, Burke had rejected Knox's suggestion of a system of
requisitions and quotas. Now Burke's efforts at appeasement along
similar lines were stillborn. Parliament applauded his speech of
March 22 but voted down his specific proposals overwhelmingly.

It was certainly ironic that Knox and Burke, the two rival "doc-
tors of physick," prescribed identical remedies during the crisis of
the empire. Knox—by his letter to Blackburn—and Burke—by his
proposals to Parliament—attempted to initiate what seemed to be
an expedient approach to preserving imperial peace. Yet it was
equally ironic that they seemed destined to work at cross-purposes:
only one month after Knox asked Blackburn to forward his proposals to New York, Burke warned the assembly of that colony that
in his opinion North's conciliatory motion was designed only to
lure New York away from the American union.[82]

It seems likely that in later years Knox must have speculated on
many occasions, both public and private, about what might have
been. What if the North government had officially adopted his

specific proposals for concessions to America? Could such terms have provided a basis, acceptable to the colonies and Britain alike, for what Knox described as "a permanent Union & Settlement with the Colonies"? Or, at least, could official sanction of Knox's letter to Blackburn, or some similar instrument, have given New York Loyalists the moral and material bases for retaining control of the strategic colony and securing a foothold for restoring royal authority in other colonies?

There is, in fact, substantial evidence that even after hostilities broke out in America, radical leaders remained exceptionally vigilant toward such contingencies.[83] But despite the sirenlike attraction of what might have been, as well as the biographer's sympathy for Knox, the historian cannot evade the ponderous thrust of evidence which indicates that by the early part of 1775, even before sustained hostilities had erupted, propitious circumstances no longer existed for mutually acceptable concessions and reconciliation. The reform and restoration of the imperial system by consent required trust and good will on both sides of the Atlantic. For several decades, however, the attitudes and opinions of Britons and Americans had been conditioned by word and deed to mutual suspicion of motives and actions. In essence, Americans were increasingly oriented toward interpreting British official behavior as tyrannical, while Britons were generally persuaded that Americans, especially the radical elements, were bent on total independence.

In this respect, then, Knox's avowed moderation and his various attempts at reconciliation assuredly remain significant. But the significance rests upon the tragic irony that for years he had contributed, by his private expressions as much as his public admonitions, to a growing suspicion in Britain of the motives behind American opposition to imperial policies. In earlier years, his schemes for an empire of mutual obligations and advantages might have held some promise, but by 1775 mutual distrust effectively undermined any such proposals appearing in the form of last-minute peace plans. Parliamentary reaction against North's timid conciliatory resolution demonstrated that His Majesty's government—divided as it was between coercion and concession—had gone as far as it could until the aroused hostility toward America abated within the political nation. Simultaneously, moderates in America found that their efforts toward imperial reconciliation were frustrated by evidence that Britain was determined to enforce its "tyranny." Particularly in

New York, where the royal officials had real—though exaggerated —grounds for optimism, the Loyalists' tenuous control over moderate opinion in the province was progressively weakened by the hard fact that fellow Americans in Massachusetts Bay were under threat of military conquest. New York officially received North's limited resolution only after news of Lexington and Concord had decisively tipped the political balance in the colony toward the forces opposing imperial reunion.[84]

William Knox was again at Spa when he learned of the outbreak of hostilities in America.[85] Almost two months after the shot heard round the world, Pownall wrote his colleague that "after a long dearth of American Intelligence we have been alarmed with a strange and in many parts unintelligible Account of an affair between the King's troops . . . and some of the provincials who . . . felt rather bolder than I thought they would." Although no official dispatches had been received from General Gage, Pownall warned that "the dye is cast and more mischief will follow." Two weeks later, he informed Knox that not only was Boston invested by rebels but also that the situation was equally "wretched" in New York, where "the fears of the Council, and the folly of their advice under the influence of them ruin all our measures and disconcert our whole plan." Pownall alerted his colleague that the American Department would begin its "meetings of Consultation" the next evening.

A few weeks after he received news of Lexington and Concord, Knox attempted to resign his post in the American Department, apparently in the desperate hope that such a gesture would preserve his colonial properties from reprisals. Dartmouth was sympathetic, but he refused Knox's resignation with the comment that "the ruin threatened to your Plantations in Carolina [Georgia] is the strongest Reason why you should not relinquish the share you have in the Plantations here."[86] With the spread of the rebellion to New York and Georgia, Knox's worst fears were realized: his New York office was abolished, and before the end of 1775 he learned that his Georgia estates were in rebel hands.[87] By August 1775, his frame of mind was such that he found it necessary once again to seek respite away from Whitehall and London. He informed Dartmouth of his retreat in a pathetic note which fathomed the depth of his despair: "I intend next week to try the Effect of the Salt Water. I wish it may prove the water of oblivion, for I have nothing to recollect that does not make me sick."[88]

Knox could not have forestalled the disasters which befell his properties in America even if he had resigned in 1775. Dartmouth in fact had accurately assessed Knox's position: with the outbreak of war, his public duty and his private interests became inseparable. Henceforth the restoration of his personal fortune depended upon the reestablishment of British authority in America by any means.

6. "Wrath My Dear Lord Is Gone Forth": The American War, 1775–1778

After Lexington, Lord Dartmouth gave outward signs of being fully aroused to promoting vigorous military action against the Continental colonies. Throughout the spring of 1775, he received encouraging accounts of substantial disaffection with the patriot cause throughout the southern provinces, and by summer he had made plans for a southern campaign for the following year.[1] Equally remarkable was his immediate response to reports that the Americans were attempting to employ Indians against British forces: putting aside the scruples of evangelical humanitarianism, he authorized royal agents in America to negotiate military alliances with various Indian tribes.[2]

These displays of firmness and resolution were nonetheless more apparent than real. Dartmouth was in fact entirely unsuited to executing a policy of military coercion. The pacific old Whig longed for a negotiated settlement of the conflict, even as he admitted that the immediate prospects for an honorable peace were depressing.

As early as June 14, 1775, Hutchinson reported that Dartmouth was so disturbed about the affairs of America that he "hinted at the puzzle the Opposition would be in, if Administration should leave the reins to them."[3] When the so-called Olive Branch Petition of the American Congress provided no concession to Dartmouth's susceptibilities concerning parliamentary authority, his personal distress was complete. Both Knox and Pownall prodded their chief to undertake firm measures for either war or peace; however, Dartmouth abandoned Whitehall for the solace of his country estate with increasing frequency, while the direction of American affairs passed into the hands of his more belligerent colleagues in the cabinet.[4]

Under these circumstances, during the fall of 1775, the ill-fated southern campaign of 1776 was initiated—an early harbinger of the decentralized, dysfunctional, and disastrous mode of wartime administration, which North would justify as government by departments. Dartmouth had originally envisioned the campaign as a limited incursion into North Carolina to mobilize erstwhile Loyalism in the South. However, by the fall of 1775 the invasion had been transmuted—by the piecemeal actions of several separate authorities—into a complex, full-scale campaign requiring the coordination of extensive naval and land forces, the latter including Loyalists and Indians as well as regular troops operating from bases in both Europe and America.[5] Although Knox and Pownall made futile gestures toward asserting the responsibility of their office for coordinating the coming campaign, in Dartmouth's absence the details of planning and execution fell largely to other departments. By September, Knox followed his master into retreat, this time to take the waters at Tunbridge Wells, while from Whitehall Pownall again complained of the neglect and inconsequence of the Colonial Office.[6]

On November 10, 1775, Dartmouth was finally allowed to give up his unhappy situation in the American Department for the more congenial and less demanding post of Lord Privy Seal. On the same day, Lord George Germain was appointed as Dartmouth's successor.[7]

Once again the personal characteristics and political attitudes of the new secretary contrasted sharply with those of his predecessor.[8] Germain was strong-willed and aggressively independent. In 1759, this independence had cost him a promising military career, when at the battle of Minden—while commanding British forces on the Rhine—he disobeyed orders because of personal pique. He had been court-martialed and declared unfit to serve His Majesty in a military capacity. Subsequently, the cloud of cowardice which hung over this episode shadowed his public life. In 1761, he entered the House of Commons, where he eventually became one of the staunchest advocates of British supremacy over the colonies. As American resistance to parliamentary legislation stiffened, he argued against concessions, insisting that the colonies could be restored to obedience only if the executive asserted its power firmly and consistently. His appointment to the Colonial Office gave him the opportunity not only to act upon these political principles but also to remove the stigma of his military disgrace. To Germain, the restoration of British rule in America was a matter of personal interest as well as political principle—much as it was to Undersecretary Knox.

When Germain entered North's administration, the cabinet still remained divided between coercion and conciliation. North believed that preparations for the military conquest of the colonies should be accompanied by concrete proposals for peace. He decided to revive Pownall's idea of sending a commission to America, and in February 1776 he persuaded Admiral Lord Richard Howe, the naval commander in America, and his brother, Gen. Sir William Howe, who commanded the military forces in the rebellious colonies, to act as commissioners. In the cabinet meetings of March 1776, however, North's proposal ran into determined opposition from Germain, who argued that the colonists should be subdued militarily before negotiations for peace were initiated. North's view seemed to prevail when the cabinet agreed in principle to the Howe Commission. But during the deliberations on the commissioners' instructions, Germain insisted that the colonies be required to give up all fortifications and to acknowledge the supreme authority of Parliament as the *sine qua non* to all negotiations. North was equally determined that negotiations should not be circumscribed by such prerequisites, although he agreed that an acknowledgment of parliamentary supremacy should be an integral part of any final settlement. The cabinet dissensions over these alternatives became so serious that Dartmouth, North, and Germain threatened in turn to resign.[9]

In the midst of this stalemate, Undersecretary Knox intervened in a manner betraying not only the paradoxes of his attitudes toward American policy but also the ambiguities of his early relationship with the new secretary. Knox was aware that Germain intended to emasculate the peace commission so that he might have an opportunity to reduce the colonies militarily; consequently, Knox privately sent Dartmouth a compromise proposal designed to expedite North's conciliatory campaign. His appeal was couched in terms well calculated to inspire and move the pious and pacific earl: "Wrath my dear Lord is gone forth and the plague will follow if some Aaron does not speedily make reconciliation. I think your Lordship may yet perform that office if you this morning call upon either one of the parties and propose a little alteration in the Instructions."[10] In fact, Knox's "middle way" smacks of the civil servant's perennial answer to ministerial conflicts—verbosity conquers all. He proposed in summary:

> that the Assemblies should be called by the Governors and acquainted that they might pass an Act appointing Delegates to meet the Commissioners so soon as all Congresses, Committees or Conventions in the colony were dissolved and legal Government restored and all bodies of Armed Men disbanded, but that they could not be restored to Peace or relieved from the late Act until they made the declaration [that they acknowledged parliamentary sovereignty in all cases whatsoever].[11]

As a specific concession to be offered by the commissioners, Knox revived his proposal for colonial export duties in lieu of parliamentary taxation. He argued that his recommendations would give the peace commissioners "latitude for treating" with the rebels; at the same time, however, he pointed out to Dartmouth that if such an approach failed to bring peace it would "at least save appearances, and throw the blame on the Colonies if they do not send Delegates under those conditions."[12] In the same vein, he recommended that the New England colonies be excluded from all peace negotiations because these provinces "so despised the power of Great Britain" that they were not likely to abide by any settlement until they were subdued militarily. Above all, he believed that his scheme would pacify the southern colonies, thus splitting the American union.[13]

The cabinet did not adopt Knox's proposals. But the instructions they finally drew up for the Howe Commission during the spring of 1776 could scarcely be considered an improvement on Knox's middle way. The differences between Germain and North over matters of procedure were settled by compromise.[14] The commissioners were not allowed to initiate negotiations by advancing specific proposals to the Americans; instead, they were required to await proposals from the colonies. The declaration of parliamentary sovereignty was not required as an indispensable condition to negotiations, but unless such a declaration were included in the colonial proposals, the commission could not restore any colony to peace until it received further instructions from the British government. The colonists would also be required to dissolve their revolutionary governments and to disband their armed forces as prerequisites to peace. Once these conditions were met, the commissioners were allowed to implement North's Conciliatory Resolution, but in this respect the commissioners' instructions specifically prohibited any alternative to parliamentary taxation which provided for colonial duties on either British manufactures or colonial products used by British manufacturers.

Throughout the summer of 1776, while the American patriots energetically promoted the cause of independence, the Howe Commission vainly awaited peace overtures from the colonies in accordance with their instructions.[15] The passivity of the commission and the specific limits of their instructions had the disastrous effect of cutting the ground out from under the feet of those colonial Loyalists who had previously employed promises of real conciliation with Britain to restrain colonial moderates from plunging into the full separation advocated by American radicals. In effect, the cabinet's compromise over the instructions for the Howe Commission was as much a victory for the American radicals' campaign in behalf of a declaration of independence as it was for Germain's policy of military coercion.

Even as Germain succeeded in checking the Howe Commission, he discovered to his dismay that the legacy of Dartmouth's approach to war was as pervasive as his influence in behalf of peace campaigns. Immediately upon entering office, the new American secretary was shocked to learn that Dartmouth had ordered the evacuation of Boston. Although Germain promptly issued instructions rescinding the orders, the dispatches never arrived in America, due to some mix-up between the Colonial Office and the admiralty. During the interval, Boston was duly abandoned. An aroused secretary undoubtedly gave his two chief lieutenants some very bad moments over this misadventure—Hutchinson, on a visit to the Plantation Office, found Pownall and Knox scouring the letter books "to see by what vessels the orders went."[16]

Germain was soon equally frustrated by the ill-planned and even more poorly executed southern campaign of 1776. Reports steadily filtered in, indicating that Loyalist strongholds in North Carolina were restricted to interior regions and that consequently the land-sea operations at Cape Fear held little promise. But even the remotest chances for successful cooperation between southern Loyalists and British regulars were dashed by unconscionable delays in the sailing of the troop convoy from Cork. As early as September 1775, Pownall had issued a flurry of instructions to various officials anticipating the imminent sailing of the convoy; however, four months later transports and supply ships were still being sent to the rendezvous in Ireland. Finally, on January 20, 1776, Knox confided to Governor Hutchinson, who was visiting in the undersecretary's home, that by last report six of the seven regiments at Cork had been embarked and that the whole fleet was probably under sail for Cape Fear, where they were expected to provide support for thousands of Loyalists taking up arms in the backcountry. Knox also reported that open disaffection was spreading and that four thousand Loyalists were in arms in South Carolina.[17]

In fact, such accounts of Loyalist risings, though exaggerated, were far from visionary. By early 1776, the Scots Highlanders of the North Carolina backcountry had rallied to the royal standard in numbers large enough to constitute a serious military threat. But on February 27, as the long-delayed Cork fleet plowed its way across the Atlantic, 1,500 loyal North Carolina Highlanders, attempting to fight their way to sea and the promised reinforcements, were brought to bay and routed by a superior rebel force at Moore's Creek Bridge.[18] The upshot of this defeat was that the southern expedition of 1776, even after the arrival of the reinforcements from Cork, succeeded only in mounting an ill-conceived and ignominiously unsuccessful attack on Charleston.

By August 22, Knox dejectedly sent Dartmouth a précis of "our Southern expedition" which was admittedly not "pleasing." The undersecretary, equally sensitive to the political and military repercussions of the abortive campaign, unerringly ferreted out the ultimate mischief which as yet lay hidden behind the immediate gloom over the southern fiasco: "The worst consequence of this failure will be the shewing the rebels where their strength lies and how they may foil us again in the winter tho' our strength be greater."[19]

Although the failures of 1776 were acknowledged, Knox—along with others in the government—drew another significant lesson from the southern campaign. Loyalist support had been proven no mere chimera but a force of considerable potential which needed only to be encouraged, supported, and unleashed at the right opportunity.[20] For the balance of the war, Knox would remain an effective champion—and the primary ministerial contact—for Loyalist advocates of renewed southern operations.

During 1776, the Knox home at Soho Square, to which the family had moved a year earlier, became an increasingly prominent gathering place for American émigrés. In June, Hutchinson called

upon Knox in the company of his Massachusetts kinsman, Chief
Justice Peter Oliver, who had recently been evacuated from Boston.
During the same month, Knox also extended hospitality to Govern-
or Wright and his family, who had just arrived in London after a
narrow escape from Georgia earlier in the year. And among the later
additions to the circle of émigrés who benefited from Knox's largess
was his plantation attorney, John Graham.[21]

In the haven of Knox's Soho residence, Wright must have described to his host the curious fate which earlier in the year had
brought about the governor's arrest at the hands of Joseph Habersham—the son of their late friend, a young man who had enjoyed
Knox's hospitality in London almost a decade earlier. Certainly
Knox must have been even more sensibly affected by Graham's firsthand account of the seizure of Knoxborough by agents of the revolutionary state government of Georgia. During the course of the
numerous dinners, receptions, and teas at Knox's residence, where
the undersecretary's growing congregation of displaced Loyalists
mingled in the gay intellectual and social life for which contemporary Soho was renowned, the conversation inevitably turned to the
latest news of the war—to military victories and defeats, rumors of
troop movements and stratagems, and ultimately to plans of campaign for the expeditious restoration of royal rule and Loyalist fortunes in America.

Even though Germain remained generally sympathetic and open
to the Loyalists' schemes, which Knox regularly communicated to
him during the latter part of 1776, the American secretary provided
no immediate encouragement for the projects which emanated from
these sources. On October 19, Germain wrote Knox that although
"Genl Howe may probably during the winter think of a Sothern
Expedition," Wright's proposals (which called for eleven thousand
regular troops in addition to Indian allies) were "most extraordinary" and "of little use."[22] Howe's southern expedition did not
materialize during the winter of 1776–77, and Germain, his attention focused throughout 1777 upon Burgoyne's campaign, could
only promise his undersecretary in August that he would speculate
upon plans for renewed southern operations after news arrived from
the northern expedition.[23]

Even before the southern campaign of 1776 had run its course in
the fiasco at Charleston, Germain's frustration and displeasure had
resulted in a shake-up of his departmental staff. On May 17, at

Knox's, Hutchinson learned that Christian D'Oyley, a former deputy secretary of war, was to be appointed undersecretary in Pownall's place at the American Office. Although the elderly Pownall had for some time longed for a less demanding post and was well compensated with a lucrative excise commission, the senior undersecretary's resignation was probably precipitated by Germain's open indignation over departmental responsibility for the sad state of American affairs. Certainly Germain looked forward to working closely with D'Oyley, who not only possessed experience in the War Office but also enjoyed a close friendship with Gen. Sir William Howe, commander in chief in America.[24]

Knox, apparently escaping Germain's displeasure, remained in office. But his relations with D'Oyley were strained from the beginning. The day after Hutchinson learned of D'Oyley's appointment, he called upon the new undersecretary to tender his congratulations but found him not "over-pleased" with his situation. Hutchinson, by no means unfriendly to D'Oyley, candidly remarked, "I believe he aimed at as good an income, attended with less trouble. He and she are fond of the country in summer, and Mr. Knox's health obliges him to be in the country; but in the present state of America, there must be one of the Secretaries in town."[25]

From 1776, under Germain's aggressive leadership, the American Department steadily became the epicenter of the British war effort.[26] Although the admiralty retained control over naval operations and the War Office attended to the technical business of military logistics, the American secretary virtually monopolized the planning and the administration of military campaigns in America. The tempo of business at the Colonial Office increased steadily as the staff became responsible for the tremendous volume of orders and dispatches which passed between their chief and the military commanders in the colonies. At the same time, the American Department continued to administer the civil affairs of the rebel colonies occupied by British forces as well as those colonies which had remained loyal to the crown.

After D'Oyley's accession to the American Department, there was a distinct division of labor between the two undersecretaries: D'Oyley became Germain's chief military confidant and was entrusted with the entire conduct of departmental correspondence with commanders in the field, while Knox was left with administrative supervision of the residual business of the Colonial Office. During the period of D'Oyley's tenure, Knox's official dispatches to military commanders were few in number and were largely restricted to such matters as informing General Howe that the Society for Promotion of Christian Knowledge was sending out religious tracts for the troops or, on another occasion, that five hundred copies of an answer to the grievances of the American Declaration of Independence were being forwarded for distribution among the troops.[27] By his own account, Knox was excluded from the conferences early in 1777 wherein Germain, Burgoyne, and D'Oyley worked out plans for the general's northern campaign.[28]

There is no doubt that Knox felt a great deal of professional resentment and personal pique toward D'Oyley, who as Pownall remarked to his former colleague was "like the dog in the manger" at the American Department.[29] This fact should be kept in mind, particularly when assessing Knox's account of D'Oyley's role in the Saratoga disaster. In an often quoted passage, Knox claimed that D'Oyley had personally "settled the force and Instructions" with Burgoyne before he went out to Canada:

> When all was prepared and I had them to compare & make up Lord Sackville [Germain] came down to the office to sign the letters on his way to Stoneland, when I observed to him that there was no letter to Howe to acquaint him with the plan or what was expected of him in consequence of it. His Lordship started & D'Oyly stared, but said he would in a moment write a few lines. So says Lord Sackville my poor horses must stand in the street all the time, & I shant be to my time anywhere. Doyly then said he had better go & he would write from himself to Howe & inclose copies of Burgoynes Instructions which would tell him all that he would want to know. And with this his Lordship was satisfied as it enabled him to keep his time for he could never bear delay or disappointment, and D'Oyly sat down & writ a letter to Howe, but he neither shewd it to me or gave a Copy of it for the office, and if Howe had not acknowledged the receipt of it with the Copy of the Instructions to Burgoyne, we could not have proved that he ever saw them.[30]

Although this narrative provides a fascinating vignette of departmental personalities and procedures, the admitted rivalry between

Knox and D'Oyley raises substantial doubts about the author's objectivity.

Despite Knox's unhappiness at being excluded from the compelling business of military operations, the vastly expanded jurisdiction of the American Department provided him ample opportunity for the full development of latent administrative talents. After Pownall's resignation Knox, as senior undersecretary, became responsible for supervising the departmental staff; and although he credited Pownall's established routine as well as the competence of the veteran first clerk, Mr. Pollock, with easing his burden, the ever-increasing volume of business must have required a careful and continuous attention to the employment of human and physical resources. Occasionally, Knox found it necessary to remain late into the evening at Whitehall, awaiting some vital dispatch which required immediate attention and routing to proper officials.[31] And although he persevered in his regular late-summer holidays from the capital, he limited the duration and distance of his excursions, usually taking the waters at Tunbridge Wells within easy reach of Whitehall.

Knox's primary administrative responsibility was the preparation and dispatch of departmental correspondence with civil officials. Of course, all departmental correspondence—civil or military—was conducted according to Germain's general instructions, with the secretary personally scrutinizing important dispatches. But within a short time, Knox won Germain's entire confidence in this business, and he was permitted to draw up official communications on his own initiative before submitting them to his chief. As the war progressed, he became so adept at anticipating Germain's wishes that the secretary usually approved his lieutenant's drafts with only minor exceptions and corrections. The occasions when Germain completely rejected Knox's original drafts were remarkably rare.

Germain, in fact, soon became sufficiently confident of Knox's competence in handling civil affairs to allow him to deal directly with colonial officials. When Gen. Sir Frederick Haldimand was appointed governor of Quebec during the fall of 1777, Germain relied upon Knox to arrange the formal details of the appointment, to secure expeditious transport to Canada for Haldimand, and to personally inform the new governor of "the State of that Country, and of its civil Constitution."[32] On other occasions, Germain charged Knox with the disagreeable and time-consuming business of compelling absentee colonial officials to return to their posts—the secretary himself intervening only to dismiss recalcitrant officials who resisted the undersecretary's persistent admonitions.[33]

Most important of all, Knox was given direct responsibility for managing the crucial business of interdepartmental affairs. Germain, temperamentally unsuited to exercising the requisite arts of diplomacy, cajolery, and persuasion, willingly left interdepartmental liaison entirely to Knox. Considering the singularly heterogeneous nature of North's war ministry, Knox's management of interdepartmental business was skillful and resourceful.

Throughout the war, Knox was on particularly good terms with John Robinson, North's secretary at the Treasury.[34] Without troubling their respective superiors, Robinson and Knox cooperated regularly in dealing with such matters as the validation of financial bills and disbursements for American civil and military accounts, as well as collecting and preparing relevant information to be included in the estimates laid before Parliament. In return, Robinson frequently forwarded to Knox useful bits of intelligence gathered by Treasury agents, and on several occasions, at Knox's request, the customs department of the Treasury arranged for boxes and parcels of the Colonial Office to be delivered and dispatched from ports of entry without delay.[35]

The cooperative relationship between Knox and Robinson, who was also North's chief political agent, extended beyond the realm of administrative matters. Frequently, the two subministers acted as mediators between Germain and North when the latter were at odds over matters of policy. In 1777, Knox even employed his connection with Robinson surreptitiously to raise opposition in the cabinet against Germain's attempts to circumvent the embargo on American tobacco in behalf of a friend. There is no evidence that Germain ever learned of Knox's action, but in any event such knowledge would not have come as a complete shock, because according to Robinson all the junior officials in the American Office, including D'Oyley, had openly objected to Germain's plan.[36]

Besides the usual jurisdictional jealousies inherent in any bureaucratic organization, Knox's conduct of interdepartmental business was frequently complicated by the fact that the ancient departments, especially the admiralty and the War Office, resented the encroachments of the upstart American Department. Knox regularly complained that Sandwich at the admiralty board, who disliked Germain intensely, was particularly hostile toward requests emanating from the Colonial Office. For some time, Knox was able to mitigate the formidable difficulties of this relationship by a judicious handling of Sandwich's chief lieutenant, Philip Stephens. Again and again, Knox translated brusque and reproachful orders from Germain into carefully worded memos to Stephens, respectfully requesting that he "move the Lord Commissioners of Admiralty" to arrange transports and convoys for troops and their equipment, to arrange passage for private individuals, or (the most sensitive request of all) to expedite the sailing of overdue vessels.[37] Germain was especially appreciative of Knox's persistent and patient management of the difficult naval business, even though the undersecretary's efforts were not always rewarded with success.

In contrast to the delicate arts Knox exercised upon the admiralty, his relationship with the War Office and its subordinate Board of Ordnance illustrates his capacity for high-handedness and bullying. This distinction may be attributed to at least two factors. First, the War Office itself was generally regarded as an inferior office, with the incumbent secretary at war usually being denied cabinet status; thus it was not exceptional for Knox, in Germain's absence, to write directly to Barrington, advising him, for example, to send marching orders for the embarkation of troops.[38] Second, at the Ordnance Board, Knox dealt most frequently with the bumbling figure of John Boddington, whose incompetence was a legend among subministers.[39] Apparently it was mainly for this reason that Knox's letters to Boddington, ordering the supply and traffic of artillery, small arms, camp equipment, surgical supplies, provisions, and wagons, were usually supplemented with blunt references to the variety of dire consequences which would befall that unfortunate official who should be the cause of any delay or error. For his part, Boddington usually replied to Knox's patronizing and even callous orders in tones of abject apology, without any trace of resentment, but seldom with any evidence of improved efficiency.

The unfortunate Boddington was the central figure in a bureaucratic episode which illustrates in detail the pivotal role Knox often played in coordinating the activities of several departments, as well as the complex personal qualities this charge demanded of him. On March 31, 1777, with preparations well under way for Burgoyne's northern campaign, Boddington wrote Knox that his office was having some difficulty in obtaining seamen to man the *Lord Howe*, a storeship bound for New York.[40] Boddington asked Knox to peruse and forward an enclosed letter to Stephens at the admiralty, requesting that the navy supply a complement of seamen to avoid detaining the vessel. The distraught official obviously hoped that Knox would personally intervene on his behalf at the naval office. The next day Knox, in an unmistakably foul mood, wrote Boddington that not only had he forwarded the request, but he had also called at the admiralty that morning, only to be informed that there was no precedent for complying with such an unusual request.[41] Obviously aroused at having borne the brunt of the naval office's bureaucratic disdain, the Colonial undersecretary now turned in full wrath upon poor Boddington and bluntly remarked, "It appears indeed very extraordinary that at the instant it might be expected the Ships were ready to proceed to join the Convoy, they should be unprovided with their compliment [*sic*] of Seamen." To Knox's credit, at least as an effective administrator, he did not leave the poor man to his fate. He informed Boddington that he had learned from the staff at the admiralty that shipowners who chartered vessels to the government commonly attempted to increase their profits by having the government provide seamen. He further suggested that the proper way to handle the whole matter was by "an action for Breach of the Charter Party." He could not resist reminding Boddington that "if the Kings service is disappointed, I know not who will excuse the Department that has Charge of supplying the troops with Ammunition & stores"; nevertheless, the American undersecretary took the unusual step of giving the wretched Boddington permission to use anything he had written which might rouse the shipowners to perform their engagements. Within a fortnight, Boddington informed Knox that the *Lord Howe* was ready to sail.[42]

Among the myriad of duties which devolved upon Knox during the course of the American war, none was more demanding than the so-called Indian business. Knox's knowledge of Indians and Indian affairs dated from his firsthand experiences in Georgia during the Cherokee wars, which had ravaged the southern frontier from 1760 to 1761. At that time, he had participated personally in Governor Ellis' successful diplomatic campaign to pacify the Creek nation, which had then represented a most serious threat to the tenuous settlements in Georgia. Thus Knox was equally knowledgeable of the delicacy of Indian diplomacy and the horror of Indian warfare. On the eve of the revolution, Knox had, in fact, opposed General Gage's suggestion that Indians be used in the event of war with the colonists—his explicit objection at this date being that their employment would excite popular resentment in England.[43] Once Dartmouth decided to retaliate against reported American overtures to various tribes, however, British agents were instructed to recruit the support of Indian nations in both the northern and southern regions, and Undersecretary Pownall was given charge of administering Indian affairs at Whitehall.

When Pownall left the American Department, Knox inherited the management of the entire Indian business, including the troublesome but lucrative job of supplying the presents used to gain and retain the loyalty of Indian allies.[44] Although various agents in America persisted throughout the war in buying goods on the spot, the exorbitant expense of such purchases led the North government to restrict this practice in favor of sending the bulk of Indian supplies from Britain. Thus, after 1776 Knox, in addition to the already considerable demands of his departmental duties, found himself personally responsible for ordering a bewildering variety of goods from merchant contractors in London, arranging transportation of these supplies to America, routing them to the proper destinations, and, finally, keeping proper accounts of all expenditures. In return for his pains in this complicated enterprise, he was allowed a commission of 1.5 percent on the cost of the goods he supplied. Between 1776 and 1779, inclusive, Knox sent out goods having a gross value of more than £82,000.[45] His commission for this four-year period alone thus totaled more than £1,200.

Knox's own account of his meticulous attention to the details of the Indian business is singularly enlightening—both as testimony to his apparent concern for the public weal and as evidence of the veteran civil servant's cautious awareness of the dangers which threatened anyone who assumed charge of public expenditures.[46] According to Knox, the persons he employed to supply Indian goods were always "of the first Character in the City for Fortune & Integrity." After some early complaints on the part of Indian agents in America regarding the quality of goods sent out from Britain, Knox asked agents on leave in London to accompany him to the warehouses of merchant contractors to examine and select various articles. He subsequently required the merchants to keep patterns of the agents' selections and to insure that the requisite goods were of best quality only—at the lowest prices, of course. As a check on the merchants' compliance with these conditions, Knox required three copies of each bill: one copy he sent out with the goods to American officials "so as to detect any imposition that might be attempted"; he personally retained the second copy; and the third he laid before "some of the principal American Merchants" for certification of price and quality. Finally, Knox delivered this last set of bills, so certified—together with the bills of lading signed by the masters of the ships transporting the goods—to the Treasury, which paid the undersecretary's commission after examining the relevant documents.

From his correspondence with Indian agents in America, Knox obtained unique bits of intelligence about the course of the war, a boon which partially compensated him for his exclusion from the military business of the department.[47] On the other hand, the tenor of these eyewitness accounts was less than assuring. Agents in both the northern and the southern provinces of America sent back reports of complete misunderstanding and mismanagement of Indian affairs by British authorities in the field. A recurrent complaint was that both civil officials and army commanders continually attempted to control their Indian allies by the generous distribution of rum —an expedient which served only to render the warriors more unmanageable than ever. One report, which Knox received from a northern agent some time during the fall of 1777, gave a depressing account of the repulse in August of a detachment of Burgoyne's army before Fort Stanwix—a defeat which this informant attributed almost entirely to General St. Leger's complete misuse of his Indian forces.[48]

Even by late 1777, such reports—ominous as they are in retrospect—were in fact the exceptions in a year which had consistently brought news of immediate successes and promises of future victories in America. And with rumors flying about Whitehall regarding the plans and progress of Burgoyne's great northern campaign, Knox managed to extricate himself from the labyrinthine corridors of Georgian power in order to speculate on the problems involved in reforming and reconstructing the empire once the rebellious colonies were subdued. When news reached England of Burgoyne's early successes, government circles buzzed with predictions that the destruction of organized resistance in America was imminent. Knox decided to commit his ideas to paper. He was convinced that the

North administration did not anticipate a permanent and comprehensive settlement of the empire and that North in particular was interested only in "patching up matters with the colonies."[49] And so during the fall of 1777, Knox submitted his own proposals for a settlement to Germain, Dartmouth, and North in the form of a lengthy manuscript entitled "Considerations on the Great Question, What is fit to be done with America."[50]

The fundamental premise of Knox's "Considerations" was the argument that the old imperial constitution had contained the seeds of its own destruction. From the beginning of colonization, imperial land policy had provided the material foundation for democratic self-government. British monarchs had contributed to the further development of democracy and republicanism in America by failing to consistently support royal governors in their struggles against the ever-increasing power of colonial assemblies. After more than a century of virtually unrestricted self-government and practical immunity to royal claims of absolute jurisdiction, it was no wonder that the colonists turned to independence when Parliament attempted to enforce its sovereign authority in America.

On this basis, Knox rejected any peace settlement predicated upon a return to the imperial status quo, because such an arrangement would not eliminate the inherent defects of the old empire. He insisted that the colonial rebellion provided the British government with an exceptional opportunity for undertaking a comprehensive reformation of the imperial system. In his opinion, the American Declaration of Independence had dissolved the imperial compact, and therefore Great Britain could consider all colonial "Laws, Charters and Grants, as entirely abrogated and annulled, the whole Country, with some Exceptions, reinvested in the Crown, and the Inhabitants without other Claim than that of being deemed British Subjects upon returning to their Allegiance."

In the "Considerations," Knox's own proposals for a colonial peace settlement—though undeniably imperial in their objectives—were not essentially inspired by vindictive motives. His ultimate goal was the establishment of a "Perpetual Union with America." And he generally argued, as he had in previous years, that a permanent imperial connection could be founded only upon an equal distribution of privileges and obligations among the members of the empire. This general principle was qualified, however, by two basic considerations. First of all, Knox was determined to prevent a recurrence of rebellion in the colonies, and to this end he recommended drastic reforms in colonial society and politics. Second, he was convinced that the colonies would soon outstrip Great Britain in population and trade, and therefore he sought to provide constitutional guarantees against the inevitable economic and political domination of the empire by America.

Specifically, Knox proposed the creation of a colonial aristocracy as a counterbalance to the democratic and separatist inclinations of the Americans. First, he argued in favor of sweeping confiscations of rebel lands, with subsequent grants designed to produce a predominant class of large landholders and a dependent tenantry. Then, the constitutions of the American provinces could be altered so that men of wealth and property would dominate domestic politics. The imperial government should distribute offices and titles among the upper classes in America, not only to promote their ascendancy in the colonies but also to bind them to the British connection by ties of ambition and sentiment.

Once these ends were accomplished, the colonies could be allowed representation in Parliament, since the colonial delegations would certainly be dominated by the imperial-minded American aristocracy. Knox recommended that representation in the imperial Parliament be distributed among the members of the empire in proportion to their contributions to the imperial treasury. But he hedged against eventual American dominance in Parliament by insisting that the whole number of American representatives should remain fixed and that no individual colony should send more than four delegates to Parliament at any time. On the other hand, the American contributions to imperial expenses were not to remain static—Knox proposed that Parliament draw a perpetual revenue from the members of the empire in proportion to their populations or exports.

In respect to trade regulations, Knox called for a continuation of the colonial navigation system in principle, with specific adjustments in accordance with his goals of equality and imperial security. Members of the empire should be required to obtain manufactures and raw materials from imperial sources; however, neither British nor colonial subjects should be permitted to take advantage of trade regulations for the purpose of increasing the prices of their products. Knox again argued that the principle of imperial equality required that Ireland be admitted to full participation in the economic life of the empire. But he also recommended that American maritime strength be restricted permanently by granting British and Irish ships a perpetual monopoly of the overseas trade of the colonies.

By this plan for "a permanent Settlement and Perpetual Union with America," Knox sought to bestow immortality upon the British Empire. However, his "Considerations" was destined to serve instead as a testimonial to the death struggles of the old colonial system. On December 4, 1777, shortly after Knox submitted his scheme to the ministry, all London was stunned by the news of Burgoyne's surrender at Saratoga. Six days later, North could only reminisce pathetically in the Commons that he had hoped that the results of the past campaign would have allowed him to conciliate the colonies upon "true constitutional grounds," designed to bring about "a permanent peace and union" between Britain and America.[51] Military catastrophe and the obvious threat of French intervention in the American war, in fact, had abruptly ended speculations about imposing terms on the colonies, even on the basis of the *statu quo ante bellum*.

Word of Saratoga had scarcely arrived in Britain when recriminations erupted over responsibility for the military disaster—Burgoyne was blamed for his inflexible execution of poor strategy; Howe, for failing to assist Burgoyne; and Germain, for poor overall planning and coordination. With the opposition in Parliament aroused and invigorated, the ministry braced itself for a full parliamentary inquiry not only into the Saratoga campaign but also into the government's conduct of the entire war. Early in 1778, Attorney General Thurlow was given the formidable task of covering the ministry's political retreat from the shambles of Saratoga.[52] In turn, Thurlow relied primarily upon the American Department to support his rear-guard action.

After Saratoga, however, the Colonial Office itself was in considerable disarray. One of the first casualties was D'Oyley. Once the charges and countercharges of responsibility for Saratoga began to reverberate through Westminster and Whitehall, the junior undersecretary openly took the part of his friend Howe against both Germain and Burgoyne. On February 7, Hutchinson learned that D'Oyley was to be removed from office, and when he called upon the exundersecretary three days later, D'Oyley insisted that he had put himself out "because he sees he does not please Lord George."[53] More important, at this crucial juncture Germain himself withdrew from public business—originally because his wife was taken with a virulent attack of measles and then, following her death on January 15, because his own ministerial future became clouded in the aftermath of Saratoga.[54]

During this hiatus, Undersecretary Knox almost single-handedly sustained the integrity of his department. Not only did he carry on the routine business of the Colonial Office without further disturbing his distracted chief, but he also supplied Thurlow with adequate resources to beat back the assaults upon the ministry. Knox had not been a party to the original planning of Burgoyne's campaign; however, when Thurlow personally asked the undersecretary for information, Knox agreed to provide the attorney general with the précis of departmental correspondence that he drew up annually for cabinet ministers.[55] Within a day Thurlow returned, obviously impressed with the efficacy and quality of Knox's work, and asked the undersecretary for copies of two additional précis dealing with the operations of 1776 and 1777, because as the attorney general admitted, he could "expect nowhere else so clear a view of the whole subject."[56] For a time Knox held back these documents, apparently until he obtained Germain's permission to release them. According to Knox's account, Thurlow took the papers home and finally "came to me a few days after with a Sheet of remarks & desired me to hear him rehearse that he might know whether he understood the business." During the course of this session, Thurlow asked Knox why Burgoyne had deployed German troops, rather than English forces, to Bennington. When Knox replied that according to military protocol, the position of the Germans dictated their detachment, Thurlow shot back, "So . . . because one damn'd blockhead did a foolish thing the other blockhead must follow his example."[57] Apparently Knox's papers had given the government a firm footing for shifting the entire burden of blame for Saratoga upon the military commanders. Indeed, by July, when General Howe returned home to defend his conduct of the previous year, he complained to the king that Germain and Knox had so "loaded him with obloquy that he must therefore be allowed some means of justifying himself."[58] Both Howe and Burgoyne attempted to vindicate themselves in Parliament and the press for several years, but the North government was consistently able to supply satisfactory evidence to fore-stall any full legislative inquiry into the responsibility for Saratoga.

Although the government was thus able in the long term to wind down any political recoil from Saratoga, the immediate force of the disaster swung the pendulum of policy once again from coercion to conciliation. Early in 1778, while cabinet members engaged in re-criminations over responsibility for Burgoyne's defeat, North and a group of subministers—headed by Solicitor General Alexander Wedderburn and his protégé William Eden, undersecretary in the Northern Department—worked out a plan for restoring peace in America. The proposals which emerged from these deliberations provided for the immediate repeal of the tea duty and the coercive measures and also for the creation of a new peace commission with liberal powers for negotiating a comprehensive settlement with the colonies. On February 11, the cabinet adopted North's new com-mission without opposition, and the next day Parliament gave its approval to the scheme.[59]

Germain and Knox objected to the broad powers Eden and Wed-derburn proposed for the commission. But the influence of the American secretary and his department was in eclipse, and the North administration adopted final instructions which empowered the peace commission to concede virtually every point in dispute between Great Britain and the colonies except Parliament's general control over imperial trade.

In fact, the British peace offensive of 1778 was short-lived. When the commissioners, under the nominal leadership of the Earl of Carlisle, arrived in America on June 5, they learned that Con-gress had already approved the Franco-American treaty and had re-jected Parliament's conciliatory measures. The commissioners lingered in the colonies, but by autumn their mission was obviously moribund, since the Americans refused to treat except on the basis of complete independence.

In later years, Knox would stubbornly maintain that if the Amer-icans had agreed to the commissioners' ultimate concessions, "the People there would have had all the advantages of British Subjects without any share of the burdens of Empire."[60] Yet the fact is that during the spring of 1778, while hopes were still high for the suc-cess of the Carlisle mission, Knox himself was reconciled to the prospects of a negotiated settlement with America. On March 5, Hutchinson, who feared that the peace commission would abandon the interests of American Loyalists, recorded that Knox had assured him that all would end in "some sort of known established government over America."[61]

Knox could not have found any solace in the sequence of events which doomed the Carlisle mission. He undoubtedly shared the common reaction which Hutchinson observed in London the day after news of the Franco-American treaty appeared in the papers: "Everybody is struck dumb."[62] To Knox, the restoration of the British Empire and the recovery of his own fortunes must have seemed more distant than ever.

7. "Firmness & Temperance with a Readiness at Expedients": The American War, 1778–1782

France's entry into the American war drastically transformed its nature and transposed the focus of Great Britain's strategic considerations and commitments. No longer was the war simply a more or less remote effort to put down an inconvenient colonial rebellion across the Atlantic. Now a divided empire and nation became locked once again in a struggle for supremacy with its ancient enemy—engaged in that very war of *revanche* which Knox had foreseen with such trepidation years before. Not even in his most pessimistic moods, however, had Knox ever conjured up the specter which became reality after 1778. Great Britain found itself alone in a hostile world with its relatively thin human resources stretched even more thinly over land and sea against adversaries who menaced not only America and India but even the home islands themselves.[1]

Ironically, after the Franco-American alliance and the concomitant failure of the Carlisle Peace Commission, Germain's influence in North's divided ministry became more pronounced than ever. The American secretary and his staff expanded their jurisdiction over the planning and execution of military operations.[2] And as Germain emerged from eclipse, Knox's star became correspondingly ascendant. Germain, who had always respected the undersecretary's administrative abilities, was demonstrably grateful for Knox's loyalty during the difficult days after Saratoga. In subsequent years, the personal relationship between the American secretary and his chief lieutenant became close and cordial—even affectionate, as much as the formal aloofness of their personalities would permit. In this latter respect, Knox's attitude toward Germain seems not at all unlike his earlier affinity for the similarly strong personalities of Thomas Knox, Philip Skelton, and George Grenville. As the haughty and querulous Germain increasingly manifested confidence in his undersecretary, Knox reciprocated with unstinting loyalty and respect.

From 1778 Knox, with Germain's implicit approval, exercised predominant sway over the American Department. Even the new junior undersecretary, Thomas de Grey, a member of Parliament as well as a capable administrator, was distinctly subordinate to Knox in Colonial Office affairs.

The most important of Knox's personal responsibilities remained the coordination of interdepartmental business. He generally carried out this charge with expert ease and efficiency—even though the inept Boddington persevered in blunders which on occasion succeeded in provoking the usually unflappable American undersecretary to heights of incredulous wrath. Knox's most persistent and most frustrating failures, however, continued to come in his dealings with the admiralty. To give him credit, the essential circumstances of the growing impasse between the two departments were not of his making. Personal relations between Germain and Sandwich, which were strained from the former's entry into office, became irreparably hostile after 1778, when the two outspoken ministers quarreled in the cabinet about the strategic deployment of fleets.[3] After France entered the war, Sandwich insisted that British naval power should be concentrated in European waters to defend the British Isles from attack. Germain, on the other hand, argued pointedly—though ultimately without success—that the main goal of British naval strategy should be to pursue and attack French fleets-in-being wherever feasible in Europe or America.

Subsequently, the ever-increasing personal animus and policy differences between Sandwich and Germain substantially affected crucial business between their two departments. Sandwich, who indeed bore the main responsibility for defending Britain from French raids and possible invasion, understandably gave first priority to these contingencies in naval strategy and assignments. After 1778, however, Undersecretary Knox came to regard the admiralty as unreasonably inflexible and even hostile toward all requests from Germain's office for naval support for operations in America. Even the most subtle arts Knox could exercise in conjunction with subministers at the naval office could not mitigate the inimical hostility between the First Lord of the Admiralty and the secretary of state for America. After 1778, the American Department, openly complaining of the failure of the Navy Board to provide adequate transports, began to make separate arrangements with masters of private merchant vessels to ferry troops, equipment, and dispatches to

America.[4] But the inadequate deployment of fighting fleets for the support of land operations in America was never remedied—with fatal consequences.

The most significant testimonial to Knox's enhanced status within the ministry rests in the fact that after D'Oyley's resignation Germain consulted William regularly on military policy as well as civil affairs. To a great extent, the undersecretary served as a sounding board—or at best a devil's advocate—for the ideas of his independent-minded chief. Nevertheless, Germain was usually attentive when Knox volunteered opinions and suggestions, and the American secretary often solicited the advice of his lieutenant, even on matters of military strategy, which Germain regarded as his own particular area of competence. After Saratoga, Germain—who had never been in the colonies—especially relied upon Knox's knowledge of America and Americans. And in war as in peace, Knox provided a veritable flood of proposals and projects for restoring British authority in America.

Some time during the winter of 1777–78, Germain and Knox worked out plans for a military expedition in the southern colonies. The explicit rationale behind this particular project originated in Knox's long-held conviction that the southern environment—in both its human and physical aspects—was more propitious to the immediate success of British arms than that of the northern provinces. In the southern climate the British army could conduct year-round campaigns, especially since the ports and rivers in the South would always be open for naval support. Most important of all, Knox was also convinced that throughout the South, British forces would receive considerable support from Loyalists and Indian allies once a major campaign was undertaken.[5]

In detail, this plan—as described in a document written in Knox's hand and preserved among his manuscripts—called for an initial assault against Savannah by an expeditionary force of two thousand regulars operating in conjunction with a detachment of five hundred troops from the garrison at St. Augustine, as well as an undetermined number of southern Indians. Once Savannah was taken, loyal subjects in the province should be commissioned and armed; the five thousand small arms to be provided for such a purpose indicate the magnitude of Loyalist support which Knox and Germain anticipated. From a secure base at Savannah, a combined force of regulars, loyal provincials, and Indians might launch an attack upon Charleston. Once South Carolina and Georgia were cleared of organized rebel forces, Knox and Germain expected the immediate recovery of North Carolina and Virginia—a most sanguine assumption, as later events proved. With the South firmly under British control, a campaign of attrition including military and naval harassment as well as economic blockade could be waged against the northern colonies. To this end, the plan recommended that bases at New York and Rhode Island be retained and that an additional port be secured upon the Penobscot River in Maine; Philadelphia was to remain occupied only if an adequate number of Loyalists took up arms to relieve regular troops for operations elsewhere.

There is no need to exaggerate Knox's contributions to (and dubious credit for) the conception and implementation of the southern campaign of 1778 to 1781. One historian has described the strategy as "jumbling together old ideas of a war of expedition and a war of conquest," to which military commanders, such as Howe and Clinton, contributed as much as civil officials at Whitehall.[6] Knox's role was nonetheless crucial in that he served as the most direct channel of influence between advocates of the southern strategy —especially the American émigrés in London, who haunted his Soho residence—and the powerful American secretary. Above all, the undersecretary's prediction of aid forthcoming from Loyalist and Indian allies in the southern colonies presented a facile solution to the beleaguered ministry's most pressing problem—providing adequate military power to defend a far-flung empire.[7]

On March 8, 1778, even before the outbreak of hostilities with France, Germain sent a most secret dispatch to General Clinton, instructing the commander in chief to begin implementing the new plan for southern operations by the following fall. With France's entry into the war, Clinton temporarily shelved Germain's instructions in order to consolidate his forces against the anticipated French attack in America. But by late 1778, he was again in a position to resurrect the plan for a southern campaign.[8]

At the end of November, Clinton detached an expedition of three thousand men, under the command of Lt. Col. Archibald Campbell, to carry out the invasion of Georgia.[9] The stroke proved to be easier than even Knox could have imagined. In late December, Campbell's forces landed unopposed near Savannah, and because the fortifications of the capital—the very defenses upon which Knox had labored so diligently two decades earlier—had been allowed to fall into ruin, the British regulars overwhelmed the outnumbered American defenders within a few days. Shortly after Savannah had been taken, troops from East Florida under Gen. Augustine Prevost belatedly joined Campbell's expedition, and during a brief winter campaign Georgia was cleared of organized rebel resistance. By the early part of 1779, royal government was restored in the colony, and efforts to rally Loyalists to the imperial cause seemed very promising.[10] Knox's faith in a southern expedition appeared to be completely vindicated.

Despite these welcome successes, Knox and Germain's new strategy misfired from the very beginning in one crucial respect. With the launching of the southern campaign, Germain and Knox had determined to exact maximum results from the Indian allies of Britain. In the main theater of operations, John Stuart—the veteran superintendent of the southern Indian district—was instructed to secure the assistance of the Cherokees, Creeks, and Choctaws to protect both the lower Mississippi Valley and East Florida from rebel forays, as well as to cooperate with British forces in the reduction of Georgia and South Carolina. Simultaneously, other agents were ordered to employ various tribes against rebel occupation of interior regions throughout the Mississippi Valley.[11] Although the northern provinces were not to be a theater of major offensive operations, Knox informed General Haldimand in Canada that the government expected that Indians would be used more effectively on the northern frontiers than they had in the past campaign.[12] Finally, under pressure from the Treasury, the American Department ordered Indian agents in both the northern and southern districts to put an end to all purchases of Indian presents in America and to make subsequent requisitions through Undersecretary Knox in London.[13]

This concerted effort to reform the conduct of Indian affairs after 1778 had only minimal effects. Expenditures for Indian presents continued to mount as American agents persisted in making large purchases from provincial traders. When the home government refused to honor such bills, civil and military officials in America protested with equal anguish against the personal injustices and public catastrophes such a penurious policy would certainly produce.[14]

To Knox and Germain, the most galling fact of all was the continuing military inefficacy of British Indian policy in America.

Throughout the early part of 1779, Knox persistently attempted to persuade John Stuart to leave his base at Pensacola and lead his Indian charges to Georgia, where they might lend assistance to His Majesty's forces. Colonel Campbell reported from Georgia, however, that between December 1778 and March 1779 "he had not seen nor heard of an Indian" and had consequently been unable to open communications with backcountry Loyalists. On June 2, Germain wrote a bitter dispatch to Stuart, reproaching his failures despite "enormous" expenditures in his department and constant assurances of success.[15] Germain insisted that the aged superintendent's plight arose from his dependence upon agents who had taken advantage of his infirm health to defraud the royal government.

The American secretary unmistakably expected these rebukes to prod Stuart into effective action. But by the time this caustic dispatch reached America, the veteran Indian agent was dead. Stuart's successors, although they achieved some limited success in mobilizing Indian auxiliaries to cooperate with later British military operations in the South, were never able to raise the substantial support which Knox and Germain demanded. In assessing this failure, the overriding fact is that after 1778 officials at Whitehall—including Germain and Knox—were goaded by military necessity into expecting more than was practicable from Indian alliances. Originally, even Knox had anticipated that Indians would serve only as auxiliaries to main bodies of British regulars and Loyalist recruits. Although mismanagement by officials in America accounts in part for the ineffectual use of Indians in this capacity, Indians, no matter how well organized and supplied, could never compensate for inadequacies in the numbers and utilization of regular troops.

For much the same reason, Knox's ambitious plans and projects for rallying American Loyalism were frequently to become as frustrating as his efforts to mobilize Indian allies. During the summer of 1778, in response to a personal request from North, Knox—with the assistance of John Nutting, a Massachusetts Tory who had recently joined the undersecretary's circle in London—worked out plans for a Loyalist enclave to be erected in the strategic Penobscot region of Maine. On September 2, Germain sent a dispatch to General Clinton, directing him to establish a base on the Penobscot River suitable for a permanent settlement of American Loyalists. Nutting was personally entrusted with carrying the dispatch to Clinton and expediting the execution of the project in America.

Unfortunately, on the voyage to New York he was captured by an American privateer, and although he was quickly exchanged, he did not arrive in America until March 1779.[16]

Although Knox was concerned that Nutting's misfortune would delay the project indefinitely, in June 1779 Clinton sent a detachment of six hundred troops to take possession of the Penobscot region.[17] Before the British forces were able to erect any works, however, a substantial American naval and land expedition from Massachusetts launched an attack upon the tenuous outpost. Only the timely intervention of a British fleet under Sir George Collier turned an apparent defeat into a rout of the American rebels.

Knox's enthusiasm was fired by the providential deliverance of the Penobscot expedition, and by October 1779 he was deeply engaged in further plans for his Loyalist colony. Throughout the vicissitudes of this project, Governor Hutchinson—true to his dour New England heritage—steadfastly endeavored to dampen the undersecretary's flights of optimism. Originally, the exgovernor of Massachusetts seems to have been peeved by Knox's failure to consult him before undertaking the scheme; and although Hutchinson resolved at first "to find no fault with the most preposterous measure," upon reflection he could not resist making "Mr. Knox acquainted, in the most prudent manner I can, with my sentiments."[18] Even after the near-miraculous relief of the Penobscot garrison, when Knox told Hutchinson that he was the only man for governor of the new colony, the New Englander replied that they had better await news of Admiral d'Estaing's French fleet "before we thought any further on measures for restoring peace to America."[19]

Hutchinson's pessimism and reserve at least should have served to caution Knox against the sanguine assumption that Loyalists could be counted upon to provide a main force for putting down the rebellion in America. Knox, of course, was substantially correct in his belief that considerable numbers of Americans were disaffected from the rebel cause, but he grossly misunderstood Loyalist attitudes and overestimated the extent of active commitment forthcoming from those sympathetic to the imperial connection.[20] Although large numbers of Loyalists volunteered for military service during the early stages of the war, American Loyalism generally assumed a passive stance once the British army proved incapable of providing consistent and widespread protection for avowed Loyalists against patriot reprisals. And yet after 1778 British policy in America—particularly Knox and Germain's plan for southern military operations—was rooted in the belief that Loyalists could be relied upon not only to provide military units substantially augmenting British regular forces in expeditionary campaigns but also to hold territories once British troops were withdrawn for further campaigns against remaining rebel strongholds.

Given the relative shortage of regular military forces available to Britain following France's entry into the war, Knox and Germain's original exaggerated expectations of Loyalist support are understandable. However, their continued attachment to this illusory faith and their persistent defense of a chimerical policy in the face of mounting contradictory evidence are indefensible. Thus in March 1779, when Sir James Wright reported from Georgia that he was yet uncertain of loyalties in the occupied colony and, consequently, suggested that the province be continued under military government, Germain rejected the veteran official's eyewitness assessment and confessed to Knox that he doubted Wright's fitness to govern.[21] For his part, Knox not only provided the North ministry with a continuous stream of statistics, arguments, and position papers defending Loyalist policies in principle and practice against opposition attacks, but he also decided, according to his own account, to "set an example of confidence in support of the Government" by reestablishing at considerable expense his plantation in the recovered province of Georgia.[22]

Knox's decision to restore his American estates was in fact as much a matter of financial necessity as an issue of political confidence. The American war had had a disastrous effect upon his personal fortune. The loss of income from his office in New York was scarcely made up by the commission he earned on Indian presents, although even this fluctuating sum frequently exceeded his income as undersecretary. From 1778, the British government allowed him a pension of £1,200 per annum in compensation for his offices in Georgia and New York; nevertheless, he still suffered a considerable decline in total income, arising from the confiscation of his estates in Georgia. Undoubtedly, when the Knoxes' third child was born in July 1778, William's paternal joy was circumscribed by trepidations over the shrunken legacy which would remain to all his children.[23]

It is hardly surprising then that in 1779, even as Colonel Campbell's forces were still engaged in securing Georgia militarily, Knox leaped at the apparent opportunity to restore his private interests in the province. Although 20 of his "most valuable" blacks had been carried away by rebels, 102 slaves were recovered "or of themselves returned" to Knoxborough. Within a year, by drawing upon his diminished financial reserves and borrowing from friends, Knox was able to resettle and restock his Savannah River plantation and bring it to a flourishing condition. His agents soon estimated that Knox-borough would produce £2,000 the following year.[24]

These hopes were dashed, however, when combined Franco-American land and sea forces under Admiral d'Estaing and General Benjamin Lincoln laid siege to Savannah during September and October 1779. Knox's slaves were among those commandeered by the British defenders of Savannah to erect fortifications about the capital;[25] perhaps they were also among the large body of blacks armed and assigned to defend the British redoubts alongside regular troops during the month-long siege.[26] Eventually, after an unsuccessful assault on October 9, d'Estaing, who had become concerned about his exposed seaward flank, recalled the French troops and sailed away from Savannah. Subsequently, Lincoln was forced to evacute Georgia and retreat to Charleston.

Knoxborough, which had served as an encampment for Lincoln's troops during the siege, was again in shambles—the crops entirely destroyed and all the livestock consumed or driven away. But after the successful defense of Savannah, especially with the promising showing on the part of Loyalist military units during the campaign, Knox was encouraged to restore his estates a second time. His slaves —so recently heroes in the tenacious defense of the royal capital of Georgia—were returned in bondage to Knoxborough to rebuild structures, replant crops, and manufacture shingles. Within a year, Knox's agents remitted him £1,400 from the produce of Knox-borough and assured him a return of £2,000 for 1782.[27]

By 1780, then, Knox—deprived as he was of the mixed blessings of historical hindsight—might be forgiven if he presumed that his frequently ill-fated star was on the rise. Within two years of the debacle at Saratoga, not only did it appear that his faith in a southern campaign was vindicated, but his personal fortunes also seemed to be restored. He had attained substantial influence within the North ministry—in the making of policy as well as its execution. And such were the incongruities of the times that during this period, in the midst of a desperate global war, this undersecretary in the Colonial Office became intimately engaged in the sequence of events which saw Ireland threaten to follow the example of America.

Of course, Knox's interest in his native land and his efforts on its behalf were by no means a matter of sudden and passing fancy. For many years, he had argued that Ireland's exclusion from imperial trade was a greater inequity than any injustice, real or imagined, about which the American colonies complained. In his various publications dealing with colonial issues, he had consistently recommended that Ireland be admitted to full participation in the commercial privileges of the empire. With the outbreak of rebellion in America, he had seen an opportunity to benefit his native country. Early in 1776, almost a year after he had prepared the measure which barred American rebels from the Newfoundland fishing grounds, Knox had proposed that the British government allow Irish subjects to participate in the North American fishery. When the North administration responded favorably, Knox communicated his project to Sir John Blacquire—chief secretary to the Irish viceroy, Lord Harcourt—and also to Sir Lucius O'Brien—a prominent member of the Irish House of Commons. Knox specifically recommended that the government of Ireland grant bounties to Irish vessels engaged in the Newfoundland fishery, and during the spring of 1776 Blacquire and O'Brien successfully piloted such a measure through the Irish Parliament. Within two years, Knox estimated that two thousand Irish seamen were annually employed in the Newfoundland fishery.[28]

By 1778, however, Ireland's new fishing industry had scarcely lightened the unfortunate impact of the American war on Irish commerce. Before the revolution, Irish merchants had successfully conducted trade with America in defiance of British commercial restrictions. But after the outbreak of war, this clandestine trade was virtually destroyed by the British embargo on American commerce and the naval blockade of rebel ports. Although Ireland's trade with America had never been great in terms of absolute volume, it was vital to a nation whose commerce and industry were generally limited by British regulations. Within a short time, the wartime embargo produced economic distress in Ireland and, in its wake, a mass revival of Irish resentment against English rule.[29]

Early in 1778, Knox, with Germain's support, persuaded North that loyal Ireland should be granted trade concessions equal to those which the Carlisle Peace Commission was empowered to offer the rebellious American colonies. On March 14, 1778, Knox wrote Sir Richard Heron, chief secretary to the new viceroy, Lord Buckinghamshire, that the time was ripe for Irish trade concessions.[30] Within a week, Buckinghamshire—acting on the basis of Knox's recommendations—officially requested that North allow Ireland to share in any commercial privileges which might be granted to the American colonies. For his part, Knox did not wait for the Irish administration to initiate specific proposals. By the end of March, he informed Heron that he had prepared two Irish trade bills: one granting Ireland free export of all native products except wool and woolen goods to the plantations in America and Africa, a second allowing Ireland to import all the products of American and African colonies.[31]

Knox excepted Irish wool and woolen goods from his export bill in an attempt to mitigate the objections which English and Scots merchants and manufacturers were certain to raise against any trade concessions for Ireland. Nevertheless, when North introduced the Irish export and import measures into Parliament early in April 1778, British merchants stirred up a storm of protest. And as North began to bend before the tempest, Knox worked desperately throughout the month of May to save the Irish concessions. He arranged meetings between Irish delegations and the agents of British manufacturers and merchants, and he acted as mediator between North and the representatives of British business interests in Parliament. On the basis of these difficult and delicate negotiations, he personally worked out "accommodations" designed to placate British fears of Irish commercial competition. He was forced to add several items, including cotton goods, to the list of products Ireland would not be allowed to export, and he also had to agree to the equalization of duties carried by the exports of Ireland and England. Although his import bill proved to be too contentious and had to be postponed until the next session of Parliament, by mid-May Knox joyously informed Heron that the export bill had passed the House of Commons without any further amendments and that he expected no serious opposition in the House of Lords.[32]

Even after Parliament passed the export bill, Knox could not take a respite from his labors. The export bill provided that none of its terms would take effect until the Irish Parliament enacted the prescribed equalization of English and Irish duties. During the last weeks of May, Knox was busily engaged in the tedious business of working out a detailed schedule of duties in consultations with British customs officials and agents of English manufacturers. The Irish executive then prepared a bill incorporating the requisite duties, and at Buckinghamshire's request North sent Knox to defend the Irish duties bill before the British Privy Council. Knox spent a good part of the summer of 1778 in attendance upon the Privy Council, explaining the bill and proposing amendments in response to objections. The Privy Council approved the Irish equalization bill late in July, and when the Irish Parliament accepted the measure, Knox's export bill became law.[33] On August 6, 1778, Heron graciously conveyed to Knox the gratitude of the Irish administration for his efforts in behalf of Ireland: "Whatever advantages may be derived to this kingdom from the laws which passed in Great Britain the last session, it had been obtained, I am persuaded principally by your judgement, industry, and zeal."[34]

By the end of 1778, Knox was justly pleased with the progress he had made toward achieving full partnership for Ireland in the imperial economy. But the Irish were not contented with the trade concessions granted by Parliament. As early as May 1778, Heron had warned Knox that the long list of exceptions to the export bill and the postponement of the import bill had caused great disappointment among the members of the Irish Parliament.[35] Knox persevered in his efforts, and late in 1778 he obtained another significant concession for Ireland when he persuaded the British government to remove its embargo on the Irish provision trade with Europe.

After years of political and economic subservience, Ireland would not be appeased by half measures. By 1779, the Irish—copying the tactics of American resistance—adopted nonimportation agreements directed against British manufacturers and also organized local associations throughout the country to enforce these agreements. In response to popular agitation, the usually subservient Irish Parliament passed measures demanding free trade for Ireland and even followed up their demands by threatening to pass a Short Money Bill, which would grant the Irish administration supplies for only six months instead of two years, as was customary.

The legislative assaults on British rule by Irish patriot politicians were accompanied as usual by mob riots, which were especially violent in Dublin. Even more ominous and effective were the activities of the Irish Volunteers. These armed paramilitary cadres had originally been organized to defend Ireland against the threat of French invasion. But in 1779, the Volunteers energetically took up the patriot cause. Volunteer units circulated propaganda calling for free trade for Ireland and also conducted armed military drills in public.

In the midst of the crisis, North seemed paralyzed. Gower, the leader of the Bedfordite faction in the administration, attempted to prod North into action. In May 1779, on his own initiative, Gower announced to Parliament that something would be done for Ireland. But North, who seemed to be cowed by the prospect of again provoking the wrath of English merchants, repudiated Gower's statement and refused to consider further relief for Irish trade. As the Irish situation continued to deteriorate, Knox, John Robinson, and king's friend Charles Jenkinson drew up proposals for new Irish trade concessions. But North took refuge in indolence, refusing even to look at Irish papers.[36]

Even by itself, the Irish problem would have seemed a most formidable tangle, but it was, in fact, only one aspect of a collective national trauma which has come to be known as the crisis of 1779. In June, following months of diplomatic bargaining and counter-bargaining between Westminster, Madrid, and Paris, Spain joined France in the war of *revanche* against Britain. Throughout the summer of 1779, the inhabitants of the southern coast of England were kept in a state of near-panic as a Franco-Spanish invasion fleet sailed freely about the Channel without any apparent opposition from the British fleet. Eventually, by early September, the combined Bourbon flotilla, its crews frustrated by poor coordination and wracked by disease, found it necessary to withdraw without even an engagement at sea. But there were few hymns of praise for Britain's deliverance. The North government was immediately treated instead to a loud chorus of abuse—charged, perhaps unfairly, with the failures of the British fleet, but most deservedly castigated for the undeniable failure of leadership ashore during the most menacing days of the invasion panic.[37]

By the end of 1779, North's paralysis in the face of consummate calamity provided the Bedfordites in the cabinet with another opportunity for a concerted effort to overthrow the prime minister.[38]

In November, Gower and Weymouth resigned. The Bedfordite conspiracy was seconded by Thurlow and Wedderburn, who insisted that they would no longer work with North. In fact, North wished desperately to give up office, but the king would not allow him to resign. George III had no intention of surrendering power to the aggressive and rapacious Bedfordites, and he certainly would not turn to the opposition, who insisted that the American war be abandoned. Almost in spite of itself, the North administration survived the crisis of 1779.

In December, once the Bedfordite plot had been thwarted, North's cabinet finally agreed to recommend additional Irish trade concessions to Parliament. In effect, the ministry adopted Knox's concept of full economic partnership for Ireland within the empire. The prohibitions on the export of Irish woolens and other manufactures were to be removed, and Ireland was to be allowed equal privileges with Britain in the colonial trade.[39] Late in December, Knox communicated the cabinet's resolutions to Irish Attorney General John Scott. But even as Scott expressed his own satisfaction with Knox's latest service for Ireland, he warned that members of the Irish administration had received the resolutions rather "coldly and dryly."[40]

The Irish government recognized that the trade concessions had come too late. By the time the British Parliament passed the cabinet's commercial resolutions during the winter of 1779–80, the Irish patriots were demanding full legislative independence from Britain. In the spring of 1780, the patriots focused their attack on the British Mutiny Act, the main source of Irish contributions to imperial defense. In the country at large, Irish magistrates responded to public pressure by refusing to enforce the British act, and in the Irish Parliament the patriots introduced a mutiny bill of their own, which in effect denied the right of the British Parliament to legislate for Ireland. The British government, which had no intention of granting legislative independence to Ireland at all, instructed Lord Lieutenant Buckinghamshire to resist the Irish mutiny bill.[41]

In the spring of 1780, Knox was sent to Ireland to assist the embattled Irish viceroy. Although the full details of Knox's role in the mutiny bill crisis are not clear, it is certain that in Ireland he acted as observer, adviser, and intermediary on behalf of the North administration. On May 26, he counseled Germain that "firmness & temperance with a readiness at expedients, will do here yet, but you must be sparing of your instructions, for it is much better, people here should use their discretion."[42] Germain agreed that he could offer little assistance to the Lord Lieutenant, and he expressed full confidence in Knox's counsels: "You that are on the spot will I am sure give him the best advice in your power."[43] Probably it was at Knox's suggestion that the Irish administration attempted to counter the patriot challenge to British legislative authority by proposing an amendment making the Irish mutiny bill perpetual. The adoption of this provision would at least have avoided annual reviews of British legislative jurisdiction in Ireland. But the Irish patriots rejected the administration's amendment and in July 1780 transmitted to Westminster a mutiny bill, which in effect challenged British parliamentary authority in Ireland.[44]

The North administration could no longer avoid direct involvement in the mutiny bill crisis. The British Privy Council had to decide whether to accept the measure as passed by the Irish Parliament or to restore the rejected amendment and resubmit the revised bill for approval. A general confrontation between the British government and the Irish patriots over legislative independence seemed unavoidable. Then, in the midst of the affair, British influence in Ireland was further jeopardized by an untimely trade dispute over the duties to be levied on English sugars imported into Ireland. Under pressure from the British government, the Irish executive recommended a low duty of 5s. 10 1/4d. per hundredweight on English sugars. The merchants of Dublin, however, demanded that the Irish Parliament adopt a higher protective duty of 16s. 7 1/2d. per hundredweight.[45]

From his vantage point in the Irish capital, Knox recognized that the sugar controversy threatened to drive the Irish mercantile interests into the arms of the patriots. At the end of May, he advised the North administration to accept a compromise duty.[46] At first, the ministry evaded his remedy, but as the mutiny bill crisis approached a climax they were forced to accept his views on the sugar duty. In August, the British Privy Council adopted a compromise duty of 9s. 2 10/12d. on English sugars imported into Ireland.[47] At the same time, the Privy Council returned the mutiny bill to the Irish Parliament with the amendment making its provisions perpetual.

With the Anglo-Irish connection virtually hanging in the balance in 1780, Knox worked skillfully and effectively behind the scenes in Ireland. During the summer, he left Dublin and took Letitia and the children on what was to all outward appearances a holiday to his childhood home at Monaghan. But even as he renewed old friendships and proudly displayed his family before the townsfolk, Knox also put to use those lessons of Irish politics learned so many years before from Sir Richard Cox. Now something of a celebrity, Knox succeeded not only in charming the powerful Blaney family, who controlled the parliamentary borough at Monaghan, but also in winning the confidence of the incumbent borough member, Gen. Robert Cunningham. In the late summer, while the British Mutiny Act was pending before the Irish Parliament, Knox expended considerable effort in instructing Cunningham about the details and the full implications of the controversial measure.[48]

Upon returning to Dublin, Cunningham warned Knox on August 10 that the patriots had bitterly attacked the mutiny bill in the Commons and threatened further public disruptions. But within the week, the tide turned in favor of the government, when the Irish Commons—just as Knox had earlier promised the North ministry—accepted the compromise duty on sugars by a vote of 119 to 38.[49] Capitalizing upon this decisive victory, the Irish government quickly secured passage of the British Mutiny Act. On August 17, with obvious relief, Lord Lieutenant Buckinghamshire reported success to Westminster and added that in the debates on the mutiny bill "Lieut. General Cunninghame also exerted himself upon the Occasion, and what he said had great Influence upon the House."[50] For the moment it seemed that Ireland—or at least a majority in the Irish Parliament—was satisfied with the privileges of imperial partnership.

The year 1780 seemed to mark a turning point for British fortunes in America as well as Ireland. During the spring, while the North administration was deeply embroiled in the Irish problems, Generals Clinton and Cornwallis successfully invaded South Carolina. Charleston fell in May, and by the summer of 1780 royal government was reestablished in the colony. When news of the conquest of South Carolina arrived in Britain, Germain confidently predicted that the restoration of British authority in the colonies south of the Hudson River was imminent. He encouraged his fellow ministers to consider plans for a settlement with America, and in August he took the initiative by personally submitting to the cabinet Knox's scheme for transforming the Loyalist refuge on the Penobscot River into a model colony.[51]

Knox had originally drawn up his proposals for the Loyalist province in 1778 at North's request.[52] Not surprisingly, the specific plans for New Ireland—the name Knox bestowed upon his model colony—were based upon the principles he had espoused before the Saratoga disaster in his "Considerations on the Great Question, What is fit to be done with America." The constitution of the new colony was to include integral checks on "the prevailing disposition of the People to Republicanism": the democratic influence of the assembly was to be balanced by an aristocratic influence embodied in a legislative council and an executive privy council. Members of these aristocratic bodies should be appointed by the crown and should hold their seats for life, unless removed by the crown for good cause upon the recommendation of the governor or a majority of the assembly. By assigning titles of honor and emoluments to seats in the privy council and by filling vacancies there from the membership of the legislative council, the colonial aristocracy would be attached to the interests of the royal government. Land policy in the colony should also be predicated upon the inseparable goals of perpetuating the provincial aristocracy and preserving the imperial connection. Original titles to land in New Ireland should be granted to the "most meritorious" Loyalists, who in turn would be allowed to lease their holdings to other settlers. Of course, the poorest Loyalists should receive land gratis from the crown. All landholders in the colony should be required to declare publicly, as a precondition to any grant, that they recognized "the King in His Parliament as the Supreme Legislature of this Province." In addition, all lands should be subject to a quitrent until the provincial legislature should provide a permanent revenue for the support of the colonial government.[53]

North's cabinet approved the New Ireland project on August 10, 1780, and the following day the king accepted Knox's plan with only minor exceptions.[54] But Attorney General Wedderburn subsequently vetoed the scheme on the grounds that the projected colony was still legally part of Massachusetts Bay. Attempts were made in the cabinet to circumvent Wedderburn's objections, but the attorney general adamantly refused to approve the project in any form. By September, Germain regretfully informed Knox that the administration could not carry his New Ireland scheme through Parliament without the support of the law officers of the crown. Of course Knox, who believed that the American colonies had abrogated all charter rights and privileges by their Declaration of Independence, had no sympathy for the attorney general's legal distinctions, and in later years he insisted that Wedderburn withheld his approval of the New Ireland scheme only because Germain had previously blocked his elevation to the peerage.[55]

Despite Knox's bitter disappointment over the New Ireland project, it was nonetheless obvious that the undersecretary exercised a considerable influence in the counsels of the North administration. And in eighteenth-century Britain, political influence—even the essentially limited form of power by proxy which subministers exercised—brought with it commensurate perquisites. Knox for some time had been allowed to share in the minor spoils of office, but by 1780 his patronage was surprisingly extensive and efficacious. He was able to obtain appointments and promotions in the fighting services, the East India Company, and the church for several relatives, friends, and their offspring. He must have been especially flattered when, in February 1780, his former patron Lord Grosvenor asked him to employ his good offices with North on behalf of Grosvenor's application for the Lord Lieutenancy of Cheshire.[56] Although Knox's petition in this instance was not successful, probably because the Grosvenor influence had provided only fickle support for the ministry, his lordship's request of itself was no mean tribute to the considerable political reputation and status Knox had achieved.

Even as Knox savored the sweet pleasures of political influence, he was also made painfully aware of its bitter aftertaste. In 1779, Philip Skelton, then living in retirement in Dublin, wrote to his former pupil requesting a church appointment for a friend.[57] Throughout the years, Knox had remained responsive to the needs and wishes of his former master, not only sending him frequent contributions for the welfare of his flocks but also exerting influence in behalf of the worthy laymen and clerics whom Skelton recommended perennially. On this single occasion, however, Knox had to reply that the position Skelton requested for his friend had already been promised to a relative. The cantankerous old man responded with a stinging rebuke, denouncing Knox as a hypocritical "courtier, who employed the little share of influence you have over the Church in serving a relation at the time you neglect a man of equal possibly of superior, attention to the duties of his function."[58] On this caustic note, Skelton brought to an end a relationship which over a period of almost fifty years had become like that between father and son rather than master and pupil. Although he was to live seven more years, this reproach for the unsatisfactory patronage of Undersecretary Knox was his final letter to his dear William.

This sad personal episode was a singularly depressing interlude in a year which saw Knox become increasingly optimistic over the course of events in America. In January 1780, he predicted to Hutchinson that "England had never been upon the eve of so many important events as at present."[59] Later in the year, once news arrived in England of "Lord Cornwallis's glorious success at Campden" during the previous August, Knox returned with his usual energy to preparing a variety of contingency plans and proposals for restoring royal authority in the conquered colonies.[60]

By this time, Knox also found himself shouldering an ever-increasing burden within the American Department. For some unspecified reason, Germain uncharacteristically delegated a larger share of his departmental responsibilities to the senior undersecretary. When Germain was in attendance at Whitehall, Knox increasingly acted as a buffer, shielding his chief from the multitude of officials and private individuals who demanded personal interviews. More significantly, Germain's absences from Whitehall became frequent, and on these occasions Knox, with the secretary's knowledge and approval, assumed considerable independence in the conduct of departmental affairs.[61]

The surviving record of Undersecretary Knox's experiences and perceptions during the period of Cornwallis' march to Yorktown provides a pointed commentary on the main responsibility the North administration must bear for the military disasters in America—above all for its failure to coordinate joint military-naval operations or to abandon such intricate projects in the face of mounting evidence that recurrent delays and disruptions in communications over thousands of miles rendered any centralized direction from Whitehall all but impossible. Early in 1781, Knox sanguinely predicted that with "the wretched state of the Rebel Military force, and the vast superiority of ours, there is a great probability of a negociation being solicited by the Inhabitants of the Revolted Provinces, if not by Congress." In April of the same year—three months after Tarleton's Loyalist Legion had been virtually wiped out at

Cowpens and one month after Cornwallis' costly engagement with
Nathanael Greene's reorganized rebel army at Guilford Court House
—Germain assured Knox that the "accounts of Lord Cornwallis'
progress are most promising as he drives the enemy before him."
Knox, nevertheless, was disturbed by subsequent reports of Greene's
persistent harassment of the southern army.[62]

Thus it was with some relief that in late July, as Cornwallis
marched toward tidewater Virginia, Knox received important intelligence at Whitehall concerning the "Plan and Intentions of the
Enemy" in America. Germain was in the country at the time, and
Knox decided that this "most certain and precise" intelligence had
to be dispatched without delay to General Haldimand, the commander in chief in Canada, so that he could undertake operations
"on the Frontiers of the Revolted Provinces in Cooperation with,
and Support of the Southern army."[63]

In a dispatch, dated July 31, 1781, Knox informed Haldimand
that Washington had been forced to give up his plan of sending
troops south to Virginia because of French objections and that instead Washington's Franco-American army would launch an offensive against General Clinton at New York, once Admiral de Grasse's
fleet arrived in the northern waters.[64] When Knox originally drew
up the dispatch, his information was in fact quite accurate, but by
the time it arrived in America it was entirely obsolete, erroneous,
and delusive. For on August 14 Washington had learned that de
Grasse was sailing to the Chesapeake rather than to New York, and
five days later the American commander sent more than six thousand French and American troops southward to join the campaign
against Cornwallis in Virginia.[65]

Within a few months, Knox's perpetual optimism was completely undermined by the unbroken succession of bad news from America, especially by reports of substantial rebel assaults upon Loyalist
settlements in Georgia and South Carolina. Under the strain and
anxiety, he finally lost all patience with the admiralty's apparent
imperviousness to the critical state of affairs in America, and on
October 31, after an especially frustrating experience at Sandwich's
office, Knox insisted that Germain take the initiative in naval affairs.[66] Germain's reply provides remarkable evidence of ministerial
responsibility for Yorktown: "It is in vain to argue upon the operations or destinations of fleets when it is impossible to know the true
situation of our naval force. If Lord Sandwich proposes or finally ap-

proves any plan we seldom want resources, on the other hand if he does not heartily adopt what other ministers think right, official difficulties occur, and the state of our fleet is such that no new measures can be pursued."[67] Not until November 4, 1781, did Germain admit his growing concern that Cornwallis' campaign would be jeopardized by a lack of naval support.[68] His alarm was well founded but monumentally tardy. A fortnight earlier on October 19, 1781, with de Grasse's fleet blockading the Chesapeake, Cornwallis had surrendered his entire army to Washington at Yorktown. News of the disaster in Virginia did not reach London until the twenty-fifth day of November.

Even after Britain learned of Yorktown, the North administration floundered on for four months, sustained mainly by George III.[69] Among the cabinet ministers, only Germain shared the king's stubborn determination to resist American independence at any cost. By the early part of 1782, however, Germain's obstinate defense of the war was becoming increasingly unpopular among the administration's supporters in Parliament, and as government strength in the Commons dwindled steadily under opposition assaults, it became increasingly clear—even to George III—that the American secretary had to go. Throughout the month of January, the business of the American Office was suspended as Germain remained in the country waiting for North to decide his fate.

Knox made a last-minute attempt to save his chief—and by the same stroke to preserve those colonies, including Georgia, still occupied by British forces. He obtained a private interview with North; and when the prime minister confided to him that it was a change in measures rather than men that he desired, Knox suggested that Germain might be persuaded to accept immediate peace with America on the basis of uti possidetis. North ended the interview without committing himself to Knox's proposal. For several days he procrastinated, but after considerable prodding by the king he agreed to a meeting with Germain, arranged by Knox and John Robinson. At this conference, on January 22, 1782, Germain offered to remain in office and negotiate a settlement with America on the basis of uti possidetis, as previously proposed by Knox. North insisted, however, that nothing short of unqualified independence would satisfy the Americans, and Germain replied that under those circumstances North would have to find someone else to head the American Department.[70]

Knox realized that Germain's removal was only the prelude to a policy of complete withdrawal from the rebel colonies. In a desperate eleventh-hour effort to save his property in Georgia, he asked Germain to send him out to America as governor of South Carolina. Knox's intentions are not clear, but in any event Germain refused his request and insisted that Knox remain in the American Department to assist the new secretary.[71] Before Germain officially gave up the seals of office at the end of January, he secured a promise from the king that the pension of £1,200, which had been granted to Knox as compensation for the loss of his offices in America, would be continued for his life and the lives of his children. But North objected that this arrangement would certainly provoke a conflict in Parliament, since the opposition seemed bent on forcing economic reforms of royal patronage. North persuaded the king to divide the pension between William and Letitia, each grant to continue at the king's pleasure rather than during their respective lives.[72]

After Germain's resignation, the days of the Colonial Office were numbered. North was unable to find a major political figure willing to assume the secretaryship. He eventually appointed Welbore Ellis, a perennial factotum in the government, to fill the post, but Ellis' brief tenure in the American Office was singularly uneventful. The fate of the American Department was finally sealed when the North administration resigned in March 1782 and was succeeded by a coalition of Rockingham Whigs and former Chathamites, now led by the Earl of Shelburne. During the course of the American Revolution, the Colonial Office had become anathema to the opposition; in 1780 they had almost succeeded in carrying a parliamentary motion calling for the abolition of the American Department. When the Rockingham government took office in 1782, the American secretaryship was left vacant. The two ancient secretaryships were reorganized into a Home Department and a Foreign Department, and jurisdiction in colonial affairs was transferred to the Home Office, headed by the Earl of Shelburne.

Knox, who recognized that his zealous role in the American Revolution made him particularly obnoxious to the new government, prepared to retire from office. But Shelburne allowed him a brief reprieve. As the weaker partner in the ministerial coalition, Shelburne was anxious to bolster his party with accessions from North's supporters. He told Knox that he intended "to select all the ability and efficiency" from the staffs of the American Office, the Board of Trade, and the Southern Department to "form out of the whole one complete establishment," and he asked Knox to assist him in the business of reorganizing his department.[73]

In later years, Knox claimed that he did not personally wish to remain in office under Shelburne. Shelburne had a reputation for being an impossible master, and more important, Knox was convinced that he would never enjoy the confidence of Shelburne or his party. He claimed that he consented to remain in office only out of a sense of loyalty to the king: "I was determined from Duty and gratitude to his M[ajesty] to submit to any situation in which H[is] M[ajesty] might be pleased to think I could render him service."[74]

Under the circumstances, it is hardly surprising that Knox's tenure under Shelburne was as difficult as it was brief. William could scarcely be expected to generate enthusiasm for an administration which seemed prepared to grant independence to Ireland as well as America. And although Shelburne was determined to preserve some semblance of the former imperial connection with the rebel states, he did not choose to take Knox into confidence. Knox was especially sensitive to the fact that after years of participating in the highest counsels of government, he was completely ostracized from the deliberations of his chief. He complained that Shelburne and his advisers treated him "rather as a spy than an Undersecretary."[75]

Their obviously strained relationship reached a crisis late one Sunday evening, when Knox received a message at his home in Soho summoning him for business at Shelburne's residence in Berkeley Square. With equal measures of injured official pride and religious piety, Knox obstinately declined to attend the secretary: "I return'd for an answer that I had never been requir'd to do any business on Sundays that did not require immediate attention; that I was then going to read Prayers to my family, according to my usual custom, but that I would attend his Lordship very early in the morning."[76] Even in the face of calamity, the righteous son of Thomas Knox and the pupil of Philip Skelton could still be aroused to assert his independence of anyone who slighted his integrity or his talents.

Late in April 1782, Shelburne finally informed Knox that his attendance at Whitehall was no longer necessary. Despite the difficult circumstances of their relationship, Shelburne expressed his gratitude for Knox's services and promised that he would be amply compensated for the loss of his office.[77] On May 1, 1782, almost twelve years after he entered the American Department, Knox took leave of the king's service.[78]

8. "I Will Do No Mischief, But I Will Stimulate the Minister to Do Good": Calamities, Public & Private, 1782–1790

During the late spring and summer of 1782, William Knox was an unhappy and impotent witness to the dissolution of Britain's old colonial empire. The policies implemented by the Rockingham government were as repugnant to Knox's public principles as they were detrimental to his private interests. At the end of May, the Rockingham administration—responding to renewed agitation among Irish patriots—granted full legislative independence to Ireland. In Georgia, British and Loyalist forces were withdrawn to Savannah in preparation for the complete evacuation of the colony. On May 4, even before the British abandoned the provincial capital, the Georgia state government confiscated Knox's estates; within a month, his plantations were sold at public auction.[1] The only sanguine interval Knox experienced in the course of this rapid sequence of public and private calamities came in the fall, when he received word that 102 of his slaves had been evacuated from Savannah to Jamaica.[2]

In the midst of his unhappiness, Knox was able to muster a perverse gratification from the increasingly obvious discomfiture of the Rockingham ministry. Within a short time, the heterogeneous factions which made up the government discovered that the withdrawal of military forces from America was more easily accomplished than the negotiation of a peace settlement satisfactory to all parties. Foreign Secretary Charles James Fox recommended that the independence of the United States be conceded before details of a peace treaty were determined. He argued that by recognizing American independence immediately Britain could regain the confidence of its former colonies, win them away from French influence, and thereby obtain an amicable and advantageous settlement with the United States. Within the cabinet, however, Fox's proposals were adamantly opposed by the Earl of Shelburne.

Shelburne was as anxious as Fox to restore good relations between

Britain and America; indeed, he was willing to allow the Americans greater concessions in trade and territory than most contemporary English considered necessary. But he also hoped that some form of imperial connection could be preserved between Britain and the Continental colonies. Above all, he was determined to resist any precipitate recognition of colonial independence, and on this point he succeeded in winning the support of a majority of Rockingham's cabinet. Fox was disgruntled, not only by Shelburne's successful opposition in matters of policy but also by the threat this able rival posed to Fox's own ambitions for party and ministerial leadership in succession to the ailing Rockingham. Thus, when Rockingham died in July 1782 and the king asked Shelburne to head the government, the foreign secretary resigned from office.[3]

At first, Knox was delighted by Shelburne's victory over Fox. He wrote to Germain early in July that "the king [had] been delivered from his bondage and the nation rescued from certain destruction by his Majesty's prudence, aided by the providential removal of the Marquis." Knox also confided to his former chief that he expected to be called upon to participate in future negotiations with the Americans.[4]

Shelburne did not avail himself of Knox's services; nevertheless, in the subsequent peace negotiations he did adopt Knox's idea of a Loyalist refuge in America. Shelburne's peace commissioners at Paris suggested that a large part of Maine be set aside for the resettlement of Loyalists.[5] Although the American negotiators resisted this particular proposal, the British government succeeded in obtaining the territory between the St. Croix and St. John rivers in the final boundary settlement. In 1783, thousands of United Empire Loyalists migrated to this region, and the following year the territory between the St. John and the St. Croix was incorporated with part of Nova Scotia to form the province of New Brunswick.

In the course of the negotiations during the summer and fall of 1782, Shelburne insisted that the United States compensate Loyalists for losses of property. He also demanded that American debts to British merchants be recognized as legal obligations. But these concessions represented the high-water mark of his demands. Although the British negotiators rejected Benjamin Franklin's suggestions that Canada be ceded to the United States, they granted the Americans the vast region between the St. Lawrence and the Ohio rivers, a region Knox and Pownall had earlier incorporated within the province of Quebec. The British delegates also agreed to allow the Americans to participate in the Newfoundland fishery. Shelburne was disappointed when he discovered that in spite of these generous concessions, his suggestions for maintaining some form of political connection between Great Britain and its former colonies fell on deaf ears. But he finally conceded full independence to the United States. In return, the American commissioners agreed to acknowledge the debts owed to British subjects and also to recommend Loyalist claims to the several states. Eventually the former promise was fulfilled, but the states refused to honor the latter provision.

Shelburne accepted these terms partly because he realized that Britain was too exhausted to continue the American war. But his generosity in conceding potentially contentious points to the Americans was primarily inspired by a radical vision of future Anglo-American relations.[6] He believed that by granting the United States extensive concessions in territory and trade, he would not only regain American good will but also establish the foundations for commercial cooperation between Britain and its former colonies. He reasoned that if the Americans were allowed to expand into the vast hinterland of the continent, they would remain primarily a nation of raw-material producers, depending upon Britain for most of their manufactured goods. Britain would thus continue to enjoy all the economic advantages of the old imperial connection without the burdens of American defense and administration. Shelburne's vision of Anglo-American economic partnership was predicated upon the principles of full economic equality and reciprocity. And although these concepts were diametrically opposed to the tenets of contemporary mercantilism, Shelburne was determined to follow up the liberal concessions of the peace treaty by granting the United States free trade with Britain and the rest of the empire.

On November 30, the British and American commissioners signed a preliminary peace treaty, and in January 1783 Shelburne laid the treaty before Parliament. The administration's policies provoked an immediate rebellion in the House of Commons. Shelburne's rival Fox, who commanded about 90 followers in the Commons, insisted that the administration had granted excessive concessions to the Americans. The faction led by North, numbering about 120 seats, was determined to resist Shelburne's matter-of-fact abandonment of the old navigation system and was equally adamant in its opposition to his plans for radical constitutional reform in Britain. Even the independent members who had previously insisted upon a quick end to the useless American war angrily criticized the humiliating terms of the preliminary treaty with the United States. In February, the Fox and North groups in the Commons joined forces to bring down Shelburne's government.[7] On February 18, the administration was defeated on the Commons address in reply to the king's speech announcing the government's policies. Three days later, the opposition passed a motion repudiating all the treaties the government had negotiated with America and the European belligerents. On February 24, Shelburne resigned.

George III regarded the union of North and Fox, who had attacked each other bitterly during the American Revolution, as an unholy alliance of unscrupulous politicians seeking to force their way into office against his wishes.[8] For more than five weeks after Shelburne's resignation, the king resisted the Fox-North coalition. During this hiatus the younger William Pitt, Shelburne's Chancellor of the Exchequer, introduced into Parliament his former leader's bill for an Anglo-American commercial agreement. This measure—which Shelburne had drawn up before his resignation, with the expert assistance of Knox's old colleague, John Pownall—would have allowed the United States virtually unrestricted participation in Britain's commercial empire. Specifically, Shelburne and Pownall's American Intercourse Bill would have permitted American ships to participate on equal terms with British vessels in the trade between the United States and Britain's colonies in the western hemisphere, in addition to establishing complete reciprocity in the direct commerce between the United States and Great Britain.[9]

The North faction in Parliament was well prepared for this challenge to Britain's old colonial system. As early as November 1782, North had invited Knox to Bushy, where the former premier's supporters—particularly the exministers Eden and Wedderburn—were pressing their leader to join Fox in opposition, as well as plotting a campaign against Shelburne's American policies. Germain, from a situation of interested semiretirement, encouraged Knox to accept North's invitation so that "his Lordship may at least have one man about him that will give him honest and true information."[10] Knox, by his own account, agreed to commit his talents and expertise to North's party when they accepted the principle "that it was better to have no colonies at all than not to have them subservient to the maritime strength and commercial interests of Great Britain."[11]

The particular contribution of Knox's creative mind to these deliberations bore fruit on March 3, 1783, when Eden delivered a devastating attack in the Commons on Shelburne's American Intercourse Bill. Employing arguments which carried Knox's unmistakable stamp, Eden predicted that American commerce with the West Indies would destroy Ireland's provision trade with the islands and that Ireland would thereby be justified in withdrawing completely from the British navigation system. He also predicted that if the United States were allowed free commerce with British colonies, the natural advantages enjoyed by American merchants would soon lead to the destruction of Britain's carrying trade and ultimately to the loss of naval supremacy. This latter point was particularly effective in swaying the opinions of an audience schooled in the principles of mercantilism; after Eden's speech of March 3, the American Intercourse Bill did not progress beyond the committee stage in the Commons. When the Fox-North coalition took office in early April 1783, Shelburne's American trade bill was finally killed on Fox's motion for an indefinite postponement.[12]

For Knox, no less than for former ministers, adherence to North's coalition with Fox was as much a matter of personal interest as a commitment to imperial principle. Besides the absolute financial losses he had suffered in America, he also discovered that the two pensions of £600 each granted to him and Letitia in 1782 produced a total of only £888 per annum in true income.[13] Furthermore, he not only found himself pressed by a considerably reduced income, but he was also painfully aware that the very existence of even that meager sum was dependent upon the king's pleasure. And this arrangement must have seemed all the more tenuous when it became clear that Rockingham's ministry was bent upon economic reform.

After leaving office, Knox had persistently petitioned to have his undersecretary's salary continued until he could be suitably compensated, as were other colleagues who had lost offices with the abolition of the American Department and the Board of Trade. He insisted that the pension he and his wife enjoyed had been awarded in compensation for the loss of his patent offices in New York and

Georgia and should in no way be held against his claim for the suppression of his undersecretaryship. With the memory of Shelburne's earlier promise of compensation, Knox was especially encouraged when his former chief succeeded Rockingham as premier. These hopes were dashed, however, when shortly before the Fox-North coalition came to power the Treasury decided that Knox's existing pensions were adequate payment for his office in the American Department.[14]

If the failure of Knox's suit for compensation from the royal bounty was not sufficient cause for his return from the political wilderness, certainly the threat of political reprisals during the administrations of both Rockingham and Shelburne must have provoked him to seek the protection of powerful allies. For several years after the Rockingham Whigs took power, political circles were periodically stirred by ominous rumors and veiled threats that the wartime ministry would be brought to account for the disasters visited upon the empire. For a while there was a distinct possibility that North would be impeached. As passions cooled, the threat to North became increasingly remote, but for Knox political retaliation became a stark reality immediately upon his resignation from office. In June 1782, his old adversary, Burke—whom he once described as a maniac—asked the Treasury to investigate the former undersecretary's accounts for Indian presents shipped to Canada during the previous year. Knox was momentarily relieved when within a single month—June 1782—Burke resigned from office and the comptroller subsequently reported that Knox's Indian accounts were in order.[15] However, the Shelburne government, which by its zeal for economic reform quickly earned a reputation for meanness, decided to pursue the issue. Understandably astounded by the huge expense for Indian supplies in Canada, which totaled £63,861.17.7 in 1781 alone, and probably sensing an opportunity to fix a charge of malfeasance in office upon a prominent member of North's war ministry, Shelburne's government launched a full investigation into Knox's stewardship of Indian presents.

Knox's meticulous attention to administrative details and procedure during his tenure as undersecretary now served him well. When Treasury commissioners raised questions regarding the prices of the Indian supplies relative to their quality, Knox was able to produce detailed bills and invoices, as well as the certificates he had obtained from independent merchants at the time of purchase, attesting to the propriety of price and quality.[16] And when the Treasury officers inquired about the reliability of such evidence, Knox was able to obtain testimonials regarding the character and integrity of the merchants who had signed the certificates.[17]

By late summer 1782, the Shelburne government had little choice but to turn its investigation of the previous year's Indian supplies toward those purchases in the field which had been carried out by agents in Canada under Governor Haldimand's command. When Haldimand replied that such purchases had been allowed to persist because his agents complained of the quality and cost of goods supplied from England, Knox drew up a rejoinder which detailed the history, conduct, and procedures of his management of the business of Indian presents.[18] In the course of this lengthy document, he not only insisted that the patterns and specifications for his Indian supplies had been provided in person by the very agents who subsequently complained of them, but he also lodged the countercharge that throughout the war Indian agents, in collusion with American traders, had profiteered on presents purchased in America. He argued that it was because of his role in frustrating this lucrative practice that the agents sought to discredit him. In a succinct conclusion, he insisted: "In respect to myself I am confident that the steps I took to prevent imposition upon the public were well calculated for the purpose and that nothing more effectual could have been done by me, or will be done by my Successor."

Since the exorbitant cost of all supplies purchased in America had achieved public notoriety even during the course of the war, the Shelburne government could now only reiterate previous instructions to Haldimand to restrict expenditures for Indian presents within his jurisdiction.[19] Haldimand himself must have been somewhat discomfited by the knowledge that the careful Knox probably possessed a copy of a letter he had sent the governor during the spring of 1782, long before the investigation had begun, detailing an attempt by Indian agents on leave in England to involve the undersecretary in a scheme to profiteer in Indian supplies.[20] Finally, in April 1783—with the Fox-North coalition in power—North personally sent Haldimand a copy of Knox's rejoinder "in vindication of his conduct" and further instructed the governor that "no waste or abuse will be made of Public Property" in the subsequent distribution of Indian presents in Canada.[21] The tone of North's dispatch indicated beyond a doubt that the new government was fully satisfied with Knox's reply to the explicit and implicit charges levied against his management of the Indian business.

Knox was undoubtedly relieved that he once again enjoyed the favor and protection of powerful patrons. This fact and the undeniable personal satisfaction of returning to the center of political power account for his willingness to serve the Fox-North coalition without office and apparently without any financial compensation. Although he hoped for an appointment, the competition for office during this administration was unusually ruthless, because a large number of places had been eliminated by the economic reforms of the Rockingham and Shelburne governments.[22] The coalition government carefully distributed the available offices with an eye to maintaining its majority in the Commons. And since Knox did not hold a seat in Parliament, he was unable to command an official position. For a while he readily accepted a situation he described as being *"about* office, tho' not belonging to *it."*[23] Ironically, as an unofficial adviser in North's department of home and colonial affairs, Knox exercised as decisive an influence over the policies of the empire as he had when he held the undersecretaryship.

Although the Fox-North coalition had cooperated in wrecking Shelburne's American program, once the two leaders attained power they demonstrated that they did not completely agree on an alternative American policy. Of course, both Fox and North—the latter guided by Knox's expert advice—accepted the fact that British commercial prosperity depended upon the restoration of Anglo-American commerce. On May 14, the administration issued an order-in-council providing for trade between Great Britain and the United States in native products carried in either British or American ships. At Knox's suggestion, a second order-in-council, on June 6, allowed the importation of certain American manufactures into Britain and also restored the prewar drawback on American tobacco reexported from Britain. Again upon Knox's recommendation, the government obtained parliamentary approval of a measure granting drawbacks for the reexport of American rice.[24]

These measures—designed to facilitate and encourage direct trade between Britain and the United States—were generally supported by both the Fox and North factions in the administration. But the two groups were divided over the question of American trade with the West Indies. Fox, as foreign secretary, was responsible for negotiating a formal commercial treaty with the United

States. He was well aware of British prejudices against American commercial rivalry in the surviving markets of the empire; nevertheless, he instructed his agents in Paris to offer the American commissioners a treaty which would allow vessels of the United States to trade directly with the British West Indies, subject only to a provision that American ships could not carry West Indian products to Great Britain.[25] To North and Knox, however, the foreign secretary's policies and proposals were no more acceptable than Shelburne's American Intercourse Bill. They were convinced that the maritime and naval strength of Great Britain could be preserved against American rivalry only if Britain maintained a complete monopoly of the colonial carrying trade. North decided to nip Fox's scheme before the American negotiations bore their bitter harvest. Late in May 1783, at North's request, Knox drew up a measure restricting trade between the British West Indies and the United States to vessels which were British-owned, British-built, and manned by British crews. Despite stiff opposition from Fox and his ally Burke, on July 2 the Northites succeeded in promulgating an order-in-council embodying Knox's proposals.[26]

Knox's order-in-council exercised a decisive influence on Anglo-American relations. It immediately wrecked Fox's negotiations for a commercial treaty with the new American republic. And although direct commerce between Great Britain and the United States subsequently flourished on an ad hoc basis, the issues of West Indian trade continued to disturb relations between the two countries for many decades.[27]

One year later, when the Pitt administration—which was known to be generally sympathetic toward freer commerce—reopened the question, Knox was summoned to testify before the Committee of the Privy Council for Trade and Plantations on March 18, 1784. Although the board included the familiar faces of many of Knox's former colleagues and friends—Lord Walsingham, Lord Frederick Campbell, and Charles Jenkinson—the council also included members who were not so sympathetic, including the board's president, Lord Sydney, formerly an avid supporter of Rockingham and a leader of Shelburne's party. Before this mixed and occasionally hostile panel, Knox openly avowed his authorship of the order-in-council of July 2, 1783, and persistently defended the mercantilist principles upon which the measure was founded. In response to questions, he admitted that the prohibition of United States vessels from the

British West Indies might work some hardship upon the loyal islands, until Britain's North American colonies were able to export provisions; however, he countered with the prediction that clandestine trade and the establishment of free ports would provide adequate relief for the islands without formally recognizing the United States' claim to share in the imperial trade. And when asked whether such a course would not provoke commercial retaliation from the United States, Knox responded, with acute prescience, that such a policy would not be likely to succeed because "whatever may be their intention either as separate States, or as united under the congress, the coercive power of their Governments is so feeble, and the general interest of the Inhabitants so directly against such a Restraint."[28]

From the perspective of postmercantilist wisdom, Knox's arguments as well as his policies might be regarded as short-sighted, vengeful, and opportunistic. From his contemporaneous point of view, however, they were above all a consistent extension of his long-held principle that imperial privileges required reciprocal imperial obligations. If any party was aggrieved by Knox's postwar policies and other like measures, it was Britain's West Indian islands, which found their particular interests increasingly ground away between the millstones of residual British imperialism and emerging American nationalism. On the other hand, the independent United States, which had repudiated the burdens of empire, especially imperial defense, could hardly be allowed to claim *by right* a share in imperial advantages. Even the popular Pitt administration was forced to recognize that the vocal majority of the country shared this general attitude during the postwar era. When the Pitt administration finally negotiated a commercial treaty with the American representative, John Jay, in 1794, the British government agreed to modify Knox's prohibition of American shipping to the West Indian colonies, but because of adverse opinion in Britain the concession was made so restrictive that it was eventually rejected outright by the United States Senate. Although Knox was a witness to the subsequent hostility between Britain and the United States—which eventually culminated in the War of 1812— throughout his later years he insisted that by the order-in-council of July 2, 1783, he saved Britain's maritime power.[29]

Knox's contribution to saving the old colonial system immediately brought him the plaudits of like-minded subjects, including those of Lord Sheffield, whose own *Observations on the Commerce of the American States* almost single-handedly rallied public opinion behind the preservation of the self-sufficient empire.[30] Nevertheless, the direct material rewards Knox anticipated were not forthcoming. Despite the valuable services he rendered the Northite faction, he received neither office nor compensation from the coalition government. By the fall of 1783, he accepted his fate and decided to give up public life.[31]

His decision was partially prompted by a remarkable improvement in the prospects of his private fortune. Throughout the latter part of 1782 and the early months of 1783, he received encouraging reports from Nathaniel Hall, who had evacuated the Knoxborough slaves from Georgia to Jamaica. In August 1782, Hall wrote from near Kingston that all the adults had arrived safely with "only two Negroe children" lost during the passage. Black laborers were at a premium on the island when the first Loyalist émigrés arrived from the rebel American provinces; before the end of the year, Hall was able to inform Knox that all his slaves had been hired out to local planters or public-works contractors. And since the provincial government seemed ready to grant public lands to the émigré masters of this new black labor force, Hall also suggested that Knox might wish to settle a plantation on the island.[32]

For Knox, even these welcome reports from Jamaica must have paled by comparison with the news that in 1783 the British government would assume responsibility for the claims of American Loyalists. The entire restoration of his personal fortune seemed assured, and within the year, apparently anticipating full compensation for his American losses, he purchased on credit a Welsh estate worth £1,000 per annum at Lanstinan in Pembrokeshire. Believing that his improved circumstances would now allow him to support a mark of royal favor for past services, Knox applied to North for a baronetcy in November 1783.[33] North, however, had fewer titles than offices at his disposal, because the king, who had refused to be reconciled with the Fox-North coalition, openly demonstrated his disapproval by withholding honors recommended by his ministers. When the administration fell from power in December 1783, Knox's request was yet unredeemed.

Knox was disappointed by the failure of his application, but within a short time after his retirement from public service he was completely absorbed in family affairs and in the life of a country gentleman. By this time there were six Knox children—the elder two, Harriot (née Henrietta) and Thomas, being in their early teens, followed in order of age by Letitia (who was five years old in 1783), George Henry, Caroline, and Wills Frederick, born in July 1783. In 1783, Knox removed his sizable brood from the house in Soho to his estate at Lanstinan, and there a year later the last of his children, John William, was born.[34]

Knox, now entering his fifties, seems to have been an attentive, indeed a dominant, parent—rather like his own father. There is some evidence that William, who had so often found himself inheriting the responsibilities of his impecunious older brothers, was rather demanding of his eldest son, Thomas—even to the point of earning a kindly warning from a friend against burdening the lad too greatly with filial obligations.[35] Knox seemed more inclined to demonstrate open affection toward his daughters than his sons—or, for that matter, toward his wife Letitia, who remains largely unnoticed in his later correspondence. Those letters he composed in the sanctuary of his Welsh retreat frequently contained prideful references to his dear Harriot and especially to little Letitia, whose vivacity and precocity were a perennial source of joy and comment among family and friends.

Once settled upon his Welsh estate, Knox took up the role of country gentleman with characteristic energy and enterprise. Lanstinan, situated in northeastern Pembrokeshire just off the road from Fishguard to Haverfordwest, was well within that region of the country where the predominant Welsh peasantry and their native culture had largely prevailed against "English" influences.[36] For this reason, the Anglicized landlords who had penetrated the region were apparently quicker to admit a newcomer, especially one of Knox's political and literary reputation, into the circle of their provincial life than might have been true elsewhere. Within a short time, Knox threw himself into the tasks of enclosing and improving his estate, pursuits to be expected of model landowners. And before long he had established himself as a leader and benefactor in the community—organizing an agricultural society in Pembrokeshire, promoting the erection of charity schools for the poor children of the county, and recommending candidates for clerical livings so that "the business of religion or at least of civility would be promoted." As early as 1784, he enjoyed sufficient standing within the county to take part in the political arrangements for the general election that year—arrangements which resulted in the uncontested return of candidates unfavorable to the government of the Younger Pitt.[37] By 1785 Knox—already referring to himself as a "Welchman"—had become so pleased with his new home that he decided to sink deeper roots, acquiring additional land and a "capital mansion house" at Slebech, on the northern extremity of Milford Haven. Undoubtedly not the least of Slebech's attractions for this erstwhile country gentleman, who still nursed hopes of obtaining a title of honor, was its history and traditions stretching back into the Norman era.[38]

Knox remained in contented retirement for almost two years, with only an occasional excursion to take the waters at Bath. In June 1784, however, he was obliged to return to London for a brief period when the Pitt government reopened the investigation of his 1782 supply of Indian presents to Canada. A board of inquiry from the Comptroller's Office conducted a month-long hearing, during which all the principals—merchants, agents, administrative officials—were examined in the presence of Knox and representatives of Governor Haldimand. This hearing generally bore out Knox's contention that the quality of goods sent to Canada had been commensurate with the prices charged. The only exception came in regard to a supply of linens and calicos—the board of inquiry concluding that a Mr. Whitelock, whom Knox had employed to select and purchase fabrics from various merchants, had charged an excessive commission for his services. Under questioning, however, Whitelock testified without reservation that Knox had received no share of his profits either directly or indirectly. The board's final report concluded that "Mr. Knox, throughout the whole, appears to have acted with uprightness towards the Public; he may have been imposed upon, but in our opinion he stands acquitted of being concerned in imposition."[39] In an era when public officials were commonly expected to use public funds for their own profit—the large personal fortunes accruing to a succession of paymasters general of the forces being the most notorious example—Knox could be satisfied that his stewardship had finally been vindicated. With his personal integrity fully exonerated, he could happily return to the interests and concerns of a country gentleman, confident that the shadow of public disgrace would no longer cloud the new-found pleasures of private life.

Within a year, however, the serenity of his rural retreat was abruptly shattered by the news that his claim for losses of American property had been summarily rejected by the government. He was completely dismayed to learn that the Treasury had classified him among those "neutrals" who rendered no service to the king during the war and on this basis had excluded him from any compensation granted to Loyalist sufferers.[40] Knox immediately petitioned the king. He even endured the humiliation of asking Hillsborough, Dartmouth, and Germain to provide him with certificates testifying to his services as undersecretary.[41] But his petition and pleas for justice went unheeded.

Even as Knox was unaccountably denied compensation for his considerable losses in America, he learned that the only property which had been spared to him was in a state of rapid decline. As early as the summer of 1783, Nathaniel Hall's reports concerning Knox's slaves in Jamaica became progressively pessimistic. The continuous arrival on the island of Loyalist émigrés bringing their slaves from the southern American provinces soon produced a glut of black laborers, as well as a considerable rise in the value and price of land. The restoration of peace, furthermore, brought an immediate decrease in the demand for labor on public works. Finally, the British government's postwar commercial policy prohibiting direct trade between the West Indian colonies and the United States marked the beginning of a long period of economic decline in Jamaica.[42] Knox was indeed hoisted upon a petard of his own making: the very order-in-council he had designed to save the British Empire ruined his personal interests. Although he never betrayed any consciousness of this new twist in that ironic fate which continually dogged his life, the sequence of misfortunes which befell his interests in Jamaica brought him to the brink of despair.

Hall informed Knox in 1783 that his slaves were all unemployed and that the prospects for an improvement in their situation in Jamaica were not promising. Since the market price for slaves in Jamaica had become considerably depressed, Hall recommended that Knox return his slaves for sale in Georgia. Knox, however, could not safely take advantage of this alternative because all his property, chattel as well as real, had been included in the Georgia decree of confiscation.[43] For over a year, he found it necessary to send goods and money to Jamaica for the support of his slaves, who remained on the island, unemployable and unmarketable.[44]

Finally, distress was turned into complete disaster between 1784 and 1786, when a succession of hurricanes brought extensive death and destruction to the beleaguered island and its unusually swollen populace. In the aftermath of these natural evils, the real threat of famine among the black inhabitants was avoided only by allowing free importation of provisions.[45] In June 1785, Hall reported that a hurricane had so devastated their miserable settlement that despite the supplies Knox had sent, his slaves were suffering badly from smallpox and yaws. The Knoxborough blacks managed to summon enough strength and courage to rebuild their shelters and replant provision crops, only to be broken materially and spiritually when a more violent hurricane struck in July.[46] Hall's account of this last horror was one of total desolation and despair: several blacks had died, many more were dying, while large numbers had fallen sick for the first time; shelters were all destroyed and provisions were all gone. The desperate overseer made it clear to Knox that there was no hope for recovery in Jamaica: "To hear of these things is very distressing, but to be an Eye Witness of them daily, & to see poor Creatures, intrusted to our Care labouring under diseases not in our power to alleviate, is to me, the most distressing of all Misfortunes. Therefore if to Liberate mine was the only means of restoring them to health, I would most chearfully do it rather than see a continuance of their Sufferings."[47]

Under the circumstances, Hall informed Knox that he intended immediately to make arrangements to return the wretched survivors to the United States for sale. The search for a safe market for Knox's slaves, their transport to Charleston, and their sale at auction took almost a year and exacted an additional toll upon the already deci-mated ranks of the Knoxborough blacks. Of the original 102 souls evacuated from Savannah in 1782, plus 30 children born in Jamai-ca, only 76 survived to be sold in 1786. And according to the Charleston merchants who conducted the auction, fewer than 25 of these were ready for the field. Consequently, the entire group brought only a minimal price of £4,320, payable in rice or indigo delivered in Charleston—minus £1,136.14.0 in costs for pro-visions and fees.[48] Knox had little recourse except to add a new fig-ure to his claims for property losses in America—hardly an optimis-tic exercise, since the Treasury adamantly continued to reject all his claims for compensation.

This unbroken succession of financial losses and personal frustra-tions soon brought him to the point of physical and emotional collapse. Late in 1785, he complained that although he was only fifty-three years of age his nervous system had been so affected by recent anxieties and misfortunes that his hearing and his eyesight were impaired and he could "seldom sleep without an opiate."[49] There is some evidence suggesting that Knox, who in his *Three Tracts* had prophesied awesome divine retribution for those masters who neglected the spiritual and material welfare of their black charges, was now himself afflicted by feelings of remorse and guilt over the tragic fate of his own blacks.[50] Nevertheless, the stark prospect of bankruptcy was a real and sufficient source of his immediate distress. Within a year, his financial circumstances had deteriorated to such an extent that he reluctantly anticipated having to sell at least part of Slebech, including his "mansion house." He was able to preserve his estate, but late in 1787 he admitted that it was "mortgaged up to the teeth."[51]

Knox was convinced that the government's rejection of his American claims was inspired by political animosity. For over two years, he endeavored to ingratiate himself with the Pitt administration by virtually inundating various government officials with schemes and proposals on subjects ranging from the Irish packet service to relations with Spain. He was obviously encouraged late in 1785, when his former colleague, William Eden, solicited his advice on the French commercial treaty, which Eden was then negotiating on behalf of the Pitt government. Although Knox protested that he was no longer attracted to public service, he immediately responded to Eden's request with a lengthy treatise on international trade.[52] After Eden completed negotiations for the French treaty in 1786, Knox published a pamphlet defending the agreement and also promoted an address to Parliament from Pembrokeshire in support of the commercial treaty.[53] The Pembrokeshire address prompted the government to offer Knox a knighthood. But he refused the honor. With characteristic hubris, he stubbornly insisted that his application for a baronetcy was still pending before the king.[54]

Knox in fact now wanted an office more than a title, for the profits and privileges of office would certainly restore his personal fortune. And reappointment to office had also become a matter of pride to him. He complained bitterly that the Pitt administration was filled with men unfit for office, even as the ministers completely neglected a man of his own experience and proven abilities. Finally, in May 1788, Knox wrote to Lord Walsingham—formerly a collea-

gue in the American Department and for several years a member
the Pitt administration—that he had decided to place his talents at
the disposal of a party which had "sprung up from the inattention and
partiality of Mr. Pitt in disposing of offices."[55] Knox offered Walsingham the customary justification for opposing the king's government:

> I shall greatly regret [Pitt's] fall for though he has used me ill,
> I admire his talents and pray for his continuance, but I owe a
> superior duty to the King and the Country and as he will not
> avail himself of my experience and Judgment, I must carry
> them where they may be rendered useful. I want not the paltry
> Salary of Office, but I expect civility and attention . . . the
> King's servant is my Minister, be he who he may . . . I will do
> no mischief, but I will stimulate the Minister to do good.

In one sense these lines simply reflect the formal conventions of an
age which had not completely accepted the concept of His Majesty's
Loyal Opposition. But the passage is more than an example of contemporary political cant, for these lines also reveal the complexity
of those material and psychological motives which prompted
Knox's return to the maelstrom of partisan politics.

William immediately attached his fortunes to the political faction which revolved around the so-called reversionary interest of the
Prince of Wales. Acute rivalry between the Hanoverian kings and
the adult heirs to the throne had become a customary feature of
eighteenth-century politics. True to this tradition, after 1784 the
eldest son of George III organized a political following under the
leadership of his favorite, Lord Rawdon. Although the Prince of
Wales' party maintained its separate identity in Parliament, it generally cooperated with the Foxites in opposition to the Pitt administration.[56] Knox acted as a man of business for Rawdon and his
party. In 1788, he provided them with expert information on a
variety of issues before Parliament, his most notable contributions
being a defense of the slave trade and proposals for reforming the
constitution of Quebec.[57]

Apparently it was only coincidental that some time during 1788
the Treasury reconsidered Knox's claim for his property losses in
America. Ever since the Pitt government, in 1785, had passed the
measure providing compensation for Loyalist claims, there had been
continuous criticism in Parliament and press of government meanness in both allowances and procedures. Certainly Knox had played

a leading role in the Loyalist lobby. In 1785, upon the death of exgovernor Wright, William had succeeded his old friend as agent for the Loyalist claimants, and for several years thereafter he divided his time between his Welsh estate and London, where he could better direct a campaign of publicity and politics on behalf of his clients.[58] The general issue was resolved in 1788, when the Pitt government established a more equitable and efficient schedule of compensation. Subsequently, Knox was able to focus his entire attention on promoting his personal cause before the Claims Commission, which finally agreed to honor his claim some time during the spring of 1788.[59]

The settlement, although providing Knox a welcome reprieve from complete bankruptcy, was not entirely satisfactory. His total claim for £16,063 in property losses was scaled down to £7,964—a reduction which exceeded considerably the discount rate established in the compensation schedule.[60] Moreover, the government continued to regard his and Letitia's pensions as adequate recompense for his abolished undersecretaryship as well as for his sequestered patent offices in New York and Georgia.

In 1789, Knox publicly vented his pent-up disappointments and frustrations in a two-volume documentary memoir, *Extra Official State Papers*, dedicated to Rawdon and his followers. Even as he offered the lessons of his long experience in politics to those described in the subtitle as being "Associated for the Preservation of the Constitution and Promoting the Prosperity of the British Empire," Knox mustered a bitter, if not entirely accurate, summary of his own grievances against an ungrateful and unappreciative government:

> Could I, indeed, have forseen what has since come to pass, that I should not only be deprived of my estate, which remitted me from 1700 l. to 2000 l. per ann. but all of my offices, which yielded me 2500 l. more, and that a pension which pays 440 l. per ann. would be here deemed an adequate compensation not only for them but for all my services also, I confess I should have been less ambitious of displaying my disinterestedness in the eyes of my countrymen.[61]

Later in the year, he published a caustic attack on the Pitt administration in the form of a pamphlet addressed to Rawdon and his followers.[62] In this piece, Knox implied that Pitt had consciously employed royal patronage to impose "the trammels of faction and the dictatorship of democratic demagogues" upon the monarchic element of the constitution. He argued—much as he had two decades earlier—that the king could remedy the maladies which beset the nation only by creating a government composed of the "ablest and the honestest men in his dominions," men willing to restore and preserve the proper constitutional functions of the crown. Knox left no doubt where the king might find such allies who placed the public good before personal interest.

In 1788, neither parliamentary challenges nor printed attacks seemed likely to upset the Pitt administration, which in fact enjoyed the entire confidence of the king and the public. But late in the year the government was almost toppled when George III fell into one of the violent fits of insanity which chronically disturbed affairs of state in the latter part of his reign. During the ensuing crisis, it seemed obvious that once the Prince of Wales became regent he would dismiss Pitt and form a new administration headed by Rawdon and Fox. The Pitt government was saved by the sudden recovery of the king in February 1789, but since the madness or death of George III appeared imminent, the Prince of Wales and his allies anticipated an immediate assumption of power.[63]

Shortly after the king's recovery, Knox attempted to strengthen the prince's party by mediating an alliance between Rawdon and Lord Chancellor Thurlow. Years earlier, Thurlow and Knox had worked together in the North administration, and subsequently Knox had cultivated Thurlow's friendship through correspondence and occasional appearances at the chancellor's levees. When Knox informed Thurlow of his reasons for joining Rawdon's party, the chancellor confided to Knox his own disapproval of Pitt and his colleagues in the government, but he warned Knox that the king "did not feel the manacles Pitt had put upon him, or was not willing to hassard the inconvenience of attempting to break them." Shortly after the Regency Crisis of 1788–89, Knox sent Thurlow a copy of his pamphlet attacking the Pitt administration, and at a subsequent interview with the chancellor, Knox suggested an alliance between Thurlow and Rawdon. Although Thurlow reiterated his belief that the king showed no inclination toward altering the administration, he commented favorably on Knox's concept of a ministry of all talents and also expressed his wish that "Lord Rawdon and his friends would fairly come forward and avow themselves the supporters of the King."[64]

Thurlow obviously had no intention of jeopardizing his position in the government by allying himself prematurely with the Prince of Wales, but he was anxious to establish some sort of rapport with the party whose fortunes were attached to the heir apparent. Knox was convinced that in any event Thurlow would be a most valuable ally. But when he informed Rawdon of the chancellor's overtures, Rawdon rejected outright any form of connection with Thurlow.[65] Rawdon insisted that although he had no intention of injuring the interests of the king, he was personally attached to the Prince of Wales and would never enter into an alliance or take office without his approval. Furthermore, he claimed that in the past Thurlow had treated him in a treacherous and abusive manner, and for that reason alone he preferred to cooperate with Fox and his supporters, who had always conducted themselves honorably.

Knox did not share Rawdon's enthusiasm for a connection with Fox's party, and their differences in this respect came to a head late in 1789, when Knox drew up a paper which contained an unqualified condemnation of the Rockingham government of 1782. Rawdon took exception to this oblique attack on Fox and his supporters, who had, of course, played a leading role in the Rockingham ministry. He lectured Knox on the virtues of opposing measures rather than men, and he bluntly insisted, ". . . if you decide to retain that tone in your Publication I must entreat you not to do me the honor of addressing it to me and my friends."[66]

After this episode, Knox was convinced that neither his principles nor his interests recommended a further attachment to Rawdon. Although Rawdon continued to solicit Knox's expert opinion on public issues, by 1790 Knox had decided to swallow his pride and make his peace with the Pitt administration.

Undoubtedly, his sudden change of heart was accelerated by another crisis in his private fortune—this time the failure of a fishing venture in which he had invested substantial sums during 1789.[67] Apparently relying entirely upon his own limited capital, he had constructed a wharf on Milford Haven and fitted out four boats for fishing off the North American banks. By his own account his bankers enjoyed a bountiful catch; nevertheless, due to a combination of relatively high wages and American competition in the Spanish markets, the enterprise lost money.

In March 1790, Knox sent a full account of his unsuccessful fishing venture—together with extensive recommendations for the improvement and encouragement of the industry in Britain—to his old colleague Jenkinson, who as a member of the Pitt administration had been raised to the peerage in 1786 with the title of Baron Hawkesbury. Knox bravely insisted to Hawkesbury that despite his fishing losses he had the "satisfaction of introducing the business among a very hardy race of indigent men, and opening a source of benefit to themselves and of strength to the Nation." Of course, he did not lose the opportunity of reminding his lordship of the "harsh treatment" he had received in the past and "continues to suffer" at the hands of the government.

A month later, Knox, with a candid admission of his "fall from opulence to embarrassed circumstances," directly petitioned the Pitt government to exchange his and Letitia's pensions for full compensation for his British and American offices. North and Welbore Ellis agreed to present the petition to Parliament, and Rawdon graciously promised the support of his party. Although the administration rejected Knox's original proposal, within a month the Pitt government finally agreed to convert the pensions from grants at pleasure to life tenure.[68]

Knox expressed his gratitude in characteristic fashion: in 1790 he sent recommendations on colonial affairs to George Rose, secretary to the Treasury, asking him to forward these proposals to the prime minister and suggesting that if Pitt wished "to have any further communication of such information as I am possessed of or to require my services in any manner he may think I can be usefully employed, I shall at all times be ready to obey his commands."[69] The Pitt government did not choose to take advantage of this offer. Although Knox actively participated in public affairs until his death, his political career ended with his acceptance of the life pensions.

9. "I Quitted the Vortex of Politics": The Elder Statesman, 1790–1810

During the last two decades of his life, William Knox assumed the status of elder statesman—bringing to this new role, of course, his seemingly unlimited capacity for ubiquitous industry. His acceptance of life pensions in 1790 marked the end of his political career only in the sense that partisan politics ceased to be important to him as a route to officeholding. For almost forty years, public affairs had been an integral part of his life, and despite his "retirement" he could hardly be expected to remain aloof from politics, especially at a time when his country was involved in the momentous international, imperial, and domestic crises of the era of the French Revolution.

In 1790, Knox published a pamphlet criticizing William Wilberforce's efforts to abolish the slave trade within the British Empire.[1] In this latter-day defense of slavery, Knox largely reiterated in summary fashion views he had advocated publicly for several decades. Yet this apologia seems all the more significant because he no longer had a direct vested interest in slaveholding. In fact, for several years after the disastrous odyssey of the Knoxborough blacks, Knox seemed compelled to justify the institution of African bondage at every opportunity. In 1788, he had not only supplied Rawdon's party with expert information for a parliamentary defense of the slave trade, but he had also attempted to fix blame for the persistent evils of slavery upon the established church—which, he insisted, had failed to act upon his earlier admonitions to improve the spiritual and material lot of black slaves. On one occasion, after drafting a speech for a Commons debate on the slave trade, Knox boasted, "I shall save the African trade, though I bring censure upon the Bishops, but as they deserve it I have no compunction in so doing."[2] Then, in 1789, he reprinted his earlier *Three Tracts* and sent a copy to Lord Chancellor Thurlow, commenting that had the bishops shown more attention to what they recommended "much of the present outcry against the slave trade would have been prevented."[3] Finally, in his *Letter to Wilberforce*, Knox's apparent obsession with fixing responsibility for the unimproved condition of slaves produced a pathetic bit of self-justification, which in fact repressed the unpleasant reality of his own stewardship: "I never did or can consider it lawful to purchase an African negroe, but with the sincere purpose of bettering his condition both here and hereafter, and with the full conviction that we are doing so."[4]

Although the *Letter to Wilberforce* unquestionably served as a mechanism of release for the author's distressed evangelical conscience, this pamphlet was equally a tract of the times, wherein Knox expressed his initial reaction to the spirit of reform aroused in Britain during the early years of the French Revolution. For example, he warned the abolitionists to "have a care that your zeal does not outrun discretion, for more mischief has been done to the best cause by the interference of zealots, than by the indolence of supine governors."[5] And in reply to the charge that slavery violated the natural rights of mankind, Knox wrote:

> Here I should find it necessary to enter into a long discussion of the rights of men, if Mr. Burke had not fortunately for me and most happily for the public, precluded all further investigation of the subject by exposing the absurdity of founding the laws of society upon the supposed natural equality of man, when the very end and purpose of society is to counteract the *natural* inequality of men.[6]

With this remarkable tribute to the wisdom of his ancient adversary, Knox reflected the growing tendency of British conservatives to close ranks in response to the internal and external challenges of the French revolutionary era.

Once Great Britain went to war with the French republic, Knox shared the conservatives' increasing suspicion of the various British parliamentary reform organizations. In 1793 he personally persuaded the parish of St. Ann, Westminster, to pass a resolution calling upon the magistrates to withdraw the licenses of "victuallers" who allowed meetings of "seditious clubs" to be held in their houses. In the same year, he also published a pamphlet, *A Friendly Address to the Members of the Several Clubs*, which categorically condemned "that novel and most unconstitutional doctrine that the House of Commons is merely a house of delegates or representatives of the people." Such a doctrine, he insisted, would lead "directly to the establishment of democracy and anarchy."[7]

Even as Knox vehemently denounced the British "republicans" he nevertheless admitted that the majority of the parliamentary reformers were misguided rather than treasonous. He believed that rational argument, instead of blind repression, was the best method of reconciling these disaffected but loyal subjects. And so he devoted the greater part of the *Friendly Address* to a dispassionately academic history of parliamentary representation in Britain, designed to prove that representation in Parliament was constitutionally predicated upon the interests of social groups rather than upon the rights of individuals or taxpayers. He insisted that the idea of directly equating representation and taxation originated with the advocates of American independence, while the principle of universal manhood suffrage was a gift of the French philosophers, whose legacy of anarchy British subjects should not seek to impose upon their country. Knox did not completely reject parliamentary reform in the *Friendly Address*. Although he opposed democratic measures—which, he argued, would have confiscated the property rights of existing constituencies—he recommended that such "new interests" as Manchester, Birmingham, and Sheffield be granted parliamentary representation and that the more populous counties be divided, with each new division receiving the customary two seats in the Commons.

Despite Knox's categorical rejection of democracy, the conservatism he espoused in the *Friendly Address* seems remarkably rational and temperate when contrasted with the emotional reaction which generally permeated conservative ranks in Britain after the outbreak of war with France. In this respect, his response to the parliamentary reform movement was similar to his general attitude toward the American problem two decades earlier: in both instances his basic philosophy may be described as conservative—but his conservatism was essentially tempered by moderate inclinations and pragmatic considerations.

In no respect was this persistent strain of moderation and toleration more evident than in Knox's attitude toward the political and social troubles which continued to plague Ireland during the era of revolution. Legislative independence had not brought political tranquility to Ireland. The traditional domination of Parliament by the Anglo-Irish minority came to be increasingly resented not only by the disfranchised Catholic majority but also by the disgruntled Presbyterians of Ulster. Radicals in both camps, inspired by the example of France, turned to revolutionary activities. Although the revolutionary organizations attempted to avoid arousing Catholic-Protestant animosities, which remarkably had been held in check during the earlier Volunteer movement, reform agitation quickly took the seemingly inevitable Irish turn toward religious conflict. In the Irish Parliament itself, the patriot leader Henry Grattan called for a general reform of the political system, including emancipation for Catholics; however, the Anglican minority seemed prepared to maintain their privileged position even at the unpredictable cost of releasing the forces of religious passion.[8]

It was against the "evil" resurrection of "ancient animosities" in Ireland that Knox directed the main thrust of a pamphlet he published in 1792. Of course, he was unable to resist taking a few backhanded slaps at the patriots who had led Ireland into legislative independence. He pointed out that the very arguments previously employed against the right of the British Parliament to make laws for Ireland made it equally absurd to maintain that the Prostestant minority of Ireland had the right to govern the Catholic majority, and he insisted that the Protestants could only avoid being hanged upon their own rhetorical gibbet "by taking shelter again under that parental wing from which you so inconsiderately withdrew."[9]

Knox admittedly wished for a thoroughgoing union of Ireland with Great Britain. Nevertheless, his essential purpose in this pamphlet was to persuade Irish Protestants that peace and progress in Ireland depended upon freely granting timely political concessions, particularly the franchise, to Irish Catholics. He dismissed as groundless the common arguments that Catholic principles were adverse to liberty and that Catholics sought ultimately to dominate church and state. He was willing to concede that many Irish Catholics were "ignorant" and "illiterate"; however, he insisted that the shame rested not with the Catholics themselves but with those obnoxious acts which had kept them in such a condition for so long, and he predicted that with the removal of these restrictions Irish Catholics would be as informed as Protestants within a few generations. Finally, he drew upon a remarkable synthesis of historical lessons and personal experiences to counter Protestant fears that any concessions would inevitably lead to dire consequences:

> I will venture to assert, that the evils, which attended the
> yielding in *right things*, are solely to be imputed to the *not
> yielding in proper time*. Had Charles the First, I will ask, made
> the concessions two years before which he sent his Parliament
> from Oxford, would he have lost his head? Had Parliament in
> 1774 passed the Act relinquishing its claim to tax America,
> which it passed in 1780, would the Thirteen Colonies have de-
> clared themselves independent? Had Mr. Calonne advised the
> French King to call the *States*, when he called the *Notables*, and
> the King, and the Nobles and Clergy made to the *States* the
> same concessions they, by Neckar's advice, afterwards made to
> the Notables, would the French Monarchy have been over-
> turned?[10]

These rhetorical lessons might indeed have been regarded as de-
batable. But one thing is certain: the failure of sufficient concessions in *"proper time,"* such as Knox commended to his fellow subjects and coreligionists, brought an immediate renewal of the long
agony of sectarian violence in Ireland.

During the last two decades of his life, nothing gave Knox greater satisfaction than his appointment as provincial agent for the
Loyalist colony of New Brunswick. And in 1801, at the age of
sixty-nine, he even assumed the additional burden of serving as
agent for Prince Edward Island. Despite his advanced years, he enthusiastically expended a great deal of energy and thought in promoting the interests of his constituents before the imperial government. He continually prodded various officials and administrative
departments with petitions, memoranda, and recommendations
dealing with such problems as land policy, economic development,
and the state of religious institutions in New Brunswick and Prince
Edward Island.[11] And as a persistent advocate of the ancient ideal
of the self-sufficient empire, he remained especially alert to any
actions of the imperial government which threatened to sacrifice the
interests of his constituents to the advantage of the United States.
In 1804, for example, when British West Indian planters and merchants applied for legislation allowing American vessels to trade directly between the United States and the British islands, Knox petitioned the Colonial secretary, Lord Camden, to revise the measure
to the effect that trade between the United States and the West In-

dies would be discontinued whenever Britain's North American colonies were capable of supplying the British islands with the requisite commodities.[12]

It is remarkable, though hardly surprising, that Knox found no sanctuary—even in the role of elder statesman—from political controversies of the very sort which had agitated his early career. In 1798, in what must have seemed a recurrent nightmare sent to bedevil his declining years, he found himself caught in the middle of a jurisdictional dispute between the council and the assembly of New Brunswick. On this occasion, he steadfastly refused to take the part of either house before the imperial government, and in reward for this sage impartiality, so dearly bought by hard experience, the assembly informed him in a haunting phrase that "his services in future as Agent for this House must necessarily and of course be dispensed with."[13] Knox, as dogged as ever, continued to serve as agent without pay in behalf of the council, until the assembly agreed to his reappointment in 1803.[14] The final irony of ironies occurred in 1806, however, when the council of Prince Edward Island, itself locked in controversy with the lower house, lodged a complaint against Knox with the Board of Trade, headed by Knox's former colleague William Eden, now Lord Auckland.[15] Within a year Knox declined reappointment as agent for the island, and a year later, in 1808, he gave up his final official post when he resigned the New Brunswick agency.[16]

The occasional agitation and disappointments of Knox's two agencies were only minor disturbances in the relative serenity of his later years. In 1804, he finally gave up his town residence in Soho and sold part of his estate in Wales in favor of a rural retreat at Ealing, Middlesex. There he spent the last six years of his life in the happy company of his children.[17]

Knox's later correspondence with his old friends Ellis and Lyttelton proudly records the progressing fortunes of his sons and daughters—fortunes to which William himself contributed most generously with loving guidance as well a material legacies. His eldest son, Thomas, who was educated in the law and called to the bar, served for a while as joint agent with his father for New Brunswick and Prince Edward Island.[18] William apparently hoped that the experience of these offices would provide Thomas with an entry into a political or official career. But when Thomas chose instead to pursue the life of a country gentleman, William willingly granted him the remaining portion of his Lanstinan estate in Wales, as well as a legacy of two thousand pounds.[19] For two of his other sons, William made substantial provisions in the overseas empire. By 1806, George, with considerable financial support from his father, was "well settled" in Trinidad, even though the island had been conquered and formally ceded to Great Britain only a few years earlier.[20] A younger brother, Wills Frederick, chose to go to sea and for a time sought his fortune in the East Indies. But shortly before his father's death, the young man took up a tract of land in New Brunswick which had been granted to William in gratitude for his services to the colony; and before long Wills Frederick, with considerable financial assistance from his father, attained the status of a prosperous and respected member of the province.[21] William was especially pleased with the vocation of his youngest son, John, who was ordained a minister in the Church of England after taking both the Bachelor of Arts and Masters of Arts degrees at Cambridge. William's properties and influence in Pembrokeshire enabled him to provide this son with a living; and as the proud father recorded in his will, John also "through his own merit and good conduct obtained a respectable appointment at Westminster College."[22]

William provided no less generously for his precious daughters, who were the comfort and delight of his old age. His eldest child, Harriot, forty years old in 1808, remained by her father's side, not only overseeing the running of his household at Ealing but also serving as his secretary, an occupation which demanded considerable attention and labor even in the old man's last years. In his final testament, William left no doubt of his gratitude for Harriot's devotion as well as his confidence in her abilities: he bequeathed her the bulk of his estate and effects at Ealing and named her coexecutor of his will, along with her brother John.[23] For his two younger daughters, William provided a sum of five thousand pounds apiece, thereby allowing each a substantial dowry for good marriages. Shortly before his death, he gave his assent to an "agreeable" marriage between his daughter Caroline and Carew Smyth, a Dublin barrister.[24] Unfortunately, William did not live to savor the proud moment when, in 1814, his vivacious "favorite" Letitia married Gen. Sir Arthur Dillon, third baronet—thereby finally securing the old civil servant a small notice within the genealogical annals of the landed aristocracy.[25]

To the end of his days, Knox preserved much of the irrepressible

vigor of his intellect. In his late seventies, almost blind and afflicted with gout, he retained full intellectual powers and remained
acutely interested in public affairs.[26] He increasingly fixed his
mind, however, upon metaphysical considerations, publishing
theological treatises in 1796 and in 1801—the latter, his final published work, being an exhausting tome of two volumes.[27] Finally,
in 1809, his speculations prompted him to submit a remarkable
query to Sir William Herschel, one of the greatest astronomers of
the day:

> Since I quitted the Vortex of Politics and retired to this place,
> I have confined my thought to subjects much more suitable to
> my Time of Life and State of Health, but as the contemplation
> of a future State leads to astronomical disquisitions, I have met
> with some difficulties in my researches, to obtain the resolu-
> tion of which is the occasion of giving you the trouble of this
> Letter. . . . We have local descriptions of Heaven and of Para-
> dise, indeed we are told of Three Heavens, or a Third Heaven
> which implies two others, but in what part of space are we to
> look for them?[28]

Herschel's reply was as kind as it was candid. The scientist patient-
ly corrected several of Knox's astronomical calculations and finally
commented that "an attempt to assign 'a space for the seat of bliss
or the assembly of angels' does not fall to the lot of astronomers who
keep always within the range of facts that may be ascertained."[29]
Within a few months of this exchange, the *Gentleman's Magazine*
noted the death, on August 25, 1810, of "William Knox, esq.
formerly Under-Secretary of State."[30]

Shortly before Knox retired from active partisan politics, he
chose his own epitaph. In a published collection of memoirs and
"extra official" documents—a combined apologia and last testament to the public—he requested that his order-in-council of
July 2, 1783, which had cut off trade between Britain's remaining
imperial possession in the West Indies and the independent United
States, be engraved upon his tombstone.[31] There seems no doubt,
then, that Knox would have embraced the title "imperialist,"
which latter-day historians have assigned to him. Especially appropriate in this respect is Professor Richard Koebner's assessment of
Knox as an imperialist who was one of the first Britons to think and

write of the empire as an integrated constitutional, political, and economic community bound by mutually reciprocal advantages and obligations—rather than as simply a commercial union, the traditional "empire of the sea," or only a sentimental connection between common cultures.[32]

There is no need here to recapitulate all the details and summarize the evolution of Knox's imperial thought, but it does seem worthwhile in retrospect to single out, explore, and analyze the salient features of his personal contribution, in theory and practice, to eighteenth-century imperialism.

A systematic analysis of all Knox's writings, both published and private, inevitably leads to the conclusion that the expansive and intricate structure of his intellect—like the radiating fan vault of some Gothic cathedral—was supported and shaped by the pillars of an evangelical religious faith. Undoubtedly, the Calvinistic influences of his early years were persistent forces in this respect, but this Calvinism had been substantially modified by education and experience. To Knox, all facets of human history and endeavor were ultimately and unquestionably part of a divine plan for the reunion of God's creatures and the reconstitution of His creation. It was this ontological thrust which provided the moral force behind his proposals for reconciling and unifying the Catholics and Protestants of Ireland, his justification of black slavery as part of a supreme plan for civilizing and Christianizing Africans (his personal economic interests in slavery notwithstanding), and his latter-day appeal for reform of the Anglican liturgy so that "Jews, Turks, and Infidels" would be united through Christianity in a common brotherhood under the fatherhood of God.[33] Of course, in those publications which focused exclusively on imperial affairs, Knox incorporated no explicit references to his apocalyptic perspectives; nevertheless, there is little doubt that the pervasive religious imperatives of his thought gave substantial impetus, meaning, and form to his speculations upon worldly empires.

In particular, these dominant religious imperatives provide a significant clue to Knox's conceptions of imperial sovereignty and authority. For Knox, order and unity in all human affairs, including imperial relations, depended upon the preservation in ideation and behavior of an authority best described as paternalistic. Certainly the original source of this ideal was the awesome figure of his Calvinistic father, who remained throughout William's life a strong but benign figure of authority—an earthly surrogate of an Almighty Father who was the ultimate source of authority in the universe. Even in his mature personal relationships, Knox consistently evinced a preference for strong figures of authority, such as Philip Skelton, Lord George Germain, and, above all, George Grenville —with whom Knox identified more closely than anyone, except his own father.

Within the logic of Knox's imperial thought, paternalistic authority was rightly and effectively entrusted to the blessed and balanced trinity of Parliament—king, Lords, and Commons. To this corporate parent the imperial offspring and dependents owed dutiful obedience and succor. Nor was this imagery only a matter of metaphor to Knox. The transcendent concept of paternalistic authority and the moral imperatives of concomitant filial obligations were the very essence of his persistent dedication to the principle of parliamentary sovereignty and of his righteous satisfaction after the revolution in barring the ungrateful American prodigals from the familial estates.

Although Knox's concept of authority was paternalistic, his ideal was neither arbitrary nor authoritarian. To the precocious and favored son of Thomas Knox and the pupil of Philip Skelton, paternalistic authority carried with it the obligation to recognize and reward filial merit and enterprise. On more than one occasion, William demonstrated a prodigious capacity for defying any authority, individual or institutional, which ignored or slighted his talents or pretensions. Similarly, in both his publications and his counsels on colonial policy, he again and again insisted, even to the point of defying such formidable figures of authority as Grenville and Hillsborough, that the sovereign imperial Parliament was obliged to promote the welfare of the colonies by granting them concessions in such matters as governance, taxation, and trade restrictions. Only when it seemed to Knox that untoward filial defiance of imperial authority on the part of the colonies threatened the essential order and unity of the empire did he abandon the counsels of benevolence in favor of summary repression.

Although the values of apocalyptic Christianity and paternalistic authority were the preeminent integrative traits of Knox's intellect and personality, they of themselves provide neither unique nor sufficient explanations of his particular approach to imperial thought. Without a doubt, the outstanding quality of his imperial theories was his conception of the empire as an abstraction which ultimately transcended the accidents of historical time, geography, and particular interests. This idealistic conception may, of course, be partly attributed to his metaphysical and ontological cast of mind. There were, however, more immediate and pragmatic factors which contributed, ironically, to this abstract quality of Knox's concept of empire.

Throughout his life Knox remained, at best, situated upon the margins of the territorial aristocracy which dominated eighteenth-century British society. Much like his Irish countryman and rival, Burke, Knox essentially remained an outsider, depending upon talent rather than hereditary associations to penetrate the labyrinthine outer perimeter of the governing elite. But unlike Burke—who established a landed seat at Beaconsfield, at the cost of considerable personal and financial sacrifice—Knox never secured what might be properly designated a territorial base. In fact, one cannot help being struck by the restless itineracy which can be traced across the milestones of his life story: from Ireland to Georgia, back to England, and—after a relatively long period of residence at several locations in London—on to Wales and back. Indeed, if one attempted to plot the personal vectors of Knox's imperial perspectives —his emotional ties to his Irish homeland, his offices and properties in America, and his professional and social ambitions in England—the focus of these interests would have to be fixed somewhere in mid-Atlantic. It is hardly surprising, then, that Knox developed an abstract concept of the British Empire and complained that the dominant territorial elite of England and Ireland—even including his cherished leader, Grenville—continued essentially to look upon the empire as an extension of their country estates. Nor is it less surprising that his ideal vision of empire found even less favor in America among, for example, the territorial gentry of Virginia and the oligarchical elect of that secularized city-on-the-hill at Massachusetts Bay.

Ultimately, then, Knox's idealized and abstract imperial construct could not bridge the real gulf of behavioral attitudes and particular interests which separated the Anglo-American community more widely than the Atlantic itself. Thus in the end this imperialist, who had spent so much of his life attempting by word and deed to transform the first British Empire into a real constitutional, political, and commercial entity of world-wide authority, found himself ironically asking that there be carved upon his tombstone a measure by which he had only *"saved the navigation of England."*[34]

Abbreviations

Add. Mss.	Additional Manuscripts in the British Museum, London
AO.	Audit Office Papers in the Public Record Office, London
BM	British Museum, London
CO.	Colonial Office Papers in the Public Record Office, London
Dartmouth Mss.	Papers of William Legge, second Earl of Dartmouth, at the Staffordshire Record Office, Stafford
DNB	*Dictionary of National Biography*
Germain Papers	Papers of Lord George Germain at the William L. Clements Library, Ann Arbor, Michigan
HEHL	Henry E. Huntington Library, San Marino, California
HMC	Historical Manuscripts Commission
HMC, *Knox*	Historical Manuscripts Commission, *Report on Manuscripts in Various Collections*, vol. 6, *The Manuscripts of Miss M. Eyre Matcham; Captain H. V. Knox; Cornwallis Wykeham-Martin, Esq.; etc.*
HMC, *Stopford-Sackville*	Historical Manuscripts Commission, *Report on the Manuscripts of Mrs. Stopford-Sackville of Drayton House, Northamptonshire*
Knox Papers	William Knox Papers at the William L. Clements Library, Ann Arbor, Michigan
PRO	Public Record Office, London
Shelburne Papers	Papers of the Earl of Shelburne at the William L. Clements Library, Ann Arbor, Michigan
SP.	State Papers in the Public Record Office, London
T.	Treasury Papers in the Public Record Office, London
WLCL	William L. Clements Library, Ann Arbor, Michigan

Notes

Preface

1. Lewis B. Namier, "The Biography of Ordinary Men," in *Crossroads of Power*, p. 2.

2. Jack M. Sosin, *Whitehall and the Wilderness*, p. 52.

3. Lewis B. Namier, *The Structure of Politics at the Accession of George III*, p. 37, and Franklin B. Wickwire, "King's Friends, Civil Servants, or Politicians," *American Historical Review* 71 (October 1965): 18–42.

4. See, e.g., Edward Channing, *A History of the United States*, 3:68; Bernard Bailyn, ed., *Pamphlets of the American Revolution, 1750–1776*, 1:129–130; Lawrence H. Gipson, *The British Empire before the American Revolution*, 11:146–148; Richard Koebner, *Empire*, pp. 177 ff.; Edmund S. Morgan and Helen M. Morgan, *The Stamp Act Crisis*, pp. 103–104; and Margaret M. Spector, *The American Department of the British Government, 1768–1782*, p. 105.

5. Chester Martin, *Empire and Commonwealth*, pp. 48–50 and 52–55.

6. In all direct quotations, I have sought to preserve both the intensity and the integrity of the actors' points of view, reproducing the original texts—including spellings—and restricting the use of bracketed editorials to those intervals where they seemed indispensable to conveying the clear sense of the quoted material.

7. Shortly after the manuscript and citations for this study were completed, the name of the books and manuscripts section of the British Museum was changed to the British Library. To avoid errors and confusion, the original title, British Museum, and the abbreviation, BM, have been retained throughout this volume.

"The First Rudiments of My Political Education": Childhood & Youth in Ireland, 1732–1757

1. See William Knox's manuscript "Memoirs," Knox Papers (WLCL), 10:36. This document is printed in HMC, *Knox*, p. xiv.

2. "Memoirs," Knox Papers, 10:36. HMC, *Knox*, mistakenly quotes Clones as William's place of birth.

3. William Knox, *Observations Upon the Liturgy*, p. 5, and *The Revealed Will of God, the Sufficient Rule of Men*, 1:21–22. For further aspects of Knox's churchmanship and theological views, see his *Considerations on the Universality and Uniformity of the Theocracy*.

4. Knox, *The Revealed Will*, 1:19.

5. Ibid., pp. 19–22.

6. Samuel Burdy, *The Life of Philip Skelton*; William E. H. Lecky, *A History of Ireland in the Eighteenth Century*, 1:295–296; *DNB*, 52:333–334.

7. BM (Haldimand Papers) Add. Mss. 21732, f. 291b; Thomas Hastings to Knox, September 29, 1780, Knox Papers, 5:57; Burdy, *The Life of Philip Skelton*, p. 48.

8. Burdy, *The Life of Philip Skelton*, pp. 52 and 214. The close relationship between Skelton and the Knox family is detailed in numerous items in the Knox Papers; also, HMC, *Knox*, pp. 440–449.

9. Burdy, *The Life of Philip Skelton*, pp. 52–53, 67, and 118.

10. Denis C. Rushe, *Monaghan in the Eighteenth Century*, p. 90; Samuel Lewis, *A Topographical Dictionary of Ireland*, 2:384.

11. Knox, *The Revealed Will*, 1:21.

12. Skelton to Knox, June 5, 1769, July 4, 1770, and October 5, 1780, Knox Papers, 11:6, 11, and 38; HMC, *Knox*, p. 442.

13. See Philip Skelton, *Ophiomaches*.

14. Ibid., 1:64.

15. Ibid., p. 172.

16. Ibid., p. 95.

17. Thomas W. Freeman, *Ireland*, pp. 24–25, and *Pre-Famine Ireland*, pp. 270 and 305; Rushe, *Monaghan in the Eighteenth Century*, pp. 32–36. Today County Monaghan is part of the Irish Republic.

18. Knox, *Considerations on the Theocracy*, p. 178.

19. Conrad Gill, *The Rise of the Irish Linen Industry*, pp. 33, 48, 138–144, and 158; Freeman, *Ireland*, pp. 106–119 and 261; Lewis, *Topographical Ireland*, 2:382.

20. This conclusion is based upon three pieces of evidence contained in the Knox Papers: two letters from William Watson to Knox, one dated August 22, 1775 (Knox Papers, 2:29), and the other, January 4, 1781 (Knox Papers, 6:3), are endorsed "Old school friend" and "Old Irish school-friend" respectively; a letter from Matthew Hemmings to Knox, July 19, 1780 (Knox Papers, 5:40), is endorsed "Letter from an old school friend (now a parson)." The published register of Trinity College, Dublin, dates Watson's enrollment from 1748 to 1753 and Hemmings' from 1749 to 1755; the same source indicates that Watson and Hemmings had come to Trinity from different schoolmasters. The register also lists one William Knox—place of birth, County Dublin, and matriculation date, September 18, 1756—but there is no way of identifying this entry positively with the subject of the present study, and the discrepancy in the place of birth

argues against such an equation. The editors of the published register point out, however, that the lists are incomplete, particularly about the year 1750 (when Knox was most likely a "school friend" of Watson and Hemmings), and that it was quite customary for students to attend the university without submitting to the entrance examinations from which these lists were derived. See George D. Burtchaell and Thomas U. Sadleir, eds., *Alumni Dublinenses*, pp. vii–xiii, 388, 476, and 864.

21. Constantia Maxwell, *A History of Trinity College Dublin, 1591–1892*, pp. 148–150; Lecky, *A History of Ireland*, 1:320–321.

22. Maxwell, *A History of Trinity College*, pp. 135–136.

23. William Knox, *Extra Official State Papers*, 1, pt. ii, p. 1; Burtchaell and Sadleir, eds., *Alumni Dublinenses*, p. 185.

24. J. L. McCracken, "The Conflict between the Irish Administration and Parliament, 1753–6," *Irish Historical Studies* 3 (1942–1943): 160–163.

25. C. Litton Falkiner, ed., "Correspondence of Archbishop Stone and the Duke of Newcastle," *English Historical Review* 20 (July & October 1905): 528 n. 27, 539 n. 36, and 755. Cox, the grandson of a Lord Chancellor of Ireland, was a member of the Irish Parliament for the borough of Cloghanakilty and had held an Irish customs office since 1749. See *Burke's Genealogical and Heraldic History of the Peerage, Baronetage, and Knightage*, 1856, pp. 241–242; James L. J. Hughes, ed., *Patentee Officers in Ireland, 1173–1826*, p. 34.

26. C. Litton Falkiner, *Essays Relating to Ireland, Biographical, Historical, and Topographical*, p. 110, and "Stone-Newcastle Correspondence," pp. 549, 742, and 743; McCracken, "Conflict," pp. 169–171.

27. McCracken, "Conflict," pp. 171–172.

28. HMC, *Stopford-Sackville*, 1:243.

29. McCracken, "Conflict," pp. 174–177; Falkiner, *Essays*, pp. 11–14; Hughes, ed., *Patentee Officers*, p. 34.

30. J. G. Swift MacNeill, *The Constitutional and Parliamentary History of Ireland till the Union*, pp. 108–109.

31. Edward Porrit and Annie G. Porrit, *The Unreformed House of Commons*, 2:513.

32. Sir Philip Magnus, *Edmund Burke*, p. 15.

33. John Nichols, *Illustrations of the Literary History of the Eighteenth Century*, 1:477.

34. Knox Papers, 10:16; HMC, *Knox*, pp. 245–246.

"Legislators . . . That No King Can Govern Nor No God Can Please": Georgia, 1757–1762

1. W. W. Abbot, *The Royal Governors of Georgia, 1754–1775*, pp. 3–7 and 17.

2. Memorial, October 5, 1756, PRO, CO.5/645, ff. 99–101.

3. PRO, CO.5/645, ff. 104, 106, 267, and 269–270.

4. Abbot, *The Royal Governors*, pp. 44–50.

5. Great Britain, *Journal of the Commissioners of Trade and Plantations*, 1754–1758, pp. 381–383.

6. Ibid.

7. PRO, CO.5/645, ff. 85 and 94; Great Britain, *Journal of the Commissioners of Trade and Plantations*, 1754–1758, pp. 241–242, 249, 251, 252, and 254.

8. Great Britain, *Journal of the Commissioners of Trade and Plantations*, 1754–1758, p. 256; PRO, CO.5/645, ff. 97–98.

9. Reynolds to Board of Trade, March 29, 1756, PRO, CO.5/645, f. 85; Knox Papers, 10:16, HMC, *Knox*, p. 245.

10. Abbot, *The Royal Governors*, pp. 57–59.

11. Ellis to Board of Trade, May 15, 1757, PRO, CO.5/646, f. 11.

12. Knox Papers, 10:16; HMC, *Knox*, pp. 246 ff.

13. Ibid.; Lewis M. Wiggin, *The Faction of Cousins*, pp. 163–164.

14. Ellis to Board of Trade, March 11, 1757, PRO, CO.5/646, ff. 100–106; Abbot, *The Royal Governors*, pp. 34–35.

15. Abbot, *The Royal Governors*, pp. 51–53.

16. Ellis to Board of Trade, March 11, 1757, PRO, CO.5/646, ff. 95–96; Knox Papers, 10:16; HMC, *Knox*, p. 246.

17. Knox Papers, 10:16; HMC, *Knox*, p. 246.

18. Ellis to Board of Trade, March 11, 1757, PRO, CO.5/646, ff. 96–97.

19. Knox Papers, 10:16; HMC, *Knox*, p. 247. Ellis expressed similar objections regarding the detrimental influence of South Carolinians in a letter to the Board of Trade, March 15, 1759, PRO, CO.5/646, f. 224.

20. Knox Papers, 10:16; HMC, *Knox*, p. 247.

21. Abbot, *The Royal Governors*, p. 66.

22. Knox Papers, 10:16; HMC, *Knox*, pp. 246 ff.

23. Allen D. Candler, ed., *The Colonial Records of the State of Georgia*, 7:497. Knox's nomination to the council was not confirmed by Whitehall until June 29, 1758; the warrants for his appointment as provost marshal were issued by the Board of Trade on October 25, 1758 (PRO, CO.5/673, ff. 26 and 89).

24. Knox Papers, 10:16; HMC, *Knox*, pp. 248 and 249.

25. Ellis to Board of Trade, February 10, 1759, PRO, CO.5/646, ff. 212–213; Candler, ed., *Colonial Records of Georgia*, 7:591–592.

26. Ellis to Board of Trade, March 11 and May 5, 1757, PRO, CO.5/646, ff. 9 and 96–97; Knox Papers, 10:16; HMC, *Knox*, pp. 247–248.

27. For Knox's views on the balanced constitution, see in particular his "Considerations on the Great Question, What is fit to be done with America," Germain Papers, 17 (WLCL), and also his *Considerations on the Present State of the Nation*. The best general treatment of the eighteenth-century British concept of a balanced constitution is Betty Kemp, *Kings and Commons, 1660–1832*.

28. Knox Papers, 10:16; HMC, *Knox*, p. 247.

29. Knox Papers, 10:16; HMC, *Knox*, p. 248. See also Knox to Sir John Par-

nell, October 31, 1791, Knox Papers, 8:11; HMC, *Knox*, pp. 210–211.

30. Ellis to Board of Trade, May 5 and July 8, 1757, and April 24, 1759, PRO, CO.5/646, ff. 10–11, 26, and 231–239; Knox Papers, 10:16; HMC, *Knox*, p. 248; Candler, ed., *Colonial Records of Georgia*, 13:204, 210, and 217, 18:235–240.

31. Knox Papers, 10:16; HMC, *Knox*, pp. 248–249; Candler, ed., *Colonial Records of Georgia*, 13:187–188, 18:240–247.

32. Ellis to Board of Trade, May 5, 1757, PRO, CO.5/646, f. 11.

33. Knox Papers, 10:16; HMC, *Knox*, p. 249; Candler, ed., *Colonial Records of Georgia*, 16:207, 18:202–211.

34. Ellis to Board of Trade, August 1, 1757, and April 24, 1759, PRO, CO.5/646, ff. 33–34 and 234; Knox Papers, 10:16; HMC, *Knox*, p. 249; Candler, ed., *Colonial Records of Georgia*, 18:191–196.

35. Knox Papers, 10:16; HMC, *Knox*, p. 249; Candler, ed., *Colonial Records of Georgia*, 13:207, 216, and 217, 16:207 and 211, 18:197–202.

36. Knox Papers, 10:16.

37. Abbot, *The Royal Governors*, pp. 75–79.

38. PRO, CO.5/646, ff. 85–94a.

39. Candler, ed., *Colonial Records of Georgia*, 7:639–640.

40. Ellis to Board of Trade, February 10, 1759, PRO, CO.5/646, ff. 212–213.

41. Charles C. Jones, Jr., *The History of Georgia*, 1:461–466.

42. Candler, ed., *Colonial Records of Georgia*, 7:504–505, 13:266, 18:144–157; Abbot, *The Royal Governors*, p. 63.

43. Jones, *The History of Georgia*, 1:482.

44. PRO, CO.5/645, f. 94.

45. Georgia Historical Society, *Report of Sir James Wright on the Condition of the Province of Georgia on 20th Sept. 1773*, p. 172.

46. Knox to———, May 20, 1760, Knox Papers, 1:5; HMC, *Knox*, p. 84.

47. Candler, ed., *Colonial Records of Georgia*, 7:518 and 808, 8:43, 345, and 379.

48. Knox to Lyttelton, March 5, 1760, Knox Papers, 1:3; HMC, *Knox*, p. 82; Knox's Memorial to the Loyalist Claims Commission, September 18, 1783, PRO, AO.12/4, ff. 4–6; Candler, ed., *Colonial Records of Georgia*, 7:717 and 867–868, 8:20, 243–244, and 274.

49. Knox to Lyttelton, March 5, 1760, and Knox to ———, May 20, 1760, Knox Papers, 1:3 and 5; HMC, *Knox*, pp. 82 and 83–84.

50. Knox to Lyttelton, March 5, 1760, Knox Papers, 1:3; HMC, *Knox*, p. 82.

51. Ibid.; Lyttelton to Knox, March 22, 1760, Knox Papers, 1:4; HMC, *Knox*, p. 83.

52. Knox to ———, May 20, 1760, Knox Papers, 1:5; HMC, *Knox*, pp. 83–84.

53. Ibid.; Ellis to Board of Trade, April 24 and November 25, 1759, PRO, CO.5/646, ff. 246–247, and CO.5/647, f. 1.

54. *DNB*, 63:107; Abbot, *The Royal Governors*, p. 84.

55. Knox to [Robert Knox], June 28, 1761, Knox Papers, 1:7; HMC, *Knox*, p. 86; Wright to Robert Wood, November 15, 1762, PRO, CO.5/658, f. 17.

56. Wright to Board of Trade, December 28, 1761, PRO, CO.5/648, f. 131.

57. Wright to Board of Trade, July 31, 1761, in ibid., ff. 95–97.

58. See the report of the committee to the Board of Trade, in ibid., ff. 109–115.

59. Ibid.

60. PRO, CO.5/648, f. 108.

61. Ibid., ff. 161–162, 179–180, and 181–187.

62. Knox's Memorial to the Loyalist Claims Commission, September 18, 1783, PRO, AO.12/4, ff. 4–6; Candler, ed., *Colonial Records of Georgia*, 8:340–342, 383, 592, and 628.

63. Knox to [Robert Knox], June 28, 1761, Knox Papers, 1:7; HMC, *Knox*, pp. 85–86.

64. Candler, ed., *Colonial Records of Georgia*, 13:627–629.

65. Knox to Lyttelton, February 10, 1762, Knox Papers, 1:8; HMC, *Knox*, p. 86.

66. Ibid.

67. See Jack P. Greene, *The Quest for Power*.

68. Jackson T. Main, *The Upper House in Revolutionary America, 1763–1788*, p. 8; Abbot, *The Royal Governors, passim*.

69. Knox to Lyttelton, March 5, 1760, Knox Papers, 1:3; HMC, *Knox*, p. 82.

"Dancing Attendance upon People in Office": Imperial Problems & the Georgia Agency, 1762–1765

1. Ellis to Knox, April 28, 1762, Knox Papers, 1:9; HMC, *Knox*, p. 86.

2. Ellis to Knox, April 30, 1762, Knox Papers, 1:10; HMC, *Knox*, p. 87.

3. Knox Papers, 10:35; HMC, *Knox*, p. 282; Sosin, *Whitehall and the Wilderness*, pp. 56–57; John Shy, "Thomas Pownall, Henry Ellis, and the Spectrum of Possibilities, 1763–1775," in *Anglo-American Political Relations, 1675–1775*, ed. A. G. Olson and R. M. Brown, p. 159.

4. Knox Papers, 10:35; HMC, *Knox*, pp. 281–282; *DNB*, 20:169.

5. Knox Papers, 10:35; HMC, *Knox*, p. 282; Knox, *Extra Official State Papers*, 1, pt. i, p. 19. There is a draft of a defense of the Anglo-French treaty in the Shelburne Papers (WLCL), 165:309–321.

6. Knox Papers, 10:33; HMC, *Knox*, pp. 279–280; Lewis B. Namier and John Brooke, *Charles Townsend*, p. 105.

7. Namier and Brooke, *Townshend*, pp. 76–77.

8. Ibid., pp. 81–86; Namier, *Crossroads*, p. 203.

9. Knox Papers, 10:33; HMC, *Knox*, p. 280.

10. Clarence W. Alvord, *The Mississippi Valley in British Politics*, 1:157–165;

Sosin, *Whitehall and the Wilderness*, pp. 54–57.

11. See Verner W. Crane, ed., "Hints Relative to the Division and Government of the Conquered and Newly Acquired Countries in America," *Mississippi Valley Historical Review* 8 (March 1922): 370–373; also, R. A. Humphreys, "Lord Shelburne and the Proclamation of 1763," *English Historical Review* 49 (April 1934): 241–264.

12. Knox Papers, 10:35; HMC, *Knox*, pp. 282–283.

13. Shelburne Papers, 85:26–34. R. A. Humphreys ("Shelburne and the Proclamation of 1763," pp. 247–248) credited Maurice Morgann, sometime private secretary to Shelburne, with writing a portion of the manuscript; however, the essential arguments, the requisite expertise, and even the style of expression of this memorandum provide conclusive evidence that Knox was the original author, while Morgann at best transcribed the document for Shelburne's use.

14. Knox Papers, 9:2; HMC, *Knox*, p. 292; Charles L. Mowat, *East Florida As a British Province, 1763–1784*, pp. 10 and 12.

15. Knox Papers, 9:3; HMC, *Knox*, p. 292.

16. Humphreys, "Shelburne and the Proclamation of 1763," pp. 248 ff.

17. Mowat, *East Florida*, pp. 12 and 71–72.

18. Shelburne Papers, 48:475–558. There is another copy of this document in the British Museum's Liverpool Papers (Add. Mss. 38335, ff. 14–33), apparently the copy which Knox claimed his patron Lord Grosvenor gave to Lord Bute (Knox Papers, 10:35; HMC, *Knox*, p. 282). This document has been printed by Thomas C. Barrow, ed., in the *William and Mary Quarterly*, 3d ser. 24 (January 1967): 108–126.

19. Knox Papers, 10:35; HMC, *Knox*, p. 282; Knox, *Extra Official State Papers*, 2:28–29.

20. Lewis B. Namier and John Brooke, *The House of Commons, 1754–1790*, 1:221, 2:558–559, 3:638; *DNB*, 23:280.

21. Grenville to Grosvenor, October 24, 1763, Stowe 7, vol. 1, "Letterbooks of Official and Personal Correspondence, 1763–69" (HEHL); Knox Papers, 10:35; HMC, *Knox*, p. 282.

22. Knox to Townshend, August 27, 1763, Knox Papers, 1:12; HMC, *Knox*, p. 86. Also see Knox's account of his "hassardous" but abortive adventure in espionage during his stay in France (Knox Papers, 10:35; HMC, *Knox*, p. 282).

23. Knox Papers, 9:4; HMC, *Knox*, pp. 286–288.

24. Grenville to Grosvenor, October 24, 1763, Stowe 7, vol. 1, "Letterbooks."

25. Wright to Board of Trade, February 20, 1762, PRO, CO.5/648, f. 135; Knox to Lyttelton, February 10, 1762, Knox Papers, 1:8; Candler, ed., *Colonial Records of Georgia*, 18:481–483; Abbot, *The Royal Governors*, p. 96.

26. Candler, ed., *Colonial Records of Georgia*, 13:729–730 and 740, 17:5, 18:536–538.

27. Ibid., 17:35–36.

28. PRO, CO.5/648, ff. 155–156; Great Britain, *Journal of the Commissioners of Trade and Plantations*, 1759–1763, pp. 360–361, and 1764–1767, p. 129.

29. Great Britain, *Journal of the Commissioners of Trade and Plantations*, 1764–1767, pp. 9, 22, and 32; Bernhard Knollenberg, *Origin of the American Revolution, 1759–1766*, p. 170; Jack M. Sosin, *Agents and Merchants*, p. 20.

30. Sosin, *Agents and Merchants*, pp. 29–31.

31. Abbot, *The Royal Governors*, pp. 100–102.

32. Habersham to Knox, April 6, 1763, in Georgia Historical Society, *The Letters of Hon. James Habersham, 1756–1775*, pp. 10–11. Hereafter cited as *Habersham Letters*.

33. Habersham to Knox, April 19, 1763, in ibid., pp. 11–12.

34. Habersham to Knox, November 24, 1763, in ibid., pp. 13–14; Great Britain, *Journal of the Commissioners of Trade and Plantations*, 1759–1763, p. 366.

35. Habersham to Knox, November 24, 1763, *Habersham Letters*, pp. 13–15.

36. Habersham to Knox, July 2, 1764, in ibid., p. 17; Candler, ed., *Colonial Records of Georgia*, 14:86, 97–98, and 99, 18:580–582. In this context the term "job" indicates a position of public service turned to private gain.

37. Candler, ed., *Colonial Records of Georgia*, 14:218–219, 221, and 231.

38. Edmund S. Morgan, "The Postponement of the Stamp Act," *William and Mary Quarterly*, 3d ser. 7 (July 1950): 355–391; also, see Charles R. Ritcheson, *British Politics and the American Revolution*, pp. 23–24.

39. William Knox, *The Claim of the Colonies to an Exemption from Internal Taxes Imposed by Authority of Parliament, Examined*, pp. 33–35. For other accounts of this meeting, see Morgan, "Postponement of the Stamp Act," pp. 359 ff.

40. Knox, *Extra Official State Papers*, 2:24–25; Lyttelton to Knox, July 22, 1764, Knox Papers, 1:13; HMC, *Knox*, p. 89. Also, see Sosin, *Agents and Merchants*, p. 62 n.

41. Knox, *Claim of the Colonies*, pp. 36–37.

42. Knollenberg, *Origin of the American Revolution*, pp. 204–205; Morgan, "Postponement of the Stamp Act," pp. 372–373. According to Dora M. Clark, *The Rise of the British Treasury*, p. 52, as early as Walpole's administration the British Treasury was convinced that colonial assemblies could not be relied upon to provide funds for colonial defense.

43. Habersham to Knox, July 18, 1765, *Habersham Letters*, pp. 40–41; Knox, *Claim of the Colonies*, pp. 36–37.

44. Habersham to Knox, April 15, 1765, *Habersham Letters*, p. 32.

45. Habersham to Knox, July 18, 1765, in ibid., pp. 40–41.

46. Great Britain, *Journal of the House of Commons*, 30:479 and 513; *The Parliamentary History of England*, 16:136–137.

47. Knox, *Claim of the Colonies*, p. 4.

48. Ibid., p. 32.

49. See Knox to Grenville, November 8, 1765, in William J. Smith, ed., *The Grenville Papers*, 3:109–110.

50. See Knox, *Extra Official State Papers*, 2:29–30.

51. Abbot, *The Royal Governors*, p. 104.

52. Habersham to Knox, October 28, 1765, *Habersham Letters*, pp. 44–46.

53. Candler, ed., *Colonial Records of Georgia*, 14:293–294, 317–318, and 337, 17:241–242; Abbot, *The Royal Governors*, p. 109.

54. Habersham to Knox, October 28 and December 4, 1765, and January 29, 1766, *Habersham Letters*, pp. 46, 50, and 56; Abbot, *The Royal Governors*, p. 106.

55. Candler, ed., *Colonial Records of Georgia*, 14:366 and 367, 17:268, 269, 362–364, 366–367, and 372–373.

56. Ibid., 14:497, 503–507, 567, and 579, 17:392.

57. Ibid., 17:375.

"An Offer . . . Advantageous & Honourable to You": Pamphleteering & the Pursuit of Office, 1765–1770

1. Lyttelton to Knox, August 30, 1759, Knox Papers, 1:2; HMC, *Knox*, p. 81.

2. In 1803 Knox sat for a portrait executed by the Baroness de Tott. See Knox to committee of correspondence, June 1, 1803, Knox Papers, 8:29; HMC, *Knox*, p. 217; also, the Royal Academy of Arts, *A Complete Dictionary of Contributors, 1769–1904*, comp. Algernon Graves, 2:313. I have not been able to locate the original; however, the Clements Library does have a photograph of Knox's portrait, which they have kindly allowed me to use as a frontispiece.

3. PRO AO.13/36, pt. 1, f. 334; Mowat, *East Florida*, p. 37.

4. James Boswell, *London Journal, 1762–1763*, ed. Frederick A. Pottle, pp. 48 and *passim*.

5. Abbot, *The Royal Governors*, p. 24.

6. PRO, AO.12/4, ff. 10–11; *Habersham Letters*, *passim*.

7. PRO, AO.12/4, ff. 10–11.

8. Habersham to Knox, July 17 and October 30, 1765, *Habersham Letters*, pp. 36 and 47.

9. PRO AO.12/4, f. 5; Dartmouth Mss., D. 1778, 2:772; Great Britain, *Journal of the Commissioners of Trade and Plantations*, 1764–1767, pp. 176 and 178–179.

10. Habersham to Knox, March 9, 1764, *Habersham Letters*, pp. 15–16; Spector, *The American Department*, p. 116.

11. Bartholomew Zouberbuhler to the secretary of the Society for the Propagation of the Gospel, December 31, 1764, Hawks Transcripts, Georgia-Florida Mss., p. 81; Lyttelton to Knox, January 10, July 14, and October 20, 1765, Knox Papers, 1:15, 16, and 17; HMC, *Knox*, pp. 90 and 92.

12. Skelton to Knox, October 25, 1765, and May 6, 1773, Knox Papers, 11:1 and 17; HMC, *Knox*, pp. 440 and 443; PRO, AO.13/35, ff. 63–64.

13. Skelton to Knox, October 25, 1765, and July 28, 1769, Knox Papers, 11:1 and 7; HMC, *Knox*, p. 440.

14. Skelton to Knox, September 14, 1766, and Lyttelton to Knox, July 30, 1767, Knox Papers, 11:4 and 1:20; HMC, *Knox*, p. 93.

15. Michael Hanson, *Two Thousand Years of London*, p. 127; Percy Fitzgerald, "Old London Squares," in *London, As Seen and Described by Famous Writers*, ed. Esther Singleton, pp. 302–303.

16. Skelton to Knox, September 14 and October 11, 1766, Knox Papers, 11:4 and 5; HMC, *Knox*, p. 441.

17. PRO, CO.5/540, ff. 92 and 169, CO.5/544, ff. 189–190, CO.5/548, ff. 39, 43, and 164; Mowat, *East Florida*, pp. 34–35.

18. Dartmouth Mss., D. 1778, 2:1817a.

19. Grosvenor to Grenville, February 16, 1764, in *Additional Grenville Papers, 1763–1765*, ed. John R. G. Tomlinson, p. 89; *Parliamentary History*, 16:181–193; Namier and Brooke, *House of Commons*, 1:221, 2:558–559, and 3:638.

20. Knox to Grenville, November 9, 1764, Knox Papers, 1:14; HMC, *Knox*, pp. 89–90; Knox to Grenville, November 28, 1765, in Smith, ed., *Grenville Papers*, 3:109–110; Dartmouth Mss., D. 1778, 2:1817a; Great Britain, *Journal of the Commons*, 30:513.

21. Knox, *Extra Official State Papers*, 2:26 n.

22. The best treatment of Grenville's party and his leadership during this period is in John Brooke, *The Chatham Administration, 1766–1768*.

23. Keith G. Feiling, *The Second Tory Party, 1714–1832*, pp. 94–96.

24. Grenville to Knox, October 7, 1767, Knox Papers, 1:22; HMC, *Knox*, p. 94; Knox to Grenville, October 10, 1767, Knox Papers, 1:22a; also, Knox Papers, 10:17; HMC, *Knox*, pp. 250–251.

25. Lyttelton to Knox, December 9, 1767, Knox Papers, 1:23; HMC, *Knox*, p. 94.

26. Brooke, *The Chatham Administration*, pp. 28 ff.

27. Knox Papers, 10:25; HMC, *Knox*, p. 270.

28. Knox, *Extra Official State Papers*, 2:34–35.

29. Wiggin, *The Faction of Cousins*, pp. 159 and 313.

30. During the summer of 1768, Knox went to the considerable trouble of sending Mrs. Grenville "some Summer Ducks" and "a Red Bird from Georgia for her Closet Window"; and when he learned from Grenville that the ducks had "miscarried," he sent replacements along with a "Virginia Nightingale." Grenville to Knox, July 28 and September 11, 1768, Knox Papers, 1:31 and 34.

31. Grenville to Knox, October 7, 1767, Knox Papers, 1:22; HMC, *Knox*, p. 94.

32. Knox to Grenville, August 4, 1768, BM (Grenville Papers) Add. Mss. 42086, ff. 86–87; Knox to Grenville, August 9, 1768, in Smith, ed., *Grenville Papers*, 4:335–336.

33. Grenville to Knox, June 27, 1768, Knox Papers, 1:27; HMC, *Knox*, pp. 95–96.

34. Knox to Grenville, July 7, 1768, BM (Grenville Papers) Add. Mss. 42086, f. 52.

35. Italics mine.

36. Grenville to Knox, July 15, 1768, Knox Papers, 1:30; HMC, *Knox*, p. 97.

37. Knox, *Extra Official State Papers*, 2:33.

38. Ibid., p. 32.

39. Knox to Grenville, September 27 and October 4, 1768, in Smith, ed., *Grenville Papers*, 4:367–368.

40. Knox to Grenville, September 8, September 27, and October 4, 1768, in ibid., pp. 359 and 367–369.

41. Knox to Grenville, October 15, 1768, BM (Grenville Papers) Add. Mss. 42086, f. 149.

42. See William Knox, *The Present State of the Nation . . . Addressed to the King and Both Houses of Parliament*.

43. Ibid., p. 18.

44. Ibid., pp. 16–17.

45. Ibid., pp. 34–37.

46. Ibid., pp. 37–38.

47. Ibid., pp. 38–39.

48. Ibid., pp. 34–36.

49. Ibid., p. 17.

50. Ibid., p. 32.

51. Ibid., pp. 46–47.

52. Grenville to Knox, October 9, 1768, Knox Papers, 1:36; HMC, *Knox*, pp. 101–102.

53. *Gentleman's Magazine* 38 (November 1768): 529–532.

54. Dartmouth Mss., D. 1778, 2:1817a; Knox to Grenville, November 1, 1768, in Smith, ed., *Grenville Papers*, 4:394–395.

55. Whately to Grenville, October 27 and October 28, 1768, in Smith, ed., *Grenville Papers*, 4:390–392.

56. See Edmund Burke, *Observations on a Late State of the Nation*.

57. Burke, e.g., in questioning Knox's statistics on the decline of the "carrying trade," included all British shipping in his definition, whereas Knox restricted this term to the transport by British ships of "foreign commodities from one foreign country to another." Again, in respect to the increased costs of imperial defense, the differences between Knox's figures and those of Burke stemmed from the fact that Knox wrote about the increase in the "military guard," excluding the navy and other items, whereas Burke referred to the entire defense establishment. Knox pointed out these distinctions in his subsequent *An Appendix to the Present State of the Nation*. Here he defended most of the statistics included in the *Present State of the Nation* and challenged several of Burke's figures. Knox admitted to some errors in his earlier work but replied that they had been corrected in later editions and insisted that these errors in no way invalidated his general conclusions.

58. Burke, *Observations*, p. 51.

59. *Gentleman's Magazine* 39 (March 1769): 152–154. In fact, Adam Smith's library contained a volume wherein Knox's *Present State of the Nation* and Burke's *Observations* were bound together with two pamphlets by Josiah Tucker (Koebner, *Empire*, p. 358 n.).

60. *Gentleman's Magazine* 39 (May 1769): 254–255.

61. Knox to Grenville, May 24, 1768, in Smith, ed., *Grenville Papers*, 4:297–299; Grenville to Knox, July 15, 1768, Stowe 7, vol. 2, "Letterbooks"; Knox to Grenville, July 23, 1768, BM (Grenville Papers) Add. Mss. 42086, ff. 70–71.

62. Knox to Grenville, July 7 and August 4, 1768, and January 9, 1769, BM (Grenville Papers) Add. Mss. 42086, ff. 55b and 86–87, and Add. Mss. 42087, ff. 5–6; Dartmouth Mss., D. 1778, 2:1817a.

63. Knox to Grenville, August 9, 1768, in Smith, ed., *Grenville Papers*, 4:335–336.

64. See particularly Grenville's lengthy dissertation upon taxation and representation in Grenville to Knox, August 15, 1768, Knox Papers, 1:33.

65. See William Knox, *The Controversy Between Great Britain and her Colonies Reviewed*.

66. Ibid., pp. 21–22.

67. Knox, *Extra Official State Papers*, 2:11.

68. J. Harry Bennett, Jr., *Bondsmen and Bishops*, p. 88; Leland J. Bellot, "Evangelicals and the Defense of Slavery in Britain's Old Colonial Empire," *Journal of Southern History* 37 (February 1971): 27 ff.

69. See William Knox, *Three Tracts Respecting the Conversion and Instruction of the Free Indian and Negroe Slaves in the Colonies*.

70. Ibid., pp. 14–15.

71. Ibid., p. 36.

72. Ibid, p. 39.

73. Frederick Campbell to Knox, November 7, 1768, Knox Papers, 1:38; Skelton to Knox, June 5, 1769, Knox Papers, 11:6; Lyttelton to Knox, August 5, 1769, Knox Papers, 1:41; HMC, *Knox*, p. 104.

74. Ellis to Knox, December 30, 1767, Knox Papers, 1:25; HMC, *Knox*, p. 95; Brooke, *The Chatham Administration*, pp. 18–19.

75. Knox to Grenville, August 20 and September 8, 1768, BM (Grenville Papers) Add. Mss. 42086, ff. 106 and 120; Knox to Grenville, September 15, 1768, in Smith, ed., *Grenville Papers*, 4:364.

76. Ritcheson, *British Politics and the Revolution*, pp. 122 and 129–130.

77. Knox to Grenville, October 18, 1769, in Smith, ed., *Grenville Papers*, 4:468–469; Grenville to Knox, October 22, 1769, Knox Papers, 1:43, and in Smith, ed., *Grenville Papers*, 4:471–472; Knox to Grenville, October 24, 1769, in Smith, ed., *Grenville Papers*, 4:475–476; Grenville to Knox, October 29, 1769, Knox Papers, 1:44; HMC, *Knox*, pp. 104–105; Knox to Grenville, November 10, 1769, in Smith, ed., *Grenville Papers*, 4:479–480.

78. Lyttelton to Knox, August 29 and December 9, 1767, and March 14, 1768, Knox Papers, 1:21, 23, and 26; HMC, *Knox*, p. 94.

79. Knox to Grenville, August 9 and August 20, 1768, BM (Grenville Papers) Add. Mss. 42086, ff. 98 and 109b; Clare to Knox, October 10, 1768, Knox Papers, 1:37; HMC, *Knox*, p. 102; also, see the registered copy of Knox's will, dated December 10, 1806, preserved at Somerset House, London.

80. Lyttelton to Knox, January 5, 1770, Knox Papers, 1:45; HMC, *Knox*, p. 105; also, see PRO, AO.13/36, pt. 1, ff. 332b and 434, for copies of Thomas' birth certificate.

81. Skelton to Knox, May 27, 1766, and Clare to Knox, June 28 and October 10, 1768, Knox Papers, 11:2 and 1:28 and 37; HMC, *Knox*, pp. 96 and 442.

82. Skelton to Knox, October 11, 1766, June 5, July 26, and October 25, 1769, and July 4, 1770, Knox Papers, 11:5, 6, 7, 9, and 11; HMC, *Knox*, pp. 441–442.

83. Knox to [Pownall], [February 5, 1770], and Pownall to Knox, February 9, 1770, Knox Papers, 1:46 and 47; HMC, *Knox*, p. 105.

84. Knox, *Extra Official State Papers*, 2:39–43.

85. Ibid.

86. Ibid.

87. Charles Lloyd to Grenville, July 3, 1770, in Smith, ed., *Grenville Papers*, 4:521–522.

88. *DNB*, 33:408.

89. Grenville to Knox, July 19, 1770, Knox Papers, 1:48; HMC, *Knox*, p. 106.

"The Dye Is Cast & More Mischief Will Follow": Conflicts of Interest & the Coming of the American Revolution, 1770–1775

1. Ellis to Knox, August 7, 1770, Knox Papers, 1:49; HMC, *Knox*, p. 106.

2. Spector, *The American Department*, pp. 19–20.

3. Mark A. Thomson, *The Secretaries of State, 1681–1782*, p. 58.

4. John C. Miller, *Origins of the American Revolution*, p. 262.

5. Knox to Grenville, May 24, 1768, BM (Grenville Papers) Add. Mss. 42086, ff. 42–45.

6. Knox to Grenville, November 10, 1769, in Smith, ed., *Grenville Papers*, 4:480–481.

7. Spector, *The American Department*, pp. 34–40, 111–112, and 115–116.

8. Charles M. Andrews, *Guide to Materials for American History, to 1783, in the Public Record Office of Great Britain*, 1:84–95.

9. Franklin B. Wickwire, "John Pownall and British Colonial Policy," *William and Mary Quarterly*, 3d ser. 20 (October 1963): 541–554.

10. Knox Papers, 10:21; HMC, *Knox*, p. 257.

11. Habersham to Knox, October 9, 1770, *Habersham Letters*, pp. 87–88.

12. Habersham to Knox, December 1, 1770, in ibid., pp. 97–99.

13. Habersham to Knox, March 13, 1771, and Habersham to Henry Laurens, June 3, 1771, in ibid., pp. 122 and 133.

14. Habersham to John Nutt, November 28, 1771, and Habersham to James Wright, November 30, 1771, in ibid., pp. 152 and 155–156; Skelton to Knox, January 30, 1772, Knox Papers, 11:12.

15. Habersham to Knox, February 11 and July 24, 1772, and Habersham to Nutt, July 31, 1772, *Habersham Letters*, pp. 164 and 194–196.

16. PRO, AO. 12/4, f. 5.

17. Habersham to Knox, July 24, 1772, and August 12, 1773, *Habersham Letters*, pp. 194 and 232.

18. Bellot, "Evangelicals and the Defense of Slavery," pp. 31–34.

19. Habersham to Knox, August 12, 1773, *Habersham Letters*, pp. 231–232.

20. PRO, AO. 12/4, ff. 1–14, and AO. 13/36, pt. 1, ff. 335–338; Knox to Shelburne, April 23, 1782, Knox Papers, 6:44; HMC, *Knox*, p. 183.

21. Spector, *The American Department*, pp. 50–58. Knox eventually succeeded in having the office of provost marshal of Georgia granted to his sons during their lives (ibid., pp. 63–64). And in 1772 William's brother Robert was granted the lucrative East Florida agency, which he retained until Britain gave up the colony in 1782 (Mowat, *East Florida*, p. 35).

22. Knox to Shelburne, April 23, 1782, Knox Papers, 6:44; HMC, *Knox*, pp. 183–184; PRO, AO. 13/36, pt. 1, ff. 330–331.

23. Dartmouth Mss., D. 1778, 2:772.

24. Knox Papers, 10:19; HMC, *Knox*, pp. 253–255; Thomson, *The Secretaries of State*, p. 58; Ritcheson, *British Politics and the Revolution*, pp. 144–146.

25. See Bradley D. Bargar, *Lord Dartmouth and the American Revolution*.

26. Dartmouth Mss., D. 1778, 2:448.

27. Pownall to Knox, September 19, September 21, and October 3, 1772, and Ellis to Knox, October 17, 1772, Knox Papers, 1:52, 53, 56, and 57; HMC, *Knox*, pp. 107–109.

28. Knox to Dartmouth, September 24, 1773, Dartmouth Mss., D. 1778, vol. 1, pt. ii, p. 883.

29. Extract from Dartmouth to Tryon, December 9, 1772, enclosed in Knox to Dartmouth, October 6, 1773, in ibid., p. 887.

30. Pownall to Dartmouth, October 6, [1773], in ibid., p. 886.

31. Knox to Dartmouth, October 6, 1773, in ibid., p. 887.

32. Knox Papers, 10:19 and 22; HMC, *Knox*, pp. 254 and 256.

33. Thomson, *The Secretaries of State*, pp. 58–59; Ritcheson, *British Politics and the Revolution*, pp. 149–150. For a contrasting interpretation, see Bargar, *Dartmouth and the American Revolution*, pp. 65–66.

34. Wickwire, "Pownall," pp. 549–553.

35. Pownall to Knox, October 3, 1772, Knox Papers, 1:56; HMC, *Knox*, p. 109.

36. PRO, CO.5/250, ff. 30–31. There is a comprehensive treatment of British policy and the Carib War in Gipson, *The British Empire*, 9:255–266.

37. Pownall to Knox, October 3, 1772, Knox Papers, 1:56; HMC, *Knox*, p. 109. Colonial Office documents provide substantial evidence of Rochford and Suffolk's encroachments upon Dartmouth's jurisdiction during the latter's absences from Whitehall. See PRO, CO.5/243, ff. 20–21, and CO.5/250, ff. 30–31.

38. *Parliamentary History*, 17:568 ff.

39. PRO, CO.5/241, ff. 222–224 and 225; Pownall to Knox, December 21 and December 26, 1772, Knox Papers, 1:58 and 59; HMC, *Knox*, p. 110.

40. *Parliamentary History*, 17:722–741.

41. Pownall to Knox, July 23, 1773, Knox Papers, 2:2; HMC, *Knox*, p. 110.

42. Pownall to Knox, August 31, 1774, Knox Papers, 2:15; HMC, *Knox*, p. 115.

43. Pownall to Knox, December 3, 1773, and Ellis to Knox, July 15, 1774, Knox Papers, 2:4 and 9; HMC, *Knox*, pp. 111–112.

44. Knox Papers, 10:25; HMC, *Knox*, p. 269.

45. Dartmouth to Mr. Reed, n.d., in Great Britain, HMC, *Eleventh Report, Appendix, Part V*, pp. 354–355.

46. Knox Papers, 10:21 and 25; HMC, *Knox*, pp. 257 and 269–270.

47. Bernard Donoughue, *British Politics and the American Revolution*, pp. 50–66; Benjamin W. Labaree, *The Boston Tea Party*, pp. 174–176.

48. Knox Papers, 10:25; HMC, *Knox*, p. 270.

49. Knox Papers, 10:21; HMC, *Knox*, p. 257. Knox's claim that he personally advocated limited sanctions against Massachusetts Bay is credible because he composed this manuscript memoir in 1775, at a time when he could not have expected to derive any particular advantage from identifying himself with a policy of moderation.

50. Peter O. Hutchinson, ed., *The Diary and Letters of Thomas Hutchinson, Esq.*, 1:183. See also Ritcheson, *British Politics and the Revolution*, pp. 160–163, and Donoughue, *British Politics and the American Revolution*, pp. 66–71.

51. Knox Papers, 10:21; HMC, *Knox*, p. 257.

52. Dartmouth to Reed, n.d., in Great Britain, HMC, *Eleventh Report, Appendix, Part V*, pp. 354–355.

53. PRO, CO.5/242, f. 4.

54. Lawrence H. Gipson, *The Coming of the Revolution, 1763–1775*, p. 227; Carl B. Cone, *Burke and the Nature of Politics*, 1:263–264. Professor Cone argues that Burke was ignorant of conditions in Quebec and was, in fact, unduly partial to the small English minority in Canada.

55. Dartmouth Mss., D. 1778, 2:1817a; William Watson to Knox, July 23, 1774, Knox Papers, 2:11.

56. See William Knox, *The Justice and Policy of the Late Act of Parliament for . . . the Province of Quebec*.

57. Donoughue, *British Politics and the American Revolution*, pp. 125 and 146 ff.; Namier and Brooke, *House of Commons*, 1:73–80.

58. Pownall to Knox, August 31 and September 13, 1774, Knox Papers 2:15 and 17; HMC, *Knox*, pp. 114–116.

59. Hutchinson, ed., *Diary*, 1:177, 184, and 192.

60. Ellis to Knox, July 15, 1774, and George Cressner to Knox, August 28, September 20, and November 10, 1774, Knox Papers, 2:9, 14, 18, and 19; HMC, *Knox*, pp. 112–116.

61. Pownall to Knox, August 31 and September 13, 1774, Knox Papers, 2:15 and 17; HMC, *Knox*, pp. 114–116.

62. Hutchinson, ed., *Diary*, 1:261 and 267–268.

63. Ibid., pp. 267–268.

64. Knox Papers, 9:13.

65. Hutchinson, ed., *Diary*, 1:272–273 and 289.

66. Ibid., p. 295.

67. Knox to Dartmouth, November 15, 1774, Dartmouth Mss., D.1778, 2:994.

68. William Knox, *The Interest of the Merchants and Manufacturers of Great Britain*, pp. 49–50.

69. Dartmouth Mss., D. 1778, 2:1817a; Sosin, *Agents and Merchants*, pp. 218–221.

70. Knox Papers, 10:21; HMC, *Knox*, p. 258; Hutchinson, ed., *Diary*, 1:310; *Parliamentary History*, 18:33–34.

71. Bargar, *Dartmouth and the American Revolution*, pp. 133 ff.

72. Knox Papers, 10:21; HMC, *Knox*, p. 258; Knox to [Dartmouth], August 5, 1775, Dartmouth Mss., D. 1778, 2:1424.

73. Ritcheson, *British Politics and the Revolution*, p. 178; Donoughue, *British Politics and the American Revolution*, pp. 214 ff.

74. Hutchinson, ed., *Diary*, 1:392–393.

75. Knox to John Blackburn, February 15, 1775, Knox Papers, 2:21; Hutchinson, ed., *Diary*, 1:391.

76. Knox to Dartmouth, November 15, 1774, Dartmouth Mss., D. 1778, 2:994.

77. Bargar, *Dartmouth and the American Revolution*, pp. 133–138.

78. Bernard Mason, *The Road to Independence*, pp. 42–49.

79. Weldon A. Brown, *Empire or Independence*, pp. 45–48.

80. *Parliamentary History*, 18:319 ff.

81. Donoughue, *British Politics and the American Revolution*, pp. 248–260; Cone, *Burke*, 1:287–288.

82. Ritcheson, *British Politics and the Revolution*, pp. 189–191.

83. Brown, *Empire or Independence*, pp. 133 ff.

84. Mason, *Road to Independence*, pp. 29–30; Miller, *Origins of the Revolution*, p. 407.

85. Pownall to Knox, June 2 and June 13, 1775, Knox Papers, 2:23 and 24; HMC, *Knox*, p. 118.

86. Dartmouth to Knox, July 3, 1775, Knox Papers, 2:25; HMC, *Knox*, p. 119.

87. Cressner to Knox, September 25, 1775, Knox Papers, 2:31; Knox to Shelburne, April 23, 1782, Knox Papers, 6:44; "Mr. Knox's Case," May 5, 1787, Knox Papers, 7:36; HMC, *Knox*, pp. 184 and 196; Georgia Historical Society, *Proceedings of the Georgia Council of Safety*, pp. 115–116; Candler, ed., *Colonial Records of Georgia*, 19:126–127.

88. Knox to [Dartmouth], August 5, 1775, Dartmouth Mss., D. 1778, 2:1424.

"Wrath My Dear Lord Is Gone Forth": The American War, 1775–1778

1. PRO, CO.5/243, ff. 41 and 42–46.
2. PRO, CO.5/242, ff. 45–46.
3. Hutchinson, ed., *Diary*, 1:470.
4. Dartmouth to Knox, August 6, 1775, Knox Papers, 2:28; HMC, *Knox*, p. 121; Bargar, *Dartmouth and the American Revolution*, pp. 176–177.
5. Piers G. Mackesy, *The War for America, 1775–1783*, pp. 43–45.
6. Pownall to Knox, October 10, 1775, Knox Papers, 2:32; HMC, *Knox*, p. 122.
7. PRO, CO.5/242, f. 48; Hutchinson, ed., *Diary*, 1:576.
8. For divergent treatments of Germain's life and career, compare Alan Valentine, *Lord George Germain*, and Gerald S. Brown, *The American Secretary*; also, see Mackesy, *War for America, passim*.
9. Knox Papers, 10:23; HMC, *Knox*, p. 259.
10. Dartmouth Mss., D. 1778, 2:1667.
11. Knox Papers, 10:23 and 24; HMC, *Knox*, p. 259.
12. Dartmouth Mss., D. 1778, 2:1667.
13. Knox Papers, 10:23; HMC, *Knox*, p. 259.
14. Ritcheson, *British Politics and the Revolution*, pp. 203–207.
15. Brown, *Empire or Independence*, pp. 108 ff.
16. Hutchinson, ed., *Diary*, 2:44–45.
17. PRO, CO.5/243, ff. 41–42; Hutchinson, ed., *Diary*, 2:8; Mackesy, *War for America*, p. 63.
18. Christopher Ward, *The War of Revolution*, 2:663–664.
19. Knox to Dartmouth, August 22, 1776, in Great Britain, HMC, *Fourteenth Report, Appendix, Part X*, 2:424–425.

20. Paul H. Smith, *Loyalists and Redcoats*, p. 30.

21. Ellis to Knox, August 13, 1777, Knox Papers, 3:26; Hutchinson, ed., *Diary*, 2:70 and 72; *DNB*, 63:108–109.

22. Germain to Knox, October 19, 1776, Knox Papers, 2:58; HMC, *Knox*, p. 126.

23. Spector, *The American Department*, p. 142.

24. Hutchinson, ed., *Diary*, 2:55; Spector, *The American Department*, pp. 105–106; Wickwire, "Pownall," p. 553.

25. Hutchinson, ed., *Diary*, 2:56.

26. Brown, *American Secretary*, pp. 45 ff.; Spector, *The American Department*, pp. 74–75 and 85–86.

27. PRO, CO.5/243, ff. 81 and 88.

28. Knox Papers, 10:34; HMC, *Knox*, p. 277.

29. Pownall to Knox, November 13, 1776, Knox Papers, 2:66; HMC, *Knox*, p. 127.

30. Knox Papers, 10:34; HMC, *Knox*, p. 277.

31. Dartmouth Mss., D. 1778, 2:1793; Knox, *Extra Official State Papers*, 1, pt. i, pp. 24–25.

32. Germain to Knox, August 29 and September 16, 1777, Knox Papers, 3:34 and 36; HMC, *Knox*, pp. 137 and 138.

33. PRO, CO.5/251, ff. 58, 107, and 150–151.

34. See PRO, CO.5/258, *passim*.

35. Knox to Edward Stanley, August 2, 1776, PRO, CO.5/251, f. 15.

36. Robinson to Dartmouth, March 2 and [March 3], 1777, Dartmouth Mss., D. 1778, 2:1739 and 1740.

37. See PRO, CO.5/254, *passim*.

38. See PRO, CO.5/261, *passim*; also Spector, *The American Department*, pp. 85–86.

39. Pownall to Stephens, July 24, 1775, PRO, CO.5/250, f. 113.

40. Boddington to Knox, March 31, 1777, PRO, CO.5/256, ff. 72–73.

41. Knox to Boddington, April 1, 1777, PRO, CO.5/261, ff. 48–49.

42. Boddington to Knox, April 11, 1777, PRO, CO.5/256, f. 74.

43. Knox to Dartmouth, November 15, 1774, Dartmouth Mss., D. 1778, 2:994.

44. Knox to Evan Nepean, December 28, 1782, BM (Haldimand Papers) Add. Mss. 21705, f. 114b; Spector, *The American Department*, pp. 56–57.

45. Knox Papers, 10:2.

46. Knox to Nepean, December 28, 1782, BM (Haldimand Papers) Add. Mss. 21705, ff. 108–114.

47. See PRO, CO.5/78, *passim*.

48. D. W. Claus to Knox, October 16, 1777, in ibid., ff. 222–227.

49. [Knox] to [Dartmouth], [1777], Dartmouth Mss., D. 1778, 2:1817b; Dartmouth to Knox, October 15, 1777, Knox Papers, 3:49.

50. There are complete copies of this manuscript in the Germain Papers (17)

and in the Dartmouth Manuscripts (D. 1778, 2:1817b), as well as a copy of the first part of the document in the Gower Papers at the Public Record Office (30/29/3/6, ff. 556–573).

51. *Parliamentary History*, 19:592.

52. Valentine, *Germain*, pp. 279–280.

53. Hutchinson, ed., *Diary*, 2:184.

54. Brown, *American Secretary*, p. 145.

55. Knox Papers, 10:25; HMC, *Knox*, p. 270.

56. Thurlow to Knox, January 20, 1778, and Germain to Knox, January 23, 1778, Knox Papers, 4:2 and 4; HMC, *Knox*, p. 142.

57. Knox Papers, 10:25; HMC, *Knox*, pp. 270–271.

58. Sir John Fortescue, ed., *The Correspondence of King George the Third from 1760 to December 1783*, 4:176.

59. Ritcheson, *British Politics and the Revolution*, pp. 233 ff.

60. Knox Papers, 10:34; HMC, *Knox*, pp. 277–278.

61. Hutchinson, ed., *Diary*, 2:185–186 and 190.

62. Ibid., pp. 192–193.

"Firmness & Temperance with a Readiness at Expedients": The American War, 1778–1782

1. Mackesy, *War for America*, pp. 237 ff.

2. Brown, *American Secretary*, p. 173.

3. Gerald S. Brown, "The Anglo-French Naval Crisis, 1778: A Study of Conflict in the North Cabinet," *William and Mary Quarterly*, 3d ser. 13 (January 1956): 3–25.

4. PRO, CO.5/254, ff. 127–128, 147–148, 152, and 166.

5. See the manuscript "Plan for carrying on the war in America," Knox Papers, 9:21.

6. William B. Willcox, *Portrait of a General*, pp. 223 and 293.

7. Smith, *Loyalists and Redcoats*, p. 115.

8. Mackesy, *War for America*, pp. 156–159 and 233–234.

9. Willcox, *Portrait of a General*, pp. 222 and 293.

10. Eric Robson, *The American Revolution in Its Political and Military Aspects, 1763–1783*, pp. 191–192.

11. PRO, CO.5/242, ff. 159–164. Also see John R. Alden, *John Stuart and the Southern Colonial Frontier*.

12. Knox to Haldimand, April 6, 1779, BM (Haldimand Papers) Add. Mss. 21703, ff. 79–80.

13. PRO, CO.5/242, f. 124; BM (Haldimand Papers) Add. Mss. 21705, ff. 29–30.

14. Stuart to Knox, October 9, 1778, PRO, CO.5/80, ff. 3–8; Haldimand to Germain, October 23, 1781, Knox Papers, 10:5; HMC, *Knox*, pp. 294–295.

15. PRO, CO.5/80, f. 89.

16. North to Knox, August 8, 1778, Knox Papers, 4:20; HMC, *Knox*, p. 146; Germain to Clinton, September 2, 1778, PRO, CO.5/243, ff. 134–136; Hutchinson, ed., *Diary*, 2:217–218; Smith, *Loyalists and Redcoats*, pp. 175–177.

17. Knox to Germain, October 31, 1778, Knox Papers, 4:39; HMC, *Knox*, p. 154; Hutchinson, ed., *Diary*, 2:285–286.

18. Hutchinson, ed., *Diary*, 2:218.

19. Ibid., pp. 290–291.

20. Smith, *Loyalists and Redcoats*, *passim*.

21. Germain to Knox, March 12, 1779, Knox Papers, 4:56; HMC, *Knox*, p. 156.

22. Knox Papers, 7:36; HMC, *Knox*, p. 196.

23. PRO, AO.12/4, ff. 14–15; Germain to Knox, July 23, 1778, Knox Papers, 4:17.

24. PRO, AO.12/4, f. 2; Knox to Ellis, September 6, 1780, Knox Papers, 5:53; HMC, *Knox*, p. 171.

25. PRO, AO.13/87, f. 177.

26. Ward, *War of Revolution*, 2:688–694.

27. PRO, AO.12/4, f. 2, and AO.13/36, pt. 1, ff. 345–346.

28. Knox to Blacquire, March 22, 1776, and Knox to Heron, May 26, 1778, in Knox, *Extra Official State Papers*, 1, pt. ii, appendix, pp. 10–15 and 127; O'Brien to Knox, April 2, 1776, Knox Papers, 11:41; HMC, *Knox*, pp. 231–232; Blacquire to Knox, May 14, 1776, Knox Papers, 11:42; HMC, *Knox*, p. 232. Much of the evidence regarding Knox's work on Irish trade concessions rests upon the correspondence he published in the *Extra Official State Papers*; the surviving manuscripts of this correspondence in the Knox Papers substantially corroborate the account contained in the printed version.

29. Herbert Butterfield, *George III, Lord North, and the People, 1779–80*, pp. 77 ff. For a detailed study of developments in Ireland during this period, see Maurice R. O'Connell, *Irish Politics and Social Conflicts in the Age of the American Revolution*.

30. Knox to Heron, March 14, 1778, HEHL, PE 221; Knox, *Extra Official State Papers*, 1, pt. ii, pp. 6–7 and 79–81.

31. Buckinghamshire to North, March 20, 1778, Heron to Knox, March 21, 1778, and Knox to Heron, March 28, 1778, in Knox, *Extra Official State Papers*, 1, pt. ii, appendix, pp. 82–90.

32. Knox to Heron, April 21, May 4, May 14, May 19, and May 26, 1778, in ibid., pp. 93–121.

33. Knox to Heron, May 26, 1778, Heron to Knox, July 4, 1778, Knox to Heron, July 16, July 23, and July 31, 1778, in ibid., pp. 122–151.

34. Heron to Knox, August 6, 1778, in ibid., pp. 154–155.

35. Heron to Knox, May 22, 1778, Knox Papers, 11:49; HMC, *Knox*, p. 234.

36. Knox to Lord———, November 14, 1779, Knox Papers, 11:58; HMC, *Knox*, p. 237; manuscript endorsed "Papers respecting Irish Affairs, November 1779," Knox Papers, 11:59; Butterfield, *George III, Lord North, and the People*, pp. 88–90, 103, and 148–149.

37. Mackesy, *War for America*, pp. 279 ff.

38. Butterfield, *George III, Lord North, and the People*, pp. 120–138.

39. Vincent T. Harlow, *The Founding of the Second British Empire, 1763–1793*, 1:524.

40. Scott to [Knox], December 28, 1779, Knox Papers, 5:20.

41. PRO, SP.63/469, ff. 101–102, 165–167, and 205–206.

42. Knox to Germain, May 26, 1780, HMC, *Stopford-Sackville*, 1:270.

43. Germain to [Knox], June 1, 1780, Knox Papers, 11:61; HMC, *Knox*, p. 238.

44. Germain to Knox, May 27, 1780, Knox Papers, 5:37; Buckinghamshire to Hillsborough, July 3, 1780, PRO, SP.63/470, f. 48.

45. PRO, SP.63/469, ff. 250 and 254.

46. Germain to Knox, May 27, 1780, Knox Papers, 5:37.

47. PRO, SP.63/470, f. 258.

48. Matthew Hemmings to Knox, July 19, 1780, and Cunningham to Knox, August 10, 1780, Knox Papers, 5:40 and 11:62; HMC, *Knox*, pp. 238–239. Also see Denis C. Rushe, *Historical Sketches of Monaghan*, p. 116, and Porrit and Porrit, *Unreformed House of Commons*, 2:337–339.

49. PRO, SP.63/470, f. 258.

50. Ibid., ff. 267–268.

51. Germain to Knox, August 7, 1780, Knox Papers, 5:43; HMC, *Knox*, p. 169.

52. North to Knox, August 15, 1778, Knox Papers, 4:21; HMC, *Knox*, p. 146; Hutchinson, ed., *Diary*, 2:217–218.

53. Shelburne Papers, 66:513–528.

54. Germain to Knox, August 11, 1780, Knox Papers, 5:44. The manuscript "New Ireland" is endorsed "approved in Cabinet the 10th Aug. 1780 and by the King the 11th" (Shelburne Papers, 66:513–528).

55. Germain to Knox, September 18, 1780, and Knox to Edward Cooke, January 27, 1808, Knox Papers, 5:54 and 8:51; HMC, *Knox*, p. 228.

56. Knox to North, February 8, 1780, Knox Papers, 5:25; HMC, *Knox*, p. 165.

57. Skelton to Knox, December 13, 1779, Knox Papers, 11:35; HMC, *Knox*, p. 448.

58. Skelton to Knox, October 5, 1780, Knox Papers, 11:38; HMC, *Knox*, p. 449.

59. Hutchinson, ed., *Diary*, 2:327.

60. Knox to James Simpson, November 9, 1780, PRO, CO.5/242, ff. 175–177.

61. See, e.g., PRO, CO.5/251, ff. 101, 132, 137–138, and CO.5/252, ff. 62 and 66–67, as well as Knox's correspondence in 1781 with military commanders and civil officials in America, preserved in the Germain Papers at the Clements Library.

62. Knox to Simpson, March 7, 1781, PRO, CO.5/242, ff. 179–180; Germain to Knox, April 16, 1781, Knox Papers, 6:7; HMC, *Knox*, p. 175; Knox to Mr. Shaw, June 6, 1781, PRO, CO.5/242, f. 182.

63. Knox to Haldimand, July 31, 1781, BM (Haldimand Papers) Add. Mss. 21704, ff. 136–137. There are copies of this dispatch in PRO, CO.5/263, f. 115, and Germain Papers, Secret Dispatch Book, pp. 282–284.

64. Ibid.

65. Howard H. Peckham, *The War for Independence*, pp. 167–170.

66. Knox to Germain, October 31, 1781, Germain Papers.

67. Germain to Knox, November 1, 1781, Knox Papers, 6:25; HMC, *Knox*, p. 180.

68. Germain to Knox, November 4, 1781, Knox Papers, 6:26; HMC, *Knox*, p. 180.

69. Ian R. Christie, *The End of North's Ministry, 1780–1782*, pp. 267 ff.

70. See Knox's account of Germain's resignation in Knox Papers, 10:31; HMC, *Knox*, pp. 272–276. Also, George III to North, January 17 and January 21, 1782, in Fortescue, ed., *Correspondence of George III*, 5:331 and 334; Knox, *Extra Official State Papers*, 1, pt. i, p. 40.

71. Knox Papers, 10:31; HMC, *Knox*, p. 276; Germain to Knox, February 7, 1782, Knox Papers, 6:36; HMC, *Knox*, p. 183.

72. Germain to Knox, February 7, 1782, Knox Papers, 6:36; HMC, *Knox*, p. 183; North to Germain, February 16, 1782, HMC, *Stopford-Sackville*, 1:77–78; Knox to Shelburne, April 23, 1782, Knox Papers, 6:44; HMC, *Knox*, p. 184; George Rose to Knox, May 22, 1790, Knox Papers, 8:5; HMC, *Knox*, p. 209; PRO, AO.13/36, pt. 1, f. 379.

73. Knox Papers, 10:35; HMC, *Knox*, pp. 283–286.

74. Ibid.

75. Ibid.

76. Ibid.

77. Ibid.

78. Knox to George III, May 1, 1782, Knox Papers, 6:45.

"I Will Do No Mischief, But I Will Stimulate the Minister to Do Good": Calamities, Public & Private, 1782–1790

1. Allen D. Candler, ed., *The Revolutionary Records of the State of Georgia*, 1:373–397 and 413–417.

2. PRO, AO.12/4, f. 2; Hall to Knox, July 14, August 12, and September 13, 1782, PRO, AO.13/36, pt. 1, ff. 345, 351–352, 396–397, and 400b.

3. John Norris, *Shelburne and Reform*, pp. 151 ff.; Harlow, *Founding of the Second British Empire*, 1:277 ff.

4. Knox to Germain, July 6, 1782, Germain Papers.

5. The Shelburne Papers (66:513–528) at the Clements Library contain a manuscript copy of Knox's New Ireland scheme, corrected and endorsed in his handwriting. Also, see Harlow, *Founding of the Second British Empire*, 1:291.

6. For a comprehensive treatment of Shelburne's concept of Anglo-American relations, see Harlow, *Founding of the Second British Empire*, 1:308 ff.

7. Norris, *Shelburne and Reform*, pp. 246–249 and 265–268; Feiling, *Second Tory Party*, pp. 147–152.

8. Richard Pares, *King George III and the Politicians*, pp. 122–125. Also, see John Cannon, *The Fox-North Coalition, passim*.

9. Harlow, *Founding of the Second British Empire*, 1:310 and 448–450; Wickwire, "Pownall," p. 554.

10. Lord Sackville [Germain] to Knox, November 11, 1782, Knox Papers, 6:57; HMC, *Knox*, p. 189.

11. Knox, *Extra Official State Papers*, 2:53–54.

12. Harlow, *Founding of the Second British Empire*, 1:450–459. This was neither the first nor the last occasion when Eden availed himself of Knox's ideas and advice. In 1781, Eden, who was then serving as secretary to the Irish victory, asked Knox for advice on establishing a national bank in Ireland (Eden to Knox, November 28, 1781, Knox Papers, 11:64; HMC, *Knox*, pp. 239–240), and in 1785 Eden solicited Knox's ideas on the commercial treaty which Eden was then negotiating with France (Eden to Knox, December 27, 1785, Knox Papers, 7:25; HMC, *Knox*, p. 194).

13. PRO, Rodney Papers, 30/20/15.

14. Knox to Shelburne, April 23, 1782, Knox Papers, 6:44; HMC, *Knox*, pp. 183–184; George Rose to Knox, March [?], 1783, PRO, AO.13/bundle 34, f. 502; also, Knox Papers, 10:35; HMC, *Knox*, p. 285.

15. PRO, T.1/573, ff. 333–334; Knox to Edward Cooke, May 14, 1807, PRO, CO.226/22, f. 152.

16. PRO, T.1/573, ff. 335–336 and 340–341. Also, see BM (Haldimand Papers) Add. Mss. 21705, ff. 115 and 120–126.

17. PRO, T.1/573, ff. 344–345.

18. Knox to Nepean, December 28, 1782, BM (Haldimand Papers) Add. Mss. 21705, ff. 108–114.

19. Thomas Townshend to Haldimand, February 28, 1783, in ibid., f. 93.

20. Knox to Haldimand, April 23, 1782, in ibid., ff. 48–49.

21. North to Haldimand, April 10, 1783, in ibid., ff. 106–107.

22. John Scott to Knox, May 17, 1783, Knox Papers, 7:5; HMC, *Knox*, p. 190; Norris, *Shelburne and Reform*, p. 273.

23. Knox to Edmund Sexten Pery, September 12, 1783, HEHL, PE 223.

24. George Augustus North to Knox, [May 1783], Knox Papers, 7:6; HMC, *Knox*, p. 190; Harlow, *Founding of the Second British Empire*, 1:472 and 480.

25. Harlow, *Founding of the Second British Empire*, 1:472.

26. George Augustus North to Knox, [May 1783], Sheffield to Knox, July 3, 1783, Sackville to Knox, July 4, 1783, and Knox to Walsingham, August 20, 1787, Knox Papers, 7:6, 8, 9, and 38; HMC, *Knox*, pp. 190, 191, and 199.

27. Charles R. Ritcheson, *Aftermath of Revolution*, *passim*.

28. BM (Liverpool Papers) Add. Mss. 38388, ff. 21b–27b.

29. Knox to Walsingham, August 20, 1787, Knox Papers, 7:38; HMC, *Knox*, p. 199.

30. Sheffield to Knox, July 3, 1783, Knox Papers, 7:8; HMC, *Knox*, p. 191.

31. Sackville to Knox, September 20, 1783, Knox Papers, 7:12.

32. Hall to Knox, August 12, August 29, September 2, and September 13, 1782, PRO, AO.13/36, pt. 1, ff. 351–352, 398, 400, and 400b; Lowell J. Ragatz, *The Fall of the Planter Class in the British Caribbean, 1763–1833*, pp. 129–130 and 194–196.

33. Sackville to Knox, September 20, 1783, Knox to North, November 8, 1783, Lord Earlsfort to Knox, May 28, 1784, Knox Papers, 5:12, 14, and 17; HMC, *Knox*, pp. 192–193.

34. Those sources supplying fragmentary details regarding Knox's children are too numerous and varied for specific citations. There is a complete listing of the children in Knox's will, preserved at Somerset House, London.

35. Thomas Hastings to Knox, March 14, 1789, Knox Papers, 11:72.

36. Samuel Lewis, *A Topographical Dictionary of Wales*, 2:105; Ronald M. Lockley, *Pembrokeshire*, *passim*.

37. Knox to Eden, October 1, 1783, BM (Auckland Papers) Add. Mss. 34419, ff. 276–277; Knox to George III, October 4, 1785, in Arthur Aspinall, ed., *The Later Correspondence of George III*, 1:189; Lord Westcote to Knox, October 15, 1786, Knox Papers, 7:34; Knox Papers, 8:8.

38. John Fisher to Knox, September 1, 1785, and Westcote to Knox, January 10, 1787, Knox Papers, 7:23 and 35; HMC, *Knox*, p. 196; Lockley, *Pembrokeshire*, pp. 28 and 119.

39. PRO, AO.17/56, pp. 302–309.

40. Knox to George III, July 6, 1785, Knox Papers, 7:20; HMC, *Knox*, p. 193; PRO, AO.13/36, pt. 1, ff. 363–364. The Loyalist Claims Commission, though acknowledging Knox's sizable losses of property in America, was inclined for the moment to allow his existing pensions to stand as sufficient compensation for all his losses (PRO, AO.12/99, ff. 302b–303).

41. Knox Papers, 7:21; HMC, *Knox*, p. 193.

42. Ragatz, *Fall of the Planter Class*, pp. 190 and 196.

43. Hall to Knox, February 20, June 5, and September 8, 1783, PRO, AO.13/36, ff. 407–408, 411–412, and 424b.

44. Hall to Knox, April 28 and June 5, 1783, in ibid., pt. 1, ff. 409 and 412.

45. Ragatz, *Fall of the Planter Class*, p. 191.

46. Hall to Knox, June 14 and September 8, 1785, PRO, AO.13/36, pt. 1, ff. 422–425.

47. Hall to Knox, September 10, 1785, in ibid., ff. 361–362.

48. Ibid., ff. 367, 371, 428, and 433–434.

49. Knox to Eden, December 27, 1785, Knox Papers, 7:26; HMC, *Knox*, p. 195.

50. Bellot, "Evangelicals and the Defense of Slavery," pp. 34–35.

51. Westcote to Knox, January 10, 1787, and Knox to Rose, December 9, 1787, Knox Papers, 7:33 and 42; HMC, *Knox*, p. 196.

52. Eden to Knox, December 27, 1785, Knox Papers, 7:25; HMC, *Knox*, p. 194; Knox to Eden, January 7, 1786, BM (Auckland Papers) Add. Mss. 34420, ff. 351–358 (copy in Knox Papers, 7:26; HMC, *Knox*, p. 195).

53. Eden to Knox, June 7, 1787, and Knox to George III, October 5, 1787, Knox Papers, 7:37 and 41; HMC, *Knox*, pp. 197–198 and 200; William Knox, *Helps to a Right Understanding of the . . . Treaty with France*.

54. Knox to George III, October 5, 1787, Knox Papers, 7:41; HMC, *Knox*, p. 200.

55. Knox to Walsingham, May 25, 1788, Knox Papers, 7:44; HMC, *Knox*, pp. 201–202.

56. Archibald S. Foord, *His Majesty's Opposition, 1714–1830*, p. 409.

57. Knox to Walsingham, May 25, 1788, Knox Papers, 7:44; HMC, *Knox*, p. 202; Knox's manuscript, "Speech on the Slave Trade," May 25, 1788, Knox Papers, 9:35; Patrick C. Lipscomb III, "William Pitt and the Abolition of the Slave Trade," pp. 519–524; Bellot, "Evangelicals and the Defense of Slavery," pp. 34–35.

58. Knox to Sydney, June [?], 1788, Knox Papers, 7:46; Lorenzo Sabine, *Biographical Sketches of the Loyalists of the American Revolution*, 1:107–112 and 608 and 2:459.

59. PRO, AO.12/19, ff. 15–16, and AO.13/36, pt. 1, ff. 381–389 and 392–393.

60. PRO, AO.12/109, ff. 76b–77; Sabine, *Biographical Sketches*, 1:107–112.

61. Knox, *Extra Official State Papers*, 1, pt. ii, pp. 11–12.

62. See Knox, *Considerations on the Present State of the Nation*.

63. Foord, *His Majesty's Opposition*, p. 410.

64. Knox Papers, 10:34; HMC, *Knox*, p. 278.

65. Rawdon to Knox, December 19, 1789, Knox Papers, 7:54; HMC, *Knox*, pp. 203–205.

66. Rawdon to Knox, December 29, 1789, Knox Papers, 7:55; HMC, *Knox*, pp. 205–208.

67. Knox to Hawkesbury, March 24, 1790, BM (Liverpool Papers) Add. Mss. 38225, ff. 98–103 (copy in Knox Papers, 8:1, dated February 1790).

68. Knox to Rose, April 23 and May 15, 1790, Rawdon to Knox, [spring 1790], Rose to Knox, May 22, 1790, Knox Papers, 8:2, 3, 4, and 5; HMC,

Knox, p. 209. There is a printed copy of the petition which Knox circulated among members of Parliament in PRO, Rodney Papers, 30/20/15.

69. Knox to Rose, November 18, 1790, Knox Papers, 8:10.

"I Quitted the Vortex of Politics": The Elder Statesman, 1790–1810

1. See William Knox, *A Letter from W. K., Esq. to W. Wilberforce, Esq.*

2. Knox to Walsingham, May 25, 1788, Knox Papers, 7:44; HMC, *Knox*, p. 202; Bellot, "Evangelicals and the Defense of Slavery," pp. 34–35.

3. Knox to Thurlow, May 26, 1789, Knox Papers, 7:50; HMC, *Knox*, p. 203.

4. Knox, *Letter to Wilberforce*, p. 19.

5. Ibid., p. 17.

6. Ibid., pp. 10–11.

7. See William Knox, *A Friendly Address to the Members of the Several Clubs in the Parish of St. Ann.*

8. J. Steven Watson, *The Reign of George III, 1760–1815*, pp. 392–393.

9. William Knox, *A Letter to the People of Ireland*, p. 23.

10. Ibid., pp. 27–28.

11. The Colonial Office Papers at the Public Record Office, London, provide extensive documentation of Knox's work on behalf of New Brunswick (PRO, CO.188) and Prince Edward Island (PRO, CO.226).

12. Knox to Camden, June 9, 1804, Knox Papers, 8:35; HMC, *Knox*, pp. 219–220.

13. PRO, CO.188/9, f. 214.

14. PRO, CO.188/12, ff. 87 and 88.

15. PRO, CO.226/22, ff. 96–97.

16. Knox to Cooke, May 14, 1807, in ibid., f. 152; PRO, CO.188/14, f. 123.

17. Lyttelton to Knox, April 18, 1803, and Ellis to Knox, November 27, 1804, Knox Papers, 8:28 and 38. I have not found any reference to Mrs. Knox in either the printed or manuscript sources appropriate to this later period.

18. PRO, CO.188/12, ff. 87 and 88, and CO.226/17, ff. 64–65.

19. See the codicil to Knox's will, August 17, 1809.

20. See Knox's will, December 10, 1806.

21. Codicil to Knox's will, August 17, 1809; George Leonard to Knox, June 23, 1798, November 23, 1809, and March 31, 1810, Knox Papers, 8:19, 58, and 59.

22. Knox's will, December 10, 1806; J. A. Venn, ed., *Alumni Cantabrigienses*, pt. 2, vol. 4, p. 69.

23. Hastings to Knox, January 12, 1789, Knox Papers, 7:48; Knox's will, December 10, 1806. In Knox's will Harriot is, of course, identified by her real name, Henrietta, rather than the pet name by which she was more commonly known among family and friends.

24. Codicil to Knox's will, August 17, 1809.

25. *Burke's Peerage, Baronetage, and Knightage*, 1956, p. 600.

26. Knox to George III, October 5, 1787, and Lyttelton to Knox, April 18, 1803, Knox Papers, 7:41 and 8:28.

27. Knox, *Considerations on the Theocracy* and *The Revealed Will*.

28. Knox to Herschel, October 9, 1809, Knox Papers, 8:56; HMC, *Knox*, p. 230.

29. Herschel to Knox, October 13, 1809, Knox Papers, 8:57; HMC, *Knox*, p. 231.

30. *Gentleman's Magazine* 80, pt. ii (August 1810): 197.

31. Knox, *Extra Official State Papers*, 2:56–57.

32. Koebner, *Empire*, pp. 177 ff.

33. Knox, *Observations Upon the Liturgy*, pp. 49–50.

34. Knox, *Extra Official State Papers*, 2:57.

Bibliography

Manuscript Collections

British Museum, London
    Auckland Papers (Add. Mss. 34412–34471)
    Grenville Papers (Add. Mss. 42083–42088)
    Haldimand Papers (Add. Mss. 21661–21892)
    Liverpool Papers (Add. Mss. 38190–38489)
Church Historical Society Library and Archives, Austin, Texas
    Hawks Transcripts, Georgia-Florida Manuscripts
Henry E. Huntington Library, San Marino, California
    Miscellaneous Knox items
    Stowe Collections—George Grenville Letterbooks
Public Record Office, London
    Audit Office Papers 12 and 13 (Loyalist Claims Commission)
    Audit Office Papers 17
    Colonial Office Papers 5 (America and the West Indies)
    Colonial Office Papers 188–191 (New Brunswick)
    Colonial Office Papers 226–229 (Prince Edward Island)
    Rodney Papers
    State Papers 63 (Ireland)
    Treasury Papers
Somerset House, London
    William Knox, will dated December 10, 1806, and codicil dated
    August 17, 1809
Staffordshire Record Office, Stafford
    Dartmouth Manuscripts
William L. Clements Library, Ann Arbor, Michigan
    Germain Papers
    Knox Papers
    Shelburne Papers

Bibliography

William Knox's Published Writings (in chronological order)

The *DNB*, 31:337, attributes to Knox *A Letter to a Member of Parliament, wherein the Power of the British Legislature and the Case of the Colonies are Briefly and Impartially Considered* (London, 1764). This claim seems to be based solely upon a bit of conjecture in the *Grenville Papers*, 3:109–110, where the editor, William J. Smith, speculated that Knox referred to the *Letter to a M.P.* when in 1765 he sent Grenville a pamphlet he had recently published. The *Letter to a M.P.*, however, contains a wholesale indictment of Grenville's administration, and Knox would scarcely call Grenville's attention to his authorship of such a piece. He was probably referring instead to the *Claim of the Colonies*, which he published in 1765. The tone, style, and specific arguments of the *Letter to a M.P.* are, in fact, incompatible with those in the *Claim of the Colonies*. Halkett and Laing's *Dictionary of the Anonymous and Pseudonymous Literature of Great Britain* attributed the *Letter to a M.P.* to Knox only after the publication of the *DNB*.

1765. *The Claim of the Colonies to an Exemption from Internal Taxes Imposed by Authority of Parliament, Examined: In a Letter from a Gentleman in London to his Friend in America.* London.

1768. *Three Tracts Respecting the Conversion and Instruction of the Free Indians and Negroe Slaves in the Colonies Addressed to the Venerable Society for the Propagation of the Gospel in Foreign Parts.* 2d ed. 1789. London.

1768. *The Present State of the Nation, Particularly with respect of its Trade, Finances, etc., etc., Addressed to the King and Both Houses of Parliament.* London.

1769. *An Appendix to the Present State of the Nation, Containing a Reply to the Observations on that Pamphlet.* London.

1769. *The Controversy Between Great Britain and her Colonies Reviewed, the Several Pleas of the Colonies in Support of their Right to all the Liberties and Privileges of British Subjects and to Exemption from the Legislative Authority of Parliament Stated and Considered, and the Nature of their Connection with and Dependence on Great Britain Shewn upon the Evidence of Historical Facts and Authentic Records.* London & Boston.

1774. *The Justice and Policy of the Late Act of Parliament for Making more Effectual Provision for the Government of the Province of Quebec Asserted and Proved, and the Conduct of Administration Respecting that Province Stated and Vindicated.* London.

1774. *The Interest of the Merchants and Manufacturers of Great Britain in the Present Contest with the Colonies Stated and Considered.* London.

1778. *Considerations on the State of Ireland.* Dublin.

1787. *Helps to a Right Understanding of the Merits of the Commercial Treaty with France.* London.

1789. *Extra Official State Papers Addressed to the Right Hon. Lord Rawdon and Other Members of Parliament Associated for the Preservation of the Constitution and*

Promoting the Prosperity of the British Empire. By a Late Under Secretary of State. 2 vols. London.

1789. *Considerations on the Present State of the Nation Addressed to the Right Hon. Lord Rawdon and the Other Members of the Two Houses of Parliament Associated for the Preservation of the Constitution and Promoting the Prosperity of the British Empire. By a Late Under Secretary of State.* London.

1789. *Observations Upon the Liturgy with a Proposal for its Reform upon the Principles of Christianity as Professed and Taught by the Church of England; and an Attempt to Reconcile the Doctrines of the Angels' Apostacy and Perpetual Punishment, Man's Fall and Redemption, and the Incarnation of the Son of God to our Conceptions of Divine Nature and Attributes. By a Layman of the Church of England, Late an Under Secretary of State.* London.

1790. *A Letter from W. K., Esq. to W. Wilberforce, Esq.* London.

1792. *A Letter to the People of Ireland upon the Intended Application of Roman Catholics to Parliament for the Exercise of the Elective Franchise.* London.

1793. *A Friendly Address to the Members of the Several Clubs in the Parish of St. Ann, Westminster Associated for the Purpose of Obtaining a Reform in Parliament.* London.

1796. *Considerations on the Universality and Uniformity of the Theocracy, by a Layman of the Church of England.* London.

1801. *The Revealed Will of God, the Sufficient Rule of Men.* 2 vols. London.

Printed Primary Sources

Almon, John. *Biographical, Literary and Political Anecdotes of Several of the Most Eminent Persons of the Present Age.* Vol. 2. London: T. N. Longman & L. B. Seeley, 1797.

Aspinall, Arthur, ed. *The Later Correspondence of George III.* 2 vols. Cambridge, Eng.: Cambridge University Press, 1962–1963.

Barrow, Thomas C., ed. "A Project for Imperial Reform: 'Hints Respecting the Settlement for our American Provinces,' 1763." *William and Mary Quarterly*, 3d ser. 24 (January 1967): 108–126.

Boswell, James. *London Journal, 1762–1763.* Edited by Frederick A. Pottle. New York: McGraw-Hill, 1950.

Burdy, Samuel. *The Life of Philip Skelton.* Reprinted from the 1792 ed. Oxford: Clarendon Press, 1914.

Burke, Edmund. *Observations on a Late State of the Nation.* London: J. Dodsley, 1769.

Candler, Allen D., ed. *The Colonial Records of the State of Georgia.* 26 vols. Atlanta: Franklin-Turner, 1906–1911.

———. *The Revolutionary Records of the State of Georgia.* 3 vols. Atlanta: Franklin-Turner, 1908.

Bibliography

Crane, Verner W., ed. "Hints Relative to the Division and Government of the Conquered and Newly Acquired Countries in America." *Mississippi Valley Historical Review* 8 (March 1922): 370–373.

Falkiner, C. Litton, ed. "Correspondence of Archbishop Stone and the Duke of Newcastle." *English Historical Review* 20 (July & October 1905): 508–542 and 735–763.

Fortescue, Sir John, ed. *The Correspondence of King George the Third from 1760 to December 1783.* 6 vols. London: Macmillan, 1928.

Gentleman's Magazine. 103 vols. London, 1731–1833.

Georgia Historical Society. *The Letters of Hon. James Habersham, 1756–1775.* Vol. 6 of the *Collections of the Georgia Historical Society.* Savannah, 1904.

———. *Proceedings of the Georgia Council of Safety.* Vol. 5 of the *Collections of the Georgia Historical Society.* Savannah, 1901.

———. *Report of Sir James Wright on the Condition of the Province of Georgia on 20th Sept. 1773.* Vol. 3 of the *Collections of the Georgia Historical Society.* Savannah, 1873.

Great Britain. *Journal of the Commissioners of Trade and Plantations.* 14 vols. April 1704–May 1782. London: H.M.S.O., 1920–1938.

———. *Journal of the House of Commons.* Vol. 30. January 10, 1765–September 16, 1766.

———. Historical Manuscripts Commission. *Eleventh Report, Appendix, Part V: The Manuscripts of the Earl of Dartmouth.* London: H.M.S.O., 1887.

———. ———. *Fourteenth Report, Appendix, Part X: The Manuscripts of the Earl of Dartmouth.* 3 vols. London: H.M.S.O., 1895.

———. ———. *Report on Manuscripts in Various Collections.* Vol. 6: *The Manuscripts of Miss M. Eyre Matcham; Captain H. V. Knox; Cornwallis Wykeham-Martin, Esq.; etc.* Dublin: H.M.S.O., 1909.

———. ———. *Report on the Manuscripts of Mrs. Stopford-Sackville of Drayton House, Northamptonshire.* 2 vols. London: H.M.S.O., 1904–1910.

Hutchinson, Peter Orlando, ed. *The Diary and Letters of Thomas Hutchinson, Esq.* 2 vols. London: Sampson Low, Marston, Searle, & Rivington, 1883.

Hutton, Arthur Wollaston, ed. *Arthur Young's Tour in Ireland (1776–1779).* 2 vols. London: George Bell & Sons, 1892.

Labaree, Leonard Woods, ed. *Royal Instructions to British Colonial Governors, 1670–1776.* 2 vols. New York: D. Appleton–Century, 1935.

The Parliamentary History of England. 36 vols. London: T. C. Hansard, 1806–1820.

Skelton, Philip. *Ophiomaches: Or, Deism Revealed.* 2 vols. London: A. Millar, 1749.

Smith, William James, ed. *The Grenville Papers.* 4 vols. London: John Murray, 1852–1853.

Tomlinson, John R. G., ed. *Additional Grenville Papers, 1763–1765.* Manchester: Manchester University Press, 1962.

Secondary Sources

Abbot, W. W. *The Royal Governors of Georgia, 1754–1775*. Chapel Hill: University of North Carolina Press, 1959.

Alden, John Richard. *John Stuart and the Southern Colonial Frontier: A Study of Indian Relations, War, Trade, and Land Problems in the Southern Wilderness, 1754–1775*. First published 1944. New York: Gordian Press, 1966.

Alvord, Clarence W. *The Mississippi Valley in British Politics: A Study of the Trade, Land Speculation, and Experiments in Imperialism Culminating in the American Revolution*. 2 vols. First published 1916. New York: Russell & Russell, 1959.

Andrews, Charles M. *Guide to Materials for American History, to 1783, in the Public Record Office of Great Britain*. 2 vols. Washington, D.C.: Carnegie Institution, 1912–1914.

Bailyn, Bernard, ed. *Pamphlets of the American Revolution, 1750–1776*. Vol. 1. Cambridge, Mass.: Belknap Press of Harvard University Press, 1961.

Bargar, Bradley D. *Lord Dartmouth and the American Revolution*. Columbia: University of South Carolina Press, 1965.

Bayse, Arthur Herbert. *The Lords Commissioners of Trade and Plantations Commonly Known as the Board of Trade, 1748–1782*. Yale Historical Publications, vol. 14. New Haven: Yale University Press, 1925.

Bellot, Leland J. "Evangelicals and the Defense of Slavery in Britain's Old Colonial Empire." *Journal of Southern History* 37 (February 1971): 19–40.

Bennett, J. Harry, Jr. *Bondsmen and Bishops: Slavery and Apprenticeship on the Codrington Plantations of Barbados, 1710–1838*. Berkeley & Los Angeles: University of California Press, 1958.

Brooke, John. *The Chatham Administration, 1766–1768*. London: Macmillan, 1956.

Brown, Gerald Saxon. *The American Secretary: The Colonial Policy of Lord George Germain, 1775–1778*. Ann Arbor: University of Michigan Press, 1963.

———. "The Anglo-French Naval Crisis, 1778: A Study of Conflict in the North Cabinet." *William and Mary Quarterly*, 3d ser. 13 (January 1956): 3–25.

Brown, Weldon S. *Empire or Independence: A Study in the Failure of Reconciliation, 1774–1783*. First published 1941. Port Washington, N.Y.: Kennikat Press, 1966.

Burke's Genealogical and Heraldic History of the Peerage, Baronetage, and Knightage. London, 1826–.

Burtchaell, George Dames, and Thomas Ulick Sadleir, eds. *Alumni Dublinenses: A Register of the Students, Graduates, Professors, and Provosts of Trintiy College in the University of Dublin, 1593–1860*. Dublin: Alex. Thom, 1935.

Butterfield, Herbert. *George III, Lord North, and the People, 1779–80*. London: George Bell & Sons, 1949.

Bibliography

Cannon, John. *The Fox-North Coalition: Crisis of the Constitution, 1782–84*. Cambridge, Eng.: Cambridge University Press, 1969.

Channing, Edward, *A History of the United States*. Vol. 3: *The American Revolution, 1761–1789*. First published 1912. New York: Macmillan, 1958.

Christie, Ian R. *The End of North's Ministry, 1780–1782*. London: Macmillan, 1958.

Clark, Dora Mae. *The Rise of the British Treasury: Colonial Administration in the Eighteenth Century*. New Haven: Yale University Press, 1960.

Cokayne, G. E., comp. *The Complete Peerage*. Revised by Vicary Gibb. 13 vols. London: St. Catherine Press, 1910–1959.

Cone, Carl B. *Burke and the Nature of Politics*. Vol. 1: *The Age of the American Revolution*. Lexington: University of Kentucky Press, 1957.

Dickson, R. J. *Ulster Emigration to Colonial America, 1718–1775*. London: Routledge & Kegan Paul, 1966.

Dictionary of American Biography. 12 vols. New York: Charles Scribner's Sons, 1932–1973.

Dictionary of National Biography. 63 vols. London: Oxford University Press, 1885–1901.

Donoughue, Bernard. *British Politics and the American Revolution: The Path to War, 1773–75*. London: Macmillan, 1964.

Falkiner, C. Litton. *Essays Relating to Ireland, Biographical, Historical, and Topographical*. London: Longmans, Greene, 1909.

Feiling, Keith Grahame. *The Second Tory Party, 1714–1832*. London: Macmillan, 1938.

Fitzgerald, Percy. "Old London Squares." In *London, As Seen and Described by Famous Writers*, edited by Esther Singleton. New York: Dodd, Mead, 1902.

Foord, Archibald S. *His Majesty's Opposition, 1714–1830*. Oxford: Clarendon Press, 1964.

Freeman, Thomas Walter. *Ireland: A General and Regional Geography*. 2d ed. revised. London: Methuen, 1960.

―――. *Pre-Famine Ireland: A Study in Historical Geography*. Manchester: Manchester University Press, 1957.

Gill, Conrad. *The Rise of the Irish Linen Industry*. Oxford: Clarendon Press, 1925.

Gipson, Lawrence Henry. *The British Empire before the American Revolution*. 15 vols. New York: Alfred A. Knopf, 1936–1970.

―――. *The Coming of the Revolution, 1763–1775*. New York: Harper & Bros., 1954.

Gray, Lewis Cecil. *History of Agriculture in the Southern United States to 1860*. Vol. 1. Reprinted from the 1933 ed. Gloucester, Mass.: Peter Smith, 1958.

Greene, Jack P. *The Quest for Power: The Lower Houses of Assembly in the Southern Royal Colonies, 1689–1776*. Chapel Hill: University of North Carolina Press, 1963.

Halkett, Samuel, and John Laing. *A Dictionary of the Anonymous and Pseudon-*

ymous Literature of Great Britain. 4 vols. 1st ed. Edinburgh, 1882–1888.
——. *Dictionary of Anonymous and Pseudonymous English Literature*. 7 vols. 2d ed. revised. Edinburgh & London, 1926–1934.
Hanson, Michael. *Two Thousand Years of London: An Illustrated Survey*. London: Country Life, 1967.
Harlow, Vincent T. *The Founding of the Second British Empire, 1763–1793*. Vol. 1: *Discovery and Revolution*. London: Longmans, Greene, 1952.
Hughes, James L. J., ed. *Patentee Officers in Ireland, 1173–1826; Including High Sheriffs, 1661–1684 and 1761–1816*. Dublin: Stationery Office, 1960.
Humphreys, R. A. "Lord Shelburne and the Proclamation of 1763." *English Historical Review* 49 (April 1934): 241–264.
Jones, Charles C., Jr. *The History of Georgia*. 2 vols. Boston: Houghton Mifflin, 1883.
Kemp, Betty. *King and Commons, 1660–1832*. London: Macmillan, 1957.
Knollenberg, Bernhard. *Origin of the American Revolution, 1759–1766*. Revised ed. New York: Collier Books, 1961.
Koebner, Richard. *Empire*. Cambridge, Eng.: Cambridge University Press, 1961.
Labaree, Benjamin Woods. *The Boston Tea Party*. New York: Oxford University Press, 1964.
Lecky, William Edward Hartpole. *A History of Ireland in the Eighteenth Century*. Vol. 1. London: Longmans, Greene, 1913.
Lewis, Samuel. *A Topographical Dictionary of Ireland*. 2 vols. London: S. Lewis, 1837.
——. *A Topographical Dictionary of Wales*. 2 vols. 3d ed. London: S. Lewis, 1845.
Lipscomb, Patrick Cleburne, III. "William Pitt and the Abolition of the Slave Trade." Unpublished Ph.D. dissertation, University of Texas, 1960.
Lockley, Ronald M. *Pembrokeshire*. 2d ed. London: Robert Hale, 1969.
Lonn, Ella. *The Colonial Agents of the Southern Colonies*. Chapel Hill: University of North Carolina Press, 1945.
McCracken, J. L. "The Conflict between the Irish Administration and Parliament, 1753–6." *Irish Historical Studies* 3 (1942–1943): 159–179.
Mackesy, Piers G. *The War for America, 1775–1783*. Cambridge, Mass.: Harvard University Press, 1964.
MacNeill, J. G. Swift. *The Constitutional and Parliamentary History of Ireland till the Union*. Dublin: Talbot Press, 1917.
Magnus, Sir Philip. *Edmund Burke: A Life*. London: John Murray, 1939.
Main, Jackson Turner. *The Upper House in Revolutionary America, 1763–1788*. Madison: University of Wisconsin Press, 1967.
Martin, Chester. *Empire and Commonwealth: Studies in Governance and Self-Government in Canada*. Oxford: Clarendon Press, 1929.
Mason, Bernard. *The Road to Independence: The Revolutionary Movement in New York, 1773–1777*. Lexington: University of Kentucky Press, 1966.

Bibliography

Maxwell, Constantia. *A History of Trinity College Dublin, 1591–1892*. Dublin: University Press, 1946.

Miller, John C. *Origins of the American Revolution*. Boston: Little, Brown, 1943.

Morgan, Edmund S. "Colonial Ideas of Parliamentary Power, 1764–1766." *William and Mary Quarterly*, 3d ser. 5 (July 1948): 311–341.

———. "The Postponement of the Stamp Act." *William and Mary Quarterly*, 3d ser. 7 (July 1950): 355–391.

———, and Helen M. Morgan. *The Stamp Act Crisis: Prologue to Revolution*. Revised ed. New York: Collier Books, 1963.

Mowat, Charles Loch. *East Florida As a British Province, 1763–1784*. Berkeley & Los Angeles: University of California Press, 1943.

Namier, Lewis B. "Charles Garth, Agent for South Carolina." *English Historical Review* 54 (October 1939): 632–652.

———. *Crossroads of Power: Essays on Eighteenth-Century England*. Vol. 2 of *The Collected Essays of Sir Lewis Namier*. London: Hamish Hamilton, 1962.

———. *The Structure of Politics at the Accession of George III*. 2d ed. London: Macmillan, 1957.

———, and John Brooke. *Charles Townshend*. New York: St. Martin's Press, 1964.

———. *The House of Commons, 1754–1790*. 3 vols. New York: Oxford University Press, 1964.

Nichols, John. *Illustrations of the Literary History of the Eighteenth Century*. 8 vols. London, 1817.

———. *Literary Anecdotes of the Eighteenth Century*. 9 vols. London, 1815.

Norris, John. *Shelburne and Reform*. London: Macmillan, 1963.

Norton, Mary Beth. *The British Americans: The Loyalist Exiles in England, 1774–1789*. Boston: Little, Brown, 1972.

O'Connell, Maurice R. *Irish Politics and Social Conflicts in the Age of the American Revolution*. Philadelphia: University of Pennsylvania Press, 1965.

Pares, Richard. *King George III and the Politicians*. Oxford: Clarendon Press, 1953.

Peckham, Howard H. *The War for Independence: A Military History*. Chicago: University of Chicago Press, 1958.

Porrit, Edward, and Annie G. Porrit. *The Unreformed House of Commons: Parliamentary Representation before 1832*. Vol. 2: *Scotland & Ireland*. Cambridge, Eng.: Cambridge University Press, 1909.

Ragatz, Lowell Joseph. *The Fall of the Planter Class in the British Caribbean, 1763–1833: A Study in Social and Economic History*. New York: Century, 1928.

Ritcheson, Charles R. *Aftermath of Revolution: British Policy toward the United States, 1783–1795*. Dallas: Southern Methodist University Press, 1969.

———. *British Politics and the American Revolution*. Norman: University of Oklahoma Press, 1954.

Robson, Eric. *The American Revolution in Its Political and Military Aspects, 1763–1783*. First published 1955. Hamden, Conn.: Archon Books, 1965.

Royal Academy of Arts. *A Complete Dictionary of Contributors, 1769–1904*. Compiled by Algernon Graves. 8 vols. London: Henry Graves & George Bell, 1905–1906.

Rushe, Denis Carolan. *Historical Sketches of Monaghan, From the Earliest Records to the Fenian Movement*. Dublin: James Duffy, 1895.

————. *Monaghan in the Eighteenth Century*. Dublin: M. H. Gill, 1916.

Sabine, Lorenzo. *Biographical Sketches of the Loyalists of the American Revolution*. 2 vols. Boston: Little, Brown, 1864.

Shy, John. "Thomas Pownall, Henry Ellis, and the Spectrum of Possibilities, 1763–1775." In *Anglo-American Political Relations, 1675–1775*, edited by A. G. Olson and R. M. Brown. New Brunswick, N.J.: Rutgers University Press, 1970.

Smith, Paul H. *Loyalists and Redcoats: A Study in British Revolutionary Policy*. Chapel Hill: University of North Carolina Press, 1964.

Sosin, Jack M. *Agents and Merchants: British Colonial Policy and the Origins of the American Revolution, 1763–1775*. Lincoln: University of Nebraska Press, 1965.

————. *Whitehall and the Wilderness: The Middle West in British Colonial Policy, 1760–1775*. Lincoln: University of Nebraska Press, 1961.

Spector, Margaret Marion. *The American Department of the British Government, 1768–1782*. Columbia University Studies in History, Economics, and Public Law, no. 466. New York: Columbia University Press, 1940.

Thomson, Mark A. *The Secretaries of State, 1681–1782*. Oxford: Clarendon Press, 1932.

Valentine, Alan. *Lord George Germain*. Oxford: Clarendon Press, 1962.

Venn, J. A., ed. *Alumni Cantabrigienses: A Biographical List of All Known Students, Graduates, and Holders of Office at the University of Cambridge from the Earliest Times to 1900*. Pt. 2, vol. 4. Cambridge, Eng.: Cambridge University Press, 1951.

Ward, Christopher. *The War of Revolution*. 2 vols. New York: Macmillan, 1952.

Watson, J. Steven. *The Reign of George III, 1760–1815*. Oxford: Clarendon Press, 1960.

Wickwire, Franklin B. *British Subministers and Colonial America, 1763–1783*. Princeton: Princeton University Press, 1966.

————. "John Pownall and British Colonial Policy." *William and Mary Quarterly*, 3d ser. 20 (October 1963): 541–554.

————. "King's Friends, Civil Servants, or Politicians." *American Historical Review* 71 (October 1965): 18–42.

Wiggin, Lewis M. *The Faction of Cousins: A Political Account of the Grenvilles, 1733–1763*. New Haven: Yale University Press, 1958.

Willcox, William B. *Portrait of a General: Sir Henry Clinton in the War of Independence*. New York: Alfred A. Knopf, 1964.

Index

Index

Index

Index